WHEN THE MASK CAME OFF

WHEN THE MASK CAME OFF

LOCKDOWN 2020: A PEOPLE'S HISTORY OF CRUELTY AND COMPASSION

Edited by

Harsh Mander, Natasha Badhwar and Anirban Bhattacharya

YODA PRESS
79 Gulmohar Enclave
New Delhi 110 049
www.yodapress.co.in

ISBN 9789382579298

Editors in charge: Arpita Das, Giitanjali and Himadri Agarwal
Typeset by Saanvi Graphics, Noida
Published by Arpita Das for YODA PRESS

This book is dedicated to the life and work of our beloved colleagues, Mohd Arif and Pradip Bijalwan, both of whom died after being infected by the COVID-19 virus while providing relief to communities during the second wave of the pandemic in India.

It is also dedicated to every person lost to our collective indifference, to the failure of an uncaring state, to the pandemic of our prejudice.

Contents

Acknowledgements

We dedicate this book to our colleagues, Mohd Arif and Dr Pradip Bijalwan, whose life and work were a source of great inspiration for all of us.

Dr Pradip Bijalwan was a rare human being, and the rarest of doctors.

Indifferent to money, fame and his own safety, he selflessly dedicated himself only to serve those at the very end of the line, with dignity and compassion. For nearly a decade, he led our street medicine programme for the homeless and finally our Delhi COVID-19 clinic as well. In a grotesquely unequal world, he was one who believed steadfastly in the equal worth of every life. The bitter irony is that when he became infected, his own family could not secure a hospital bed with oxygen in time for him. A quiet unsung hero, he succumbed not just to the virus but to our apathy.

Mohd Arif was one of our most *zinda dil* comrades at Karwan-e-Mohabbat, so full of life, care and hope for the future; who left us far too early, as he succumbed to the COVID-19 virus during the unforgiving second wave. A tireless voice against the forces of hate, he was the strength and solace of so many lynching-affected families and others who were marginalised in Mewat. He had grown into a charismatic leader who wanted to reclaim the idea of an India of equal citizenship. He cared little about the risks of his own exposure as he dedicated himself to COVID relief.

He didn't ask for anyone's *kagaz* while extending his hand and heart to the people of Mewat.

Preface

Rage, Rage Against the Dying of the Light[1]

HARSH MANDER

It is the spring of 2020. Shamim is 30 years old. Over the past 15 years, he has spent long months at a stretch away from his family and village, while touring states like Kerala, Tamil Nadu, Karnataka, Gujarat and Haryana to peddle his wares.

Shamim was barely 15 years old when he took over his father's profession. Like many other young men, born into impoverished and landless homes in Western Uttar Pradesh's Shamli district, he apprenticed and became a *pheri wallah* or travelling cloth salesman.

Pheri wallahs travel in groups of three or four, going door to door to sell cloth or readymade garments like salwar suits, shirts and jeans. Their *thekedars* or contractors meet them from place to place, invest in the wares and take half their earnings.

---

1 Thomas, D. (1952) 'Do Not Go Gentle Into That Good Night'. *The Poems of Dylan Thomas*. New York: New Directions.

Every month, Shamim used to send a few thousand rupees home. On a good day, he would save Rs 300 for himself. He would visit his village in Shamli once in three or four months and spend a fortnight with his family—his father, wife and four children.

Since Shamim took over the profession 15 years ago, he hasn't stopped travelling. The roads are his life, his livelihood. But the latest journey he undertook, after the imposition of a nationwide lockdown in March 2020 within a four-hour notice, is the one he will never forget.

Stranded Overnight

In March, Shamim, three other *pheri wallahs* and their contractor, had hired two rooms in the district town of Jhalod in Eastern Gujarat, not far from Banswada in Rajasthan. It was during their stay here that they heard Prime Minister Narendra Modi's announcement of the 21-day lockdown in an attempt to contain the spread of COVID-19. Everyone was directed to stay indoors, wherever they were, for three weeks.

Through the night, the four men tried to make sense of this sudden and dramatic alteration in their fortunes. In the morning, they went to the contractor's room only to find that he had checked out and disappeared, without a word. They tried to call him, but he had switched his phone off.

Shamim had barely Rs 500 in his wallet. His companions had just as little money. They had kept most of their savings with the contractor for safe-keeping. Shamim called his wife and children. They wept in fear and confusion: 'Whatever happens, just come home,' they urged him.

Shamim and his companions weighed their options. They did not have the money to pay the room rent or buy food for 21 days. They had to return home at any cost. As buses and trains had halted because of the lockdown, their only option was to walk. The distance from Jhalod to Shamli is 893 km.

The Journey

As they began the journey on foot, they saw that they were not alone. According to their estimate, there were 60,000 to 70,000 others on the highway.

The police were not unkind. They did not try to stop them. They were fortunate, as they were among the early walkers. Those who set out in the days to come would meet many roadblocks, including police batons and disinfectant sprays.

At each state border that Shamim crossed, he found health staff pressing a gadget against his forehead to check for fever. All those who showed no symptoms were allowed to keep walking.

Soon, Shamim and his companions grew weary. They had little money left for food and the heat was unbearable. The occasional hand pump or public tap would see interminable lines. There were some kind people in villages and towns who distributed packed food and water to the travellers. Sometimes, the men slept by the roadside. Most of the time, they just walked and walked. As trucks would pass, some of the travellers would hop on. Shamim too was lucky that he was able to cover some of the distance by truck.

Days and nights merged into one another, and Shamim started losing track of time. He would call his family once or twice a day, limiting the call time to save phone battery. His family would cry each time he called.

'Come home,' they would say. 'If we have to live or die, let us at least be together.' It was hearing their voices that encouraged him to keep walking.

Around 10 days later, he finally reached the boundaries of his village. He called his family, but said he would not come home directly to them. He did not want to infect them in case he had caught the virus. Instead, he went straight to the home of the village *chowkidar*, who worked with the local police. The *chowkidar* took him to a hospital, where the compounder checked his temperature, said he was fine, and told him he could go home. His children, wife and father wept when they saw him.

But soon, he was faced with a new challenge: he did not know how to feed his family. His wife had procured 25 kg wheat from the ration shop, but this was quickly exhausted. When he spoke with me, a week after his return home, he said their food stocks would last them only three or four days more.

They had no savings and Shamim's contractor had vanished with all his earnings. They owned no land, and received no government assistance. They could not turn to anyone in the village, as everyone was struggling for survival. Besides, he said, there was no way he would beg for food.

His only solace was that at least he was finally home.

The year 2020 will be remembered in the history of India and the entire planet as a period of immense humanitarian distress, hunger, loss of work, uprootment, infection, uncertainty and fear. What spurred conditions that might prove to be the gravest humanitarian crisis that most of us will see during our entire lifetimes, was the COVID-19 virus that emerged in China and quickly travelled around the world.

However, it would be a mistake to believe that this immense humanitarian catastrophe in the lives of the working poor in India was created by the virus. Many countries in the world—several poorer than India—were able to deal with the threats of the rising pandemic without unleashing a hunger and livelihood crisis of the scale and the depth that the working poor saw in India. The humanitarian crisis here was not caused by the deadly and infectious virus; it was instead the direct outcome of public policy choices made to deal with the virus, and in the decades past. As I have argued at length in my book *Locking Down the Poor: The Pandemic and India's Moral Centre*, India chose to impose, with less than four hours' notice, the largest, harshest and most comprehensive lockdown in the world and in human history, with the smallest relief package of actual transfers to the poor to help them cope with the consequences of this overnight and unprecedented shutdown of all demand and all supply in the economy. These policy decisions were taken without open public consultation with scientists, cabinet ministers, and chief ministers of various states. The devastation that such decisions wrought in the lives and livelihoods of millions of the working poor was aggravated by the consequences of decades of neo-liberal neglect and dismantling of social provisioning, social rights and security, labour rights, public health and social housing. It was these together, I argue, that were responsible for unleashing a state-created and substantially preventable humanitarian crisis of mass hunger, destruction of livelihoods and countrywide economic recession, combined with the difficulties of millions of people ravaged by the infection to be tested, isolated, treated and cared for with dignity. I am convinced that these public policy choices made in India ostensibly to deal with COVID-19 will be recognised, when the history of these times is written, as nothing short of crimes against humanity, shorn of public compassion and responsibility, pushing India into its gravest economic recession since Independence.

As I write this, economists and policy makers are unable to agree on how long it will take India to recover, to at least return to the economic situation that prevailed prior to the world's harshest lockdown, when 9 out of 10 workers were already in the informal sector without concrete labour rights or protection. They fear that recovery may take a full generation. I am convinced that recovery for the poor to the low-levels of survival will not be possible until the country changes tracks drastically, investing in a robust infrastructure of universal social rights, including free public health for all, decent education paid for by the state, universal social security, universal food security, universal and enforceable labour rights and universal social housing (ensuring well-ventilated and hygienic affordable housing with clean potable drinking water on tap). But in the mainstream of both economic discourse and public policy planning in India, we barely hear even the acknowledgement of the imperative universal social rights. If the working poor are to be protected from the recurrence of the tragedy upon which they were thrust in 2020, a comprehensive plan to build this foundation of universal social rights is imperative.

In this anthology, my colleagues, comrades and I have assembled a set of narrative essays which were researched and written during the harsh lockdown in 2020. In these essays, we have attempted to capture glimpses of what it meant to be a domestic worker, care worker, travelling cloth trader, homeless person, sex worker, migrant worker in a Kashmir locked down for years by security forces, a disabled person, a tea garden worker, widow, small farmer, survivor of hate violence in Northeast Delhi, sanitation worker, child folk singer in Rajasthan, Adivasi forest *tendu* plucker, landless farm worker, rag picker, Muslim, migrant from Northeast India travelling by train, and so on. Our attempt here is to record for history the specific experiences of some of the most disadvantaged of our working poor people, oppressed variously as labour without rights, and as people suffering discrimination and want because of their gender, caste, religious and ethnic identities. And through all of this, we are trying to map the consequences of a spectacularly uncaring state.

We begin the anthology with **Mihika Chanchani**'s encounter outside one of Bengaluru's affluent apartment buildings with a laid-off domestic worker Manish and his pregnant 19-year-old wife from Gumla district in the forested interiors of Jharkhand. Manish had moved to Hyderabad in 2015 when he was 15 years old to work in a cafeteria, leaving his wife who was two years younger than him behind in the village. In 2020, a broker found work for the couple as domestic helpers in a market in Bengaluru. Their experience thereafter of verbal insults, slurs, long working hours late into the night, low wages often withheld, sexual abuse, taunts about caste and religion became part of their daily work life. But what led Manish to rebel was when he found out that his pregnant wife was not being given even a full stomach of food. The essay traces their experience of suddenly being without work in the middle of the nationwide lockdown. They survived on community support, and by coming together in a shelter for stranded workers in the outskirts of Bengaluru. By mid-June, travel restrictions had eased slightly and Manish and Rani found their way back home. Yet by Diwali, he had no option except to return to Bengaluru.

We meet next, in the pages of this anthology, Shamsher Ali and his sons in western Uttar Pradesh. Shamsher, landless, searches for whatever casual work he can find. His eldest son, Afroz, carries cloth on his shoulders travelling across Maharashtra, Telangana, Andhra Pradesh, Gujarat and Madhya Pradesh. The lockdown found him stranded in Wardha, Maharashtra, without money and abandoned by his contractor. It took him weeks to walk or travel huddled in buses and trucks to finally reach his home in Kairana where he was forced into 14 days of isolation. His younger brother, Amjad, was stranded in Alwar where he worked making pillows. He, however, was closer home. A third brother, Jamal, had also begun working as a *pheriwala* at a young age. He then joined as an apprentice under an *ustaad* in Northeast Delhi, where he was soon caught up in the communal violence that erupted a month before the lockdown. The family lived in a congested tenement in Kairana where they had been displaced by brutal communal violence in 2013, unable to shake away the tragedy of being attacked suddenly by neighbours. And on top of all of this came the vicious propaganda of 'Corona Jihad', claiming that Muslims were deliberately spreading the Coronavirus. The contributors, **Sajid Ali and Anirban Bhattacharya**, reflect on the predicament of the family jolted by communal violence, lynching, discriminatory changes in citizenship laws, unprotected conditions of work in far corners of the country and the heartless lockdown.

Next, **Madhurima Majumdar** takes us into the lives of healthcare givers during the lockdown in Bengal. They spoke to her about how the caregivers were worried by a disease that has no cure and a system that did not care about them. The lockdown meant loss of work to most people, but the opposite for healthcare workers whose workload increased exponentially after the lockdown when they worked round-the-clock with very few breaks. Primary healthcare staff such as Accredited Social Heath Activist (ASHAs) and Auxiliary Nurse-Midwives (ANMs) were tasked with going from home to home to spread awareness about preventing community spread of the disease while nurses worked round-the-clock with little protection in hospitals. Nurses were asked to stay in special wings inside the hospital which were unfit for living, where the bathrooms were unsanitary and the rooms overcrowded while the Delhi government assigned single rooms in 5-star hotels to doctors and vehicles to facilitate their travel to-and-from work. Majumdar traces this neglect to both a gender- and caste-based perception of care work as impure.

Amitanshu Verma writes poignantly about the tragedy of being locked down in a country that is not only not one's own but where one is unwelcome: the displaced Rohingyas in India. Noorullah speaks to him of his nostalgia: 'In Burma, we used to distribute *zakat*, but here we are barely able to manage food for ourselves.' The BJP-led government in India has refused to accord even refugee rights to the 40,000 (estimated) Rohingyas in the country, and instead the party leaders often vilify them as potential threats to national security. Even in normal times, life is a continuous struggle for food, clothes, water, a roof over their heads and education for their children. 'Nothing comes as a right, it is always charity for which we should be grateful. Many survived by rag-picking, but even this is no longer possible after the lockdown.' As non-citizens, they were not entitled even to the small food relief that citizens were able to access. The lockdown has reminded them of Burma: that the needs of lives is a lot more than mere food and shelter; it is about a home rather than shelter; above all, it is about people one can call one's own.

Next, Harsh Mander describes his meeting with a group of around 15 homeless men living inside Hume pipes on a depression on the banks of the river Yamuna in North Delhi. The lockdown is at its peak. The main preoccupation of the men was to remain hidden from the eyes of the police. Even in normal times, the Yamuna banks are home to some 4000 destitute single homeless men. These numbers swelled to over 10,000 by just the second day of the lockdown, as bodies packed against each other awaited chance food charity. Initially, it was only civil society volunteers who supplied as much cooked food as they could muster. After public criticism, the state government stepped in, supplying cooked food for which people would have to stand in long lines for hours. It is not surprising that tempers frayed and altercations broke out. One of these briefly made national news, when some homeless men claimed disrespect in the distribution of food. There are many versions of what exactly happened but the shelter was set on fire. After the fire, a large posse of policepersons, wheeling their batons, descended on the banks of the Yamuna, and evicted all the thousands of men from river banks. The government stopped its food distribution and even private food charities were prohibited. The homeless men were packed into crowded school buildings where they were miserable, far more exposed to the superspreading of the virus. The state could not fathom how important the rough-hewn brotherhood of the homeless on the Yamuna banks was. Most men there are alone in the world. This was the only community they had ever known. Those who could, hid and escaped.

One group of workers worst hit by the lockdown were sex workers. **Shirin Choudhary** speaks to homeless sex workers in Northwest Delhi. Even in normal times, they describe sex work like a game of the gambling: 'On some days you get a little, and on some days you get more.' They speak of routinely enduring police harassment, client abuse, shame and stigma. But a complete shutdown of work with no support from the state and community was a new experience. As their meagre bank accounts were depleted, they were forced to choose between exposure to the virus and going without food. Many returned to sex work at even lower rates so as to be able to feed their children.

In Kashmir, the COVID-19 lockdown was only the latest in a series of prolonged shutdowns that had become part of the public life for the Kashmiri people. Lockdowns were imposed in the past numerous times to prevent uprisings, mass protests, mass funerals and militancy. However, through all of this, as **Misbah Rashid** records, migrant workers from far corners of the country have remained integral to the local economy of Jammu & Kashmir, as masons, carpenters, labourers, barbers, embroiderers and workers in gold ornaments shops. Migrant workers are estimated to constitute 80 per cent of the valley's construction work force. Migrant workers reported that they lived in successive lockdowns without fear. They walk to work even during curfews and *hartals*, and the contractors continue to provide them food and accommodation. There were also government relief camps for those migrant workers not accommodated by contractors, but these were in appalling conditions. Unlike in the rest of the country, each lockdown did not create the perils of losing their livelihoods. But instead, the sense of community in Kashmir ensured that it awoke a feeling of responsibility of the contractors to take care of the workers in these fraught and difficult times. Landlords often waived their rents. Still most migrants were unable to access public distribution, subsidised rations or other small government reliefs. A migrant worker wondered if Modiji had kept them in mind all that much when planning the lockdown.

Amartya Sen has spoken of persons with disabilities as probably the most oppressed and dispossessed communities in the world. **Radhika Alkazi**, in this anthology, speaks of the everyday life, even in normal times, of children and persons with disability as a silent pandemic and full of unseen everyday emergencies. When the global pandemic of COVID-19 fell upon these millions of isolated individuals, these invisible emergencies compounded greatly. Alkazi reminds us that we are talking of large numbers, with persons of disability amounting to at least 5 per cent of the Indian population. One of them, for instance, is Firdoz, a boy with cerebral palsy in a one-room tenement, in a labour camp in Okhla, Delhi. Unable to even lift himself or express his thoughts to others, and with no therapy, for the first six years, Firdoz mainly lay stiffly on his bed and almost never left his home. His parents dote on him; his father, a daily wage earner, and his mother were finally convinced that their son could become more independent and could be educated. They found a small ground floor room to help in his mobility, and he had recently started a new routine of visiting a centre with educators and therapists when the pandemic struck. The meagre relief package announced by the government was indifferent to people like Firdoz and millions of others who could not see, or could not walk, whose minds moved slowly, and who had no official documents. Finally, like millions across the land, Firdoz and family made their way back to their village in Bihar. With this journey, the slender chances of Firdoz's rehabilitation and education also collapsed.

Hunger at large has become part of the daily struggle of survival for tea garden workers of Assam and West Bengal, who have seen severe violations of even elementary labour rights for centuries. After the pandemic hit, and the country was locked down, the workers for their safety demanded that they be paid wages to be able to stay safe at home. But as **Banojoytsana Lahiri** records, the tea lobby leveraged an exception to the lockdown and workers were crowded in the gardens, forced to choose between hunger deaths and contamination by the virus. The hospitals and health facilities in the tea gardens are notoriously ill-equipped without qualified practitioners or even medicines. The workers' dwellings are crowded and unsanitary, and worryingly conducive to the super-spreading of the virus. Some workers had migrated to far corners of the country, but with the lockdown they struggled to return to their families even though there was no work and relief food. An advocate told Lahiri: 'successive governments over the decades have betrayed the tea garden workers.' The threat of starvation and infection has only become deeper since the lockdown.

Abdul Kalam Azad and **Kazi Sharowar Hussain** describe how the pandemic and lockdown closed all pathways for survival for Shahjahan Ali. He was born on a river island on the Brahmaputra. One year, the island was washed away by the floods. As a teenager, he was trafficked to brick kilns in Nagaland where he worked as a bonded labourer for five years before he escaped to Barpeta in Assam. He became a helper at a construction site, got married and started life in a rental one-room home. But the contractor did not pay him after the lockdown. There was no money for rent, food and he had no documents to access subsidised rations. It was during the lockdown that his wife Nafeeda gave birth to a baby boy who died within a week.

Abdul Kalam Azad and **Harsh Mander** document the situation of a 45- year-old tenant farmer in the Baksa district of Assam in the next chapter. 'I am in tension all the time,' he told us dispiritedly. 'I cannot eat, I cannot sleep. I just keep thinking about the future and it frightens me terribly.' He owned no land, but each year he would lease three *bighas* of farmland from a bigger landlord in his village. He was committed to pay him Rs 18,000 to the landlord, regardless of the fate of the harvest. Normally, his harvest would have fetched him at least Rs 50,000. In the lockdown, however, it just decomposed and putrefied. He would have to take a loan at exorbitant rates of interest to pay his landlord his agreed share and buy goods for the next harvest. We also spoke to Najeema Begum, a single mother who worked as a domestic worker in Guwahati to educate her daughter and look after her ailing mother. She lost her employment and was not entitled to subsidised ration since her name was not included in the ration card with her husband from whom she had been estranged for 14 years. She had mastered the skill of sleeping on an empty stomach for years but was tormented by the thought that her children may also have to endure the agony of hunger.

It was exactly a month after the largely working-class Muslim labourers of Northeast Delhi burnt in fires of communal violence, that the nationwide lockdown was imposed. In this month, the state had done too little for rescue and the establishment of dignified relief camps, and the rebuilding of livelihoods and property. But whatever little was being done, mostly by civil society volunteers, was decimated by the lockdown. **Varna Balakrishnan** and **Meera Viswanathan** record an account of the conditions they were living in during the lockdown. Irfan, a survivor, asked them: 'Do you think we like begging and asking for food and money from all of you? All we want is our lives back. We need jobs… . The government needs to step in.' They describe how hunger and desperation for food became widespread amidst the fear of recurring violence and incessant arrests, especially among working class Muslims, many of whom had already lost loved ones and property. This was a time when they could not even reach out to lawyers. They describe how healing and rebuilding were impossible in such an environment of apathy, fear and hostility.

Sagar Kumbhare reminds us that at the front line of the battle against the pandemic were not just doctors and health workers, but also sanitation workers who typically worked without any protective equipment and no special training in protecting themselves from infections as they handled trash. Also, without any transportation, they were required to put their lives at risk every day. For those in private employment, their fate in some ways was even worse because their employment was terminated overnight by the lockdown. A sanitation worker from Khajuraho ironically lamented that even the pandemic failed to make the government realise the worth of sanitation workers.

Imtiaz Quadri, a teacher, turns our attention to the impact of the digital divide on the capacity of students from disadvantaged backgrounds to undertake online learning. They were hampered by the lack of smartphones, internet connectivity, reading materials, a collegial environment and the distress of their families. Children from poor households were forced to drop out of schools, especially girls. They were cut off from classmates, friends and teachers, and missed a lot of the teaching because of extremely slow 2G internet speeds. According to a survey by ISA at the Delhi University, as many as 41 per cent of students did not attend classes because of internet connectivity. Children from deprived backgrounds were unable to meet friends with whom they normally shared their books and reading materials.

Balu Sunilraj and **Suresh Garimella** add to the tapestry of stories of migrant workers in Delhi. Enduring the triple whammy of informality, an uncaring government and the cruel lockdown, Mofidul works as an embroidery worker, unpaid by his contractors since the lockdown began and without a ration card. Lying awake each night, he would think 'if the market does not open and we do not get any work for months, we will die of starvation'. Abdul Wafal, like Mofidul, had migrated to Delhi from rural Bengal eight years earlier at the age of 16. As an assistant to a street vendor, he earned Rs 10,000 a day, half of which he sent to his parents in the village, and the other half paid for his food and rent for a dingy 6-by-8 room, which he shared with six other workers. He too was not paid by his employer. He longed to return to his village. 'We need to pay for everything here. In the village, we adjust and we can sustain ourselves.' Vikram, who had been a tenant farmer in Bengal and had migrated to Delhi to eke out a better existence is desperate worrying about his family back in Bengal. He says, 'They also have not been able to eat.'

In the next chapter, senior human rights defender **Nandita Haksar** describes an utterly harrowing 119-hour train journey from Goa to Manipur. Two months after the lockdown began, the government reluctantly organised a train to transport 996 people from the Northeast working in Goa; However, authorities declared that they were unable to organise food and water for the passengers on the journey. Haksar gets frantic calls from the passengers as they travel through the heart of India in the hot summer months without any replenishment of food and water and contacts volunteers along the way in stations like Pune, Sawal and Bhopal to organise water and food for the migrants on the train. People try to help, but there is too little time and widespread confusion. On the third day, the train reaches Bhopal. The travellers have only had 2 litres of water and 2 bananas each by this time. The toilets have not been cleaned and most are now no longer fit for use. No water was filled during any of the stops for the bathrooms. Haksar calls members of parliament, trying to shame them, but to no avail. In Katihar, migrants walking home are angered at the sight of the 'privileged' ones travelling by train and stone the train windows. Finally, 119 hours after they left Goa, the passengers' nightmare comes to an end as they reached Jiriba.

At a time when the government should have used all of its resources to provide food, preserve livelihoods and safe transport, as well as healthcare to India's working poor, **Buddhadev Dasgupta** describes how it was used instead as an opportunity to crush the ongoing nationwide protests against the Citizenship Amendment Act (CAA) and the National Register for Citizens (NRC). On the first day of the lockdown, the Delhi police dismantled anti-CAA art installations and graffiti in Jamia and across the city. Citizen protests inspired by Shaheen Bagh across the country were forcefully dispersed, and many young protestors found themselves arrested under extraordinary laws which denied them bail potentially for years.

Sagar Kumhare describes vividly the impact of the lockdown on tribal and other forest dwelling communities in Gadhchiroli in the next chapter. The region, without a single industry and with broken health and education services, has been the site of a Maoist insurgency for decades. Because of its remoteness, it was saved from the onslaught of the virus initially. But the majority of young men of the region are migrants, and as the national lockdown deprived them overnight of work, earnings and food, they returned to their forest habitats and brought with them the deadly virus. But the lockdown pushed the impoverished tribal people into even further penury by not just choking remittances, but by mindlessly prohibiting their other major livelihood, which was the collection of tendu and other non-timber forest produce.

The everyday precarity of waste workers is evocatively described by **Suresh Garimella** and **Balu Sunilraj**. Before the lockdown, the waste economy barely shielded them from starvation. The virus, they say, just pushed them over the already precarious edge that they hung onto. The lockdown barred them from scouring waste heaps, and residents of apartments would not allow them to collect waste. Pushed into starvation, the only state support in Kishangarh was cooked food distributed one day, which made many of them sick. The residents of Rangpur Pahadi survived on food packets distributed by the police or private charities.

In 'A Call for Help', **Niyati Sharma** describes her experiences in responding to distress calls during the lockdown. A human rights lawyer with Karwan-e-Mohabbat, she and her colleagues started receiving desperate calls for assistance with food from stranded migrant workers within days of the lockdown. They resolved to try to respond to these calls through a network of human rights and social workers of the Karwan across the country. She describes how the calls helped them bear witness to the enormous humanitarian crisis that had been unleashed by the lockdown and how an uncaring state had reduced working people around the country to helpless and desperate hunger. The small relief offered by the state required them to 'navigate unsympathetic bureaucratic procedures only to be able to eat'. The central and state governments seemed indifferent to the fact that they could access the pittance offered by the state only if they owned 'a mobile phone with sufficient balance, access to the internet, the requisite luck to actually get through to a government helpline number and have the officer hear them out, and the ability to fill online forms'.

Rights activists **Anjali Bharadwaj** and **Amrita Johri** who work in the slums of Delhi describe vividly how as a result of the lockdown, the poor in Delhi found themselves in a situation of utter indignity: total destitution and wracked by the agony of hunger. They also describe how a small economic relief package announced by the central government could not reach those who most needed it.

What was the fate of migrants detained in quarantine shelters in Delhi, who were unable to dodge the police and walk to their homes? Packed into unsanitary schools, one such migrant, Nandram Pahelwar from Lalitpur said to senior reporter **Radhika Bordia**, 'for 45 days now, I have been living like a *qaydi* (prisoner) for no fault of mine. I beg you to let me go.' The construction site which his wife and he were working in was shut down abruptly after the lockdown was announced and the police forced them into this school. His wife, Leela added with tears in her eyes, 'Please take a look at the place where we go to get drinking water, and then see the condition of the bathroom inside. On the rare day we have soap to bathe in, we don't have one to wash our clothes. But on most days, we have neither. We have lost jobs, we have run out of all our money, but the hardest thing is to be stripped of our dignity and to be made to feel like beggars and be treated like prisoners.' A policeman grumbled nearby, 'These people are never satisfied with what they are given.'

The final essay of this anthology, by filmmaker and writer **Natasha Badhwar** explores how the rage of people in millions forced to depend on food charity helped her see in perspective not only the value but also the limitations of the solidarity that we were trying to extend. When Badhwar went to distribute food rations, a young woman in her early-20s balancing a child on one hip asked Natasha, 'What is in this dry ration kit?'. She then added, 'How long will it last?' Natasha explained that it would last 10 days. 'How long will the lockdown last?' was the next question, followed by: 'What will I do when the food runs out? I have small children, how will I feed them?'

The young woman's anger was her rebellion against the indignity of a government in a city that had reduced her to a fugitive, a helpless refugee. 'Rage against the flickering of the light, young Parveen' Natasha writes, 'your anger is the energy we need.'

1

'I Cannot Eat or Sleep'

HARSH MANDER AND ABDUL KALAM AZAD

'I am in tension all the time,' Rahiz Uddin, a 45-year-old tenant farmer of Bhokowamari village in Baksa District of Assam, said to us dispiritedly. We watched the shadows pass over his face on our phone screens during the video call we made to him with the help of friends engaged in relief work in his district in Assam. 'I cannot eat,' he said. 'I cannot sleep. I just keep thinking about the future and it frightens me terribly.'

This was a good farming year before the calamity hit without any warning. Rahiz Uddin owned no land, and each year would take on lease three *bighas*, or 0.40 hectares, of farmland from a bigger landlord of his village. The terms of the lease committed him to pay the landowner Rs 18,000 regardless of the fate of the harvest. The rest of the earnings were his. As were all investments and any losses.

This year, he cultivated perishable vegetables like bitter gourd, ridge gourd, cucumber and radish. He had just reaped his harvest and was readying to sell the produce in the market. He hoped to bring in at least Rs 50,000. Even after he paid the landlord his share, he would have enough to feed his family and invest in the next paddy cultivation.

But then, without warning, a complete lockdown was announced on 24 March. He heard that an epidemic had broken out, so everyone was prohibited from moving out of their homes for three weeks. Helplessly, his heart sinking, he watched his harvest rot. His family ate some of the vegetables, they shared some with their neighbours, and fed some to the cows. However, most of it just decomposed and putrefied.

His 'tension'—he used the English word—is for many reasons. Even though he will now not earn a single rupee, he still has to pay his landlord his agreed share. Otherwise, the landlord won't lease him the land in future. To pay him, he may have to take a loan from the local moneylender at a high interest rate.

He also has to arrange for money for his next harvest, which is already due. He may have to borrow for this as well. Adding to his woes, he is unsure whether the government will even let him work in the fields. And with all of this, how will he feed his family?

On 29 and 30 March, we undertook a rapid impact assessment of the vegetable growers of four development blocks in Assam's Baksa and Barpeta districts. Our colleagues who are working with the communities spoke to 150 small farmers over the phone to understand the impact of sudden lockdown on their farming as well as on their lives.

Remittances

Rahiz Uddin has two twin sons, both 17, studying in Class 9. For years, many households in the village would send out their young sons to Kerala and other parts of the country to earn. It was their remittances which assured food on the plates of their children, spouses and parents who were left behind.

Rahiz Uddin is happy that at least his sons are with him today. Many people in their village heard desperate stories from sons, husbands and fathers who were trapped by the lockdowns in Kerala. They spoke to them on the phone many times a day. Although they were eager to return home to their villages in Assam, they were not permitted to leave Kerala.

In the first days of the lockdown, they were frantic about how they would feed themselves. But some employers promised them a little money. And the Kerala government stepped in quickly, establishing kitchens and offering them food for free. However, their families in the village were already despairing.

Those back in Assam survived on the remittances from their loved ones in Kerala and other parts of the country. When we spoke to them they had no idea how long the lockdown would continue, and even after it ended, if and how soon work would restart.

Infrastructural and Government Failures

There are other small and marginal farmers like Rahiz Uddin, who cultivate mostly small plots of land, sometimes taken on lease for one harvesting season. Of the 150 farmers we spoke to, around 75 per cent or 112 farmers cultivated land less than 0.40 hectare, 36 cultivated less than 0.81 hectare, and only two planted a little more than 2 hectares of land. These 150 farmers produce approximately 12,500 metric tons of perishable vegetables every week. The lockdown is causing them a weekly average loss of around Rs 20,000 per farmer.

Most of these farmers had cultivated in the winter months of 2019 vegetables like gourds, cucumber, tomato, brinjal, beans and ladies' finger, alternating in the kharif season with paddy. These vegetables are perishable and can't be stocked for a long time. There is no cold storage facility in the entire area. They have to sell their produce every week. Most, like Rahiz Uddin, have no access to banks. Tenants have no land papers, and therefore are ineligible for loans. Even landowners have holdings too small for them to access loans from the banks and other financial institutions. They are forced instead to knock on the doors of private moneylenders who charge exorbitant interest rates.

After the lockdown, the government of Assam promised that it would purchase the agricultural produce from the farmers. But among the 150 farmers we spoke to, not a single farmer has been able to sell their crop to the government.

In principle, the state government also exempted farm operations and procurement of agricultural produce from the lockdown. But on the ground, all farm work remained fully barred and interventions by our colleagues with senior officials could not help mitigate the crisis faced by local farmers in both Baksa and Barpeta districts.

Other Sources of Income

Many of these farmers use their income from vegetable cultivation to plant other crops, especially paddy, and to buy seeds, diesel, fertiliser and pesticide. Starting from the late 1990s, small and marginal farmers, especially from the state's *char-chapori* or river bank areas, shifted from traditional paddy cultivation to modernised cultivation practices, deploying high yielding seeds, fertilisers, pesticides and irrigation. This change resulted in a manifold increase of yield and thus, helped a large number of people come out of abject poverty over the past decades.

But it also made them far more vulnerable to risk.

The most crucial component of this new paddy cultivation is assured irrigation. For this, the fields need to be kept wet all the time, and individual farmers typically ensure this using power-pump machines and shallow tube-wells. They have mostly installed these with private loans, unsupported by the government.

Since the shock of the lockdown, farmers, for instance, are unable afford the diesel to power their pumps. Their fields are fast drying up as they run out of cash. 'This is the most crucial time for the paddy fields,' said Ainal Hoque, a farmer from Sidhuni village in Barpeta district. 'I need to run the machine every day but I don't have diesel.'

Ainal has taken 0.27 hectare or two *bighas* of land on lease, against an agreement to repay 4 quintals of rice after harvest. Now, he does not know how he will feed his five-member family if he fails to channel water into his still green paddy field. There is an unspoken fear of a long summer and a spell of hunger.

It is not surprising then that Rahiz Uddin finds it hard to sleep.

2

What Will I Do When This Food Runs Out?

NATASHA BADHWAR

There were a lot of tears during the weeks of lockdown—some solitary, some in the presence of others—but the story I want to tell today is about the first time I felt better after receiving a good yelling.

After being homebound in a suburb of Delhi for the first two weeks of the lockdown, I began to venture out regularly to distribute dry ration kits to families and groups of people who were stuck without wages and food within a 30 km radius of my home. I have been working closely with the Karwan-e-Mohabbat, a human rights campaign, and as soon as the distress of stranded workers began to flood the news, we immersed ourselves in fundraising for, and distribution of emergency relief to, as many people as we could reach.

The severe restrictions of the lockdown meant that we had to constantly innovate to find ways to procure large-scale dry rations even as wholesale markets were sealed. Distributing them in a city dotted with police check posts with instructions to restrict all movement on the roads was a daily challenge.

Many colleagues were unable to volunteer for fear of the infection of COVID-19. Our teams on the road were small and most of us were learning on our feet to identify the most vulnerable groups and reach out to them with respect and dignity.

I partnered with Ashok, who works as a driver for our family, and together we would load our Ertiga with almost a thousand kilograms of ration, divided into family kits, each weighing 16 kg. We had a verified list of names and addresses created by teams who were coordinating online and one by one we would call each person and deliver rations to them.

If we had collectively been struck by a natural disaster that had rendered a large number of people helpless, perhaps this role of being a rescue worker might have been somewhat satisfying. As things stood, we were constantly and acutely aware of the injustice inherent in the implementation of the lockdown that had decimated the ability of the otherwise resilient working class to be able to survive. While the privileged amongst us were safe at home, experimenting with new cuisines and entertainment, daily-wage workers and unorganised labourers found themselves abandoned in their battle against hunger and uncertainty.

When we met people to deliver food packets, often someone would break down from the helplessness. It was terrible to watch, especially since we could not even extend a reassuring touch as we stood awkwardly at a distance of a 'safe' 6 feet. When others thanked us, we felt awful too, because it heightened the severity of the injustice that had destroyed this person's ability to be self-reliant. The worst was when people spoke to us with fear and earnestly insisted that we check their Aadhaar cards to make sure that they were authentic victims.

I did not know it at the time but the response that would finally reassure me was anger.

Her name is Sumaiya Parveen; she is in her early 20s and along with an extended family of labourers from her village in Jharkhand, she is stranded in Kasna, an urban village near Greater Noida in Uttar Pradesh. It was past 10 pm when Ashok and I tried to find Parveen's address with the help of a set of vague instructions that included stopping near a temple on the highway. Parveen had been impatient on the phone, telling me that she wasn't sure the police would let them come out of their homes and cross the street to meet us on the highway. I was mildly amused that this young voice on the phone seemed to be scolding me for what was her personal frustration.

When we met Parveen and her group, I was startled by how young she looked even though she had a child balanced on her hip. 'What is in this dry ration kit?' she asked me.

I began to tell her that it had wheat flour, rice, *dals*, masalas, cooking oil and some soaps.

'How long will this last?' she snapped.

'Sumaiya, this should be enough to last for 10 days for a family of five,' I said.

'How long will the lockdown last, please tell me?' she said.

I hesitated before answering because at that time there were still two weeks to go before the first deadline of the lockdown. I began to explain the situation to her, telling her that millions of people were in distress across India and we barely reached a minuscule percentage of them. I was trying to suggest that she should be thankful instead of snapping at me.

'What will I do when this food runs out?' Parveen asked, cutting through my spiel. 'We have barely been in the city for a month and we are stuck here. Our landlord is cooperating but how long will he allow us to stay without rent? I have small children, how will I feed them?'

'I am sorry,' I began to say, reminding myself to listen to her rather than try to answer her rhetorical questions. And that's when Parveen gave me a sound yelling, standing by the dark highway in the middle of lockdown.

'I am not the state, Sumaiya,' I said at one point. 'You didn't vote for me. We are just some people struggling to help in this time of crisis.'

Parveen's anger stayed with me for a long time. There was something inherently perverse in this scene in which I had stepped out of my car with 10 days worth of bare minimum food and had tried to convince a desperately scared woman with little children to be thankful for it. Parveen's words tore through the semblance of normalcy I was trying to restore. Her questions washed away the absurdity of what we were trying to pass off as some form of justice.

Despite finding herself on the brink of abject poverty, Parveen would not allow herself to be diminished. She knew she had a right to demand a lot more than just meagre rations. She demanded the dignity of being able to support herself. She wanted to reject the city that had reduced her to the status of a helpless refugee. She did not want to be treated like a fugitive for no fault of hers.

Meeting Parveen restored some of the broken parts of my own self. Rage, rage against the flickering of the light, young Parveen. Your anger is the energy we need.

3

Hunger and Resilience

Stories of Survival Strategy During the Pandemic

ABDUL KALAM AZAD AND HARSH MANDER

Marjina Begum is in her early 50s, but she thinks of herself as old. Her poor health has made her infirm, but the weight and urgency of her responsibilities keep her moving.

She has worked as a domestic worker in Guwahati for 14 years to earn enough to raise and educate her daughter and look after her ailing mother. Marjina's mother and daughter live in their village, a few kilometres from Barpeta's district headquarters in Western Assam. The name of the village will be withheld as her home is on government land. Her teenaged son, who lives with her in Guwahati, used to work as a rag-picker and was an apprentice at a garage. He is now learning carpentry.

Assamese Hindu Mahajans from Barpeta town had occupied the land, and employed local labour to clear the scrub forests and make them cultivable. Marjina bought her house-site from one of them. Now, it has grown into a full-fledged village, but one which remains illegal.

Most of its residents are impoverished Bengali-origin Muslims like Marjina. Though they have lived there for several decades, most have no documents like ration cards or election cards. They remain illegal residents, a particularly dangerous status in Assam.

Every three or four months, Marjina goes on leave to visit her village and spend time with her family. She has no brothers—she buys medicines for her mother; pays for her daughter's college fees, books and clothes; and stocks the house with food and other essentials to tide them over when she returns to work.

The Lockdown

When the nationwide lockdown to contain the COVID-19 spread was announced, Marijna was in her village. She had gone there a month earlier, while her son remained in Guwahati. Our colleagues in Assam, who are striving to provide food and other essentials to the most vulnerable families in rural Assam, met Marjina at her home.

Marjina Begum understands the importance of the lockdown; she thinks people should protect themselves from the deadly virus. However, she also thinks there should be some form of government aid, in the absence of which she has faced enormous hardship.

Before the lockdown she had bought and boiled around 40 kg of paddy and pounded it into rice. But there were four mouths to feed, and two weeks into the lockdown, the stock was almost exhausted. Apart from this, her kitchen was empty. On some days, she managed to beg for leafy vegetables from neighbours' fields. On others, her family ate the rice with just water and salt. 'I had no problems before. We used to survive on what I earned,' she said. 'Now we have fallen suddenly on very bad times....There's no knowing how long this lockdown will continue.'

Through the Safety Net

After the lockdown, the government announced some protections for the poor—a direct transfer of Rs 500 to Jan Dhan account holders, free food grains for ration card holders under the National Food Security Act, and Rs 1,000 in cash. None of this has reached her.

During this period, neither a government official nor a local panchayat representative has visited her family to offer any help. She heard that the government had appealed to the families who had people employed in government, and other richer families, to support their poor neighbours. But her village hardly has any government employees and the rich have been tight-fisted.

In difficult times like these, people refuse to lend money even on interest. There are not many wealthy people in her village anyway. Almost all of the villagers are either marginal farmers or migrant workers like her.

Her mother did manage to get a ration card. But since she doesn't have a son, the officials marked her as the only member in the family. Though Marjina's daughter lives in the same house, the officials refused to include even her granddaughter's name in the ration card. Therefore, she is entitled to only 5 kg of rice per month.

A Single Mother

Marjina herself doesn't have a ration card. Her name is included in the ration card of her husband's family and they draw her share of rations. She left her husband 14 years ago, as he was violent. She hasn't seen him since. At the time, Marjina had resolved to educate her daughter at any cost, so that her daughter doesn't have to experience domestic violence and poverty.

In her younger days, Marjina used to work at more than 10 households. Now, she works full-time for one family for Rs 4,000 a month and two meals a day. Of this, she spends Rs 2,000 on her house rent.

'I have become old. Now, I can't work as much I worked during those days,' she said. 'I eat in the house where I work. I eat in the afternoon, then again at night and come home to sleep.'

One of her former employers allows her to use his ration card to buy 25 kg of rice a month. Marjina shares the ration card with his current employee, so she can use it every alternate month. The benefits of this are availed by her son in Guwahati. This amount of rice is enough to last him for two months, she said.

Ray of Hope

Marjina has no agricultural land but her home is surrounded by fields. Her neighbours in the village have sown paddy. She said people were struggling to get the water for their fields during the lockdown but Allah has showered rains. When her neighbours will bring the crop home, she hopes, they all would be able to survive.

'No one will eat full meals while his neighbour starves. He will spare some of his food for his neighbour,' she said.

Marjina herself has mastered the skill of going hungry for days. She has seen hunger and abject poverty since childhood, when floods would often destroy crops and her village would face famine-like situations. 'We have lived through difficult times. [At the time,] we cooked gruel with one handful of wheat flour and it was all we ate during the course of one day.'

She thanks Allah for keeping the villagers alive during that period. Now too, she believes, He will help them sail through this crisis. She said, 'We are Muslims. I have heard that people's souls remain alive for a week without food.'

However, she is saddened that if the lockdown continues, her children may have to endure the torment of hunger longer.

4

A Call for Help

Responding to Distress Calls during the Lockdown

NIYATI SHARMA, SWATI SINGH

'*Agar woh sach mein itne bhookhe hote toh khana nahin le lete? Ration kyun maang rahe hain?*' (If they were really that hungry, wouldn't they just take the cooked food they are being given? Why are they asking for ration?), the Community Development Officer in Mumbai sounded as incredulous as Mr Bumble did when Oliver Twist dared to ask for more gruel.

As India was placed under a stringent lockdown to deal with COVID-19, a broken system of governance that treated its poor and vulnerable as recipients of charity instead of rights-holders lay exposed. Food became difficult to access for the country's most vulnerable people—including migrant workers, daily wagers, the homeless and the poor—who found themselves suddenly and unexpectedly out of employment.[1] With the central government failing to foresee the crisis and plan any substantial measures of relief till as late as 14 May 2020,[2] it fell solely upon state governments to secure the right to food for people in distress.[3]

From 28 March onwards, some members of our team of lawyers and human rights workers at Karwan-e-Mohabbat started receiving calls for assistance with food from stranded migrant workers. Sitting in the sheltered confines of our homes, we bore telephonic witness to a humanitarian crisis unfolding right outside our gated societies.

Each call we received unravelled the enormity of the hunger crisis. One night, a migrant worker stuck in Palghar, Maharashtra, called us and said, *'Hum teen din se kuch nahin khaye hain. Hamare pet mein itna dard ho raha hai, mann kar raha hai khudkhushi kar lein. Aap aur kitna intezaar karwayenge?!'* (I haven't eaten anything for three days. My stomach's hurting so bad, I feel like killing myself. How much longer will you make me wait?!). We were a little surprised because that was the first time we were speaking to him. We asked him if he had called us before. He replied, *'Pata nahin, kuch samajh mein nahin aa raha. Kisko phone kiya, kisko nahin. Shayad kisi aur ko kiya hoga, par koi khaana nahin de raha.'* (I don't know, I can't understand anything. I'm not sure whom I called and whom I didn't. Maybe I'd called someone else, but no one's giving me food.)

Helpless and hungry people, reduced to such an existence by the lack of a coherent state policy, were being made to navigate unsympathetic bureaucratic procedures only to be able to eat. Decades after the right to food was articulated as an entitlement and an inalienable part of our right to live with human dignity,[4] the government was reminding the starving poor that this right could be exercised only if they had some or all of the following: a mobile phone with sufficient balance, access to the internet, the requisite luck to actually get through to a government helpline number and have the officer hear them out, and the ability to fill online forms.

Delhi

While the first phase of the nationwide lockdown started on 25 March, the state government had already announced a lockdown for Delhi from 23 March and its borders with the neighbouring states were sealed the same day.[5]

Soon after, we started receiving calls from migrant workers and the gist of their plea was this: '*Hum Jharkhand ke rehne waale hai aur lockdown ki wajah se Dilli mein phanse hue hain. Kaam band ho gaya hai, aur khaane ke liye kuchhh nahi hai.*' (I am from Jharkhand and I am stuck in Delhi because of the lockdown. My work has stopped and I have nothing to eat).

Initially, the Delhi government had not planned ration distribution as a part of their relief measures for people without ration cards,[6] and had limited themselves to running community kitchens. Realising belatedly that community kitchens could not handle the enormous demand for food, on 5 April, the Delhi government announced the 'e-coupon' system to enable non-ration card holders to procure ration from shops under the Public Distribution System (PDS)[7] for free for a period of three months.[8] The e-coupon scheme, even though 12 days late, had the potential to benefit lakhs of migrant workers whose income had been cut off abruptly.

To apply for an e-coupon, one had to log on to a website and submit a mobile number on which they would get a one-time password (OTP). They had to log in with the OTP to submit Aadhar card details of all their family members. After their application was processed, they would receive an SMS with a link. They would have to click on the link to download the e-coupon with which they could visit the designated distribution centre along with their Aadhar card and collect their share of ration.

A couple of days after this relief measure was launched, the website crashed because of the heavy traffic. It was restored a week later, but the website now said that they would accept new applications only after the pending applications from the first two days had been processed.

On 22 April, some of the applicants got their e-coupons and were called to a government school near them to collect ration; on arriving there, they found that the ration included only unground wheat and rice. It took the Delhi government 17 days from the date of the announcement of the scheme to even start delivering the promised ration. This is how long a migrant population with no employment, no savings and no community support, had to wait just to get wheat and rice.

The problems with this measure, however, were not just limited to the slow process but were manifold. Our relief network intended to reach the most vulnerable, so when we received a call, we would ask if the caller had a ration card. If not, we asked if they had applied for the state government's e-coupon initiative. These are some of the responses we received:

- '*Ab hum padhe-likhe nahi hai, samajh nahi aa raha ki yeh kaise karna hai.*' (We are not literate, we do not understand how to go about this process.)
- '*Uske liye toh internet wala phone chahiye hoga na? Humaare paas toh button wala phone hai.*' (For applying, we would need a phone with internet [smartphone], right? We only have a simple phone.)
- '*Kara tha, didi. Pandrah din ho gaye abhi tak message nahi aaya.*' (I had applied, sister. It has been 15 days, and I still have not received the message.)
- '*Humne toh pehle hi din apply kar liya tha. Uske chakkar mein sau rupay bhi gaye sochke ki ration mil jayega, aur ration bhi nahi mila.*' (We had applied on the very first day. We even

gave 100 rupees, because all we wanted was to secure our food supplies. But we wasted those 100 rupees and still did not get any ration.). Baffled, we asked, '*Kisko sau rupay diye?*' (Whom did you give 100 rupees to?). She said, '*Wahi jinhone humaara number coupon ke liye daala tha.*' (The same person who applied for the coupon on our behalf.)

- '*Jab bahut time ho gaya, toh main pareshan hokar OTP ke saath hi school chala gaya jahaan ration bant raha tha, yeh poochhne ke liye ki yeh kab tak hoga. Khana toh mila nahi, police ka danda aur mil gaya.*' (It had been a long while and I still had not received the link on my phone, so I went to the school where ration was being distributed by the government with only my OTP, to ask how much more time it would take. But instead of giving me any information or food, the police beat me up and chased me away).

The Delhi government took half a month to reach a fraction of the needy with something as essential as food because of a deliberately long-winded scheme which assumed that everyone in the target demography had a smartphone and access to the internet. This made the food distribution highly dependent on civil society to facilitate the process. As suggested by experts, the central government should have universalised PDS to help people tide over this period.[9] However, food security for all cannot be ensured if governments keep worrying about inclusion errors at a time when people find themselves in the middle of a hunger and employment crisis.

In April, Delhi Rozi Roti Adhikaar Abhiyaan filed a petition in the Delhi High Court, seeking directions to the state government to deliver free ration to everyone in need, as per the provisions of the National Food Security Act, 2013.[10] Over the next two months, the High Court passed orders that directed the Delhi government to, among other things, ensure proper functioning of the PDS shops to make food grains available for all, place helpline numbers on its website and widely publicise the same. Therefore, in May and June, food and ration distribution in Delhi was planned under the supervision and mandate of the High Court.

After June, the government discontinued the e-coupon scheme even though unemployment, hunger and reverse migration continued to be rampant.[11] The government relief measures, while they lasted, remained marred by challenges like beneficiaries not having enough information about their entitlements, a non-existent grievance redressal mechanism and the government's disregard for the material realities of the intended beneficiaries.

Maharashtra

Maharashtra, reported to be the state worst affected by COVID-19 in India,[12] was also placed under a lockdown by the state government even before the nationwide lockdown kicked in.[13] But unlike Delhi, we did not have a team physically distributing ration here. We were still working on our strategy for the state when we started receiving calls from migrant workers, primarily from the Mumbai Metropolitan Region, for help with food. As a first step, we decided to approach the state government functionaries to respond to the food requirements of the callers. This was far from straightforward.

For migrant workers calling from Mumbai city or the suburbs, we tried calling the helpline number advertised by the Brihanmumbai Municipal Corporation (BMC), but it was perpetually busy. We were also calling the nodal officers designated for migrant workers in the concerned districts and municipal wards for help, but that posed its own set of problems. If we managed to reach the correct officer based on the municipal ward of the caller, and they agreed to take down the details without redirecting us elsewhere, it would still take us multiple follow-up calls before the migrant workers were even contacted by the government. Actual help in the form of food/ration would take even longer to reach (if it reached at all).

In Dharavi, where work and industry had come to a standstill because of the lockdown, hunger was all-pervasive. A caller told us how they were surviving on just water and biscuits. He said, *'Kal mere bagal waalo ne sirf tamaatar paani mein ubaal kar khaya. Aap bataiye aisa kab tak chalega?'* (Yesterday, my neighbour boiled some tomatoes in water and just ate that. You tell us how long do we continue this way?). The nodal officer for Mumbai city was responsive to the initial requests for ration from Dharavi, but as the lockdown dragged on and calls from across the city went up, her office, possibly overwhelmed, stopped sending help despite repeated reminders. Our experience with government officers in other parts of Maharashtra (such as Thane, Raigad, Palghar) was not very different.

The overreliance on helplines by the government meant that the onus of arranging for food was shifted unfairly to the people and the state took on the role of a responder instead of a proactive provider. A number of migrant workers who were trying to call the BMC for food support reported in frustration, *'Number har waqt busy aata hai, hum kya karein?'* (The number is always busy, what do we do?). *'Unhone bola hafta dus din lagega ration aane mein, tab tak hum kya khayenge?'* (They said it would take a week to10 days for them to get ration. What will we eat till then?). Even those who quietly weathered the waiting period did not receive any ration. A common lament was: *'Kuch bhi nahin mila hai abhi tak. Woh phone karte hain, naam pata lete hain, par khana koi nahin deta.'* (We haven't received anything till now. They call us, take down our names and addresses, but no one gives us food.)

Many said that the officers didn't speak to them properly or hung up even before they could finish talking. Conscious of the power imbalance between them and the government officers, they would often say, *'Woh humse theek se baat nahin karte. Aap unse baat kariye.*

Woh aapki zaroor sunenge.' (They don't talk to us properly. You speak to them. They will definitely listen to you.)

Then there were other issues. A number of callers complained about the grossly insufficient quantity of food being given; some were only given rice and unground wheat. A migrant worker spoke about how it would cost him money to get the wheat ground into flour, and he wasn't even sure if any flour mill nearby would be open. These hurdles in accessing basic food only served to exacerbate the plight of the already distressed migrant workers.

A couple of days into handling distress calls, it became obvious that we would have to send direct help to the people the government was failing to reach on time, or where the food/ration provided was inadequate. So wherever possible, we started sending financial assistance to enable people to purchase ration, or connected them to individuals or local non-governmental organisations (NGOs) working in their area. While doing so, we were painfully aware that the ration so purchased would only last them a few days, and unless the government stepped in and made long-term arrangements for them, they would soon fall back into a state of deprivation.

Although the PDS had not been universalised in Maharashtra, the state government had passed a Government Resolution (GR) dated 29 March 2020, detailing the urgent measures to be taken by District Collectors and Municipal Commissioners in their respective jurisdictions to arrange for shelter and food for the homeless, displaced and stranded workers during the lockdown.[14] The government was also providing regular updates on social media on the number of migrant workers and persons in need they had reached out to. Still, a considerable number of people were slipping through the cracks because of red tape, lack of information and clarity on how to reach out to the government, poor implementation and a glaring disconnect between the policy-framers and their understanding of the needs of their people.[15]

The Bombay High Court was alerted to the above state of affairs by way of public interest litigation (PIL) petitions. In an order dated 12 May 2020, the Court, while appreciating the policy of the Maharashtra government to provide food grains to persons without ration cards, noted that it suffered from lack of publicity and proper implementation, which was compelling lakhs of migrant workers to travel to their native place by any mode of transport available or even by walking thousands of kilometres.[16] The Court passed certain directions to the state government in this regard, but this intervention came more than a month after the lockdown was first imposed in the state.

Right to Food *with Dignity?*

'Mere schemes without any implementation are of no use. What is important is that the food must reach the hungry,' the Supreme Court had observed in May 2003 in **People's Union of Civil Liberties (PDS Matters) v. Union of India & Ors.**[17] The Court further observed, 'In case of famine, there may be shortage of food, but here the situation is that amongst plenty there is scarcity. Plenty of food is available, but distribution of the same amongst the very poor and the destitute is scarce and non-existent leading to malnutrition, starvation and other related problems.'

17 years later, the situation hadn't improved in the least for the country's most vulnerable people, as they struggled to exercise their right to food in the face of a pandemic, while our godowns overflowed with grains.[18]

In both Delhi and Maharashtra, despite people's requests for dry ration, they were asked to go to their nearest food centre/community kitchen to get cooked food. Workers asked if it was reasonable to expect them to stand in lines for hours and come back with a meal for one, which would be shared by a family of five or six people. A caller told us, *'Hum toh jaise taise roz khichdi kha lete hain, lekin hamare bachche nahin kha paate. Dekhte hi rone lagte hain.'* (We somehow eat the *khichdi* (a dish of rice and lentils) every day but our kids don't like it and start crying at the very sight of it). Cooked meals were often irregular and sometimes the food would get over before their turn came. Even when the cooked food was being distributed a mere 500 metres away, they were scared to step out due to the threat of harassment by the police.[19]

Above all else, people did not want to go to food centres because of the legitimate fear of contracting COVID-19.[20] They wanted to control the hygiene and quality of the food they were consuming and avoid the lines outside such food centres which would make social distancing impossible. It's ironic that the government found nothing perverse or counterintuitive in making millions of its migrant workers and the poor stand in line for hours, twice a day in peak summer, for a small portion of *khichdi,* while shooting off missives asking people to stay at home and practise social-distancing as 'the only way' to combat the virus.[21]

As our callers narrated to us their ordeal of being shunted about from one helpline to another, from one government functionary to another, while they were made to wait endlessly for food, we wondered if we should attribute such behaviour of the government to callousness, incompetence, or just plain contempt for the poor. What court could a migrant worker move against them? What helpline could they call to register their grievance? They would eventually just give up, unless an NGO or a relief worker came to their aid. But isn't making access to food dependent on the goodwill and discretion of other people an assault on one's dignity?

Several women who called us said that they wouldn't have sought our help if it wasn't for their children. An auto-driver in Mumbai, who had reached out to us, was hesitant in going to a food centre every day because of the fear of police harassment. When we asked him if we should send him some money, he said, *'Maangne mein bhi sharm aati hai. Hum log kamaake khaane wale log hain.'* (We are ashamed of asking. We earn our own living).

Caught in the middle of the uncertainty of government help, the irregularity of access to food and the dependence on civil society for aid, the migrant workers started walking back to their home states, some thousands of kilometres away. A migrant worker, who reached his village in Uttar Pradesh after paying 3,500 rupees and spending five days cooped up in a container truck, said that he was only surviving on one meal a day in Mumbai and if he had to die of starvation, he would rather die amidst his own people than alone in the city.

Notes

1 Abi-Habib, M. & Yasir, S. (2020, March 29). 'India's Coronavirus Lockdown Leaves Vast Numbers Stranded and Hungry', *The New York Times*. Accessed 23 November 2020. https://www.nytimes.com/2020/03/29/world/asia/coronavirus-india-migrants.html; Vyas, M. (2020, May 5). 'India has a jobs bloodbath as unemployment rate shoots up to 27.1%', *Business Standard*. Accessed 23 November 2020. https://www.business-standard.com/article/opinion/the-jobs-bloodbath-of-april-2020-120050400524_1.html

2 On May 12, 2020, the Indian Prime Minister announced a special economic package of INR 20 lakh crore called 'Atmanirbhar Bharat Abhiyaan'. On May 14, 2020, Phase-II of this scheme was announced which included food support for migrant workers during May and June in the form of food grains, for which the cost was to be borne by the central government and the state governments were responsible for implementation and distribution.
Government of India. (2020). *Atmanirbhar Bharat Part-2: Poor, including migrants and farmers*. Accessed 26 July 2020. https://

cdnbbsr.s3waas.gov.in/s3850af92f8d9903e7a4e0559a98ecc857/uploads/2020/05/2020051751.pdf.

3 Sharma, S. (2020, May 18). 'Six reasons why the Modi government is singularly responsible for India's worst migrant crisis', *Scroll.in*. Accessed 26 May 2020. https://scroll.in/article/962223/six-reasons-why-the-modi-government-is-singularly-responsible-for-indias-worst-ever-migrant-crisis.

4 Francis Coralie Mullin v. Administrator, UT of Delhi (1981) 1 SCC 608; M/s Shantistar Builders v. Narayan Khimalal Totame & Ors., (1990) 1 SCC 520; Chameli Singh & Ors. v. State of UP & Anr., (1996) 2 SCC 549; People's Union for Civil Liberties (PDS Matters) v. Union of India & Ors., (2013) 2 SCC 688.

5 Health and Family Welfare Department. Order No. F.51/DGHS/PH-IV/COVID-19/2020/prsecyhfw/3064-3163 (2020). New Delhi: Government of National Capital Territory of Delhi. Accessed 25 May 2020. http://health.delhigovt.nic.in/wps/wcm/connect/deaf86804da4c3bb8687f7982ee7a5c7/lock.pdf?MOD=AJPERES&lmod=48689189&CACHEID=deaf86804da4c3bb8687f7982ee7a5c7.

6 Under the National Food Security Act, 2013 (NFSA), less than 40% of the population of Delhi were covered under the Public Distribution System as of July 2020 (71.38 lakh people of the estimated population of 1.93 crores in Delhi). GNCT of Delhi, Department of Food Supplies and Consumer Affairs. (2020). *Highlights*. Accessed 25 July 2020. https://nfs.delhi.gov.in/.

7 Under the NFSA, the Public Distribution System is relied on to distribute food grains at subsidized rates to poor households through fair price shops. The central government, through the Food Corporation of India (FCI), has the responsibility for procurement, storage, transportation and bulk allocation of food grains to the state governments. State governments then identify families, issue ration cards and supervise the functioning of fair price shops. See https://dfpd.gov.in/pd-Introduction.htm.

8 IANS. (2020, April 5). 'Delhi starts "e-coupon" for ration to non-PDS beneficiaries'. *Outlook*. Accessed 25 May 2020. https://www.outlookindia.com/newsscroll/delhi-starts-ecoupon-for-ration-to-nonpds-beneficiaries/1792372.

9 The Right to Food Campaign wrote to the Minister of Consumer Affairs, Food and Public Distribution, urging him to universalise the public distribution system for at least six months.
Newsclick Report. (2020, April 13). 'Make PDS Universal at least for 6 Months to Save People from Hunger, Activists Urge Paswan'. *Newsclick*. Accessed 25 May 2020. https://www.newsclick.in/PDS-Universal-Least-6-Months-Save-People-Hunger-Activists-Urge-Paswan.

10 Delhi Rozi-Roti Adhikar Abhiyan v. Union of India and Ors., Writ Petition (Civil) No. 2161 of 2017, Delhi High Court.

11 Press Trust of India. (2020, July 16). 'Plea to resume e-coupon ration scheme under MMCSY; HC seeks AAP govt stand'. *Outlook*. Accessed 25 July 2020. https://www.outlookindia.com/newsscroll/plea-to-resume-ecoupon-ration-scheme-under-mmcsy-hc-seeks-aap-govt-stand/1896597.

12 As per the information available on the website of the Ministry of Health and Family Welfare (https://www.mohfw.gov.in), as on July 25, 2020, Maharashtra reported 3,57,117 confirmed cases of Covid-19, with 13,132 deaths, the highest in the country.

13 Department of Revenue and Forest, Disaster Management, Relief and Rehabilitation. Notification No. DMU/2020/CR.92/DisM-1 (2020). *COVID-19 – The Epidemic Diseases Act, 1897-Lockdown – Orders*. Mumbai: Government of Maharashtra. Accessed 27 May 2020. https://cdn.s3waas.gov.in/s302522a2b2726fb0a03bb19f2d8d9524d/uploads/2020/03/2020032416.pdf.

14 Department of Revenue and Forest. Government Resolution. (2020). No. DMU/2020/CR.No.92/DISM-1. Mumbai: Government of Maharashtra. Accessed 27 May 2020. https://www.

maharashtra.gov.in/Site/Upload/Government%20Resolutions/Marathi/20200505131558 2019.pdf.

15 Others engaged in relief work in Maharashtra reported a similar experience. In a report dated May 1, 2020, the Stranded Workers Action Network (SWAN), a group of volunteers responding to distress calls from migrant workers across the country, pointed out that *"access to government rations in Maharashtra has been consistently poor"* and that as of April 26, 2020, 96% of the workers who had reached out to them did not have access to government rations. Stranded Workers Action Network. (2020). *32 Days and Counting: COVID-19 Lockdown, Migrant Workers, and the Inadequacy of Welfare Measures in India.* Accessed 27 May 2020. https://covid19socialsecurity.files.wordpress.com/2020/05/32-days-and-counting_swan.pdf.

16 Shri Sanjay s/o Shankarrao Dharmadhikari v. State of Maharashtra & Ors., Public Interest Litigation No. 13 of 2020, Bombay High Court (Nagpur Bench).

17 **People's Union of Civil Liberties (PDS Matters) v. Union of India & Ors.** (2013) 2 SCC 688. In the wake of several deaths by starvation taking place across the country, a petition was filed before the Supreme Court of India, seeking directions for the enforcement of the Famine Code, the immediate release of surplus foodgrains lying in the stocks of the Union of India for drought-affected areas, and requiring the government to frame schemes for scientific and reasonable public distribution of foodgrains. In what came to be known as the 'Right to Food' case, the Supreme Court passed a slew of directions to, among others, facilitate the distribution of foodgrains to vulnerable persons and those below poverty line, and to implement the mid-day meal scheme for children in government schools. While doing so, the Supreme Court expressed deep anguish over the fact that despite plenty of food being available, the same was not reaching the poor and the destitute, leading to malnutrition,

starvation and other related problems. See https://web.archive.org/web/20150722024407/http://www.righttofoodindia.org/orders/sum_may203.html

18 Dreze, J. (2020, April 9). 'Excess stocks of the Food Corporation of India must be released to the poor'. *The Indian Express*. Accessed 27 May 2020. https://indianexpress.com/article/opinion/columns/coronavirus-lockdown-food-for-poor-migrants-mass-exodus-jean-dreze-6353790/; Patel, A. K. (2020, May 30). 'Covid-19 lockdown: Food grains rot as poor battle hunger'. *India Today*. Accessed 25 July 2020. https://www.indiatoday.in/mail-today/story/covid-19-lockdown-food-grains-rot-as-poor-battle-hunger-exclusive-1683559-2020-05-30.

19 Commonwealth Human Rights Initiative. (2020). *CHRI's Compilation of Deaths following Alleged Police Excesses during Covid-19 Lockdown*. Accessed 26 July 2020. https://www.humanrightsinitiative.org/publication/chris-compilation-of-deaths-following-alleged-police-excesses-during-covid-19-lockdown.

20 As on July 23, 2020, Mumbai reported 1,05,829 Covid-19 cases (*see* https://stopcoronavirus.mcgm.gov.in/key-updates), and as on July 25, 2020, Delhi reported 1,28,389 Covid-19 cases(*see* https://www.mohfw.gov.in/). Mumbai and Delhi were two of the worst affected cities in India during this period.

21 India Today Web Desk (2020, March 24). 'National Lockdown: Social Distancing only option to fight coronavirus, says PM Modi'. *India Today*. Accessed 26 May 2020. https://www.indiatoday.in/india/story/national-lockdown-social-distancing-only-option-to-fight-coronavirus-says-pm-modi-1659276-2020-03-24.

5

Filthy toilets, Attacked with Stones

For North East workers from Goa, a 119-hour Nightmare on Rails

NANDITA HAKSAR

A Week before Departure

We do not know when the train from Goa will leave for Manipur. We do not know the date, timing and even the station. Desperately, we are trying to contact friends in Manipur to ensure that the train goes right up to Jiribam in Manipur and does not drop the migrants at Guwahati, which could mean quarantine in Assam, then bus via Nagaland and another quarantine in Nagaland then entry into Manipur and quarantine in Imphal and then by bus to the village where there would be another quarantine.

For the past few days, at the request of friends in Manipur, my husband Sebastian and I have been trying to help migrant workers from the North East who have been stuck in Goa, where we live, because of the lockdown to prevent the spread of COVID-19.[1]

Now, reports in the press about the train to Manipur confuse everyone. No authentic information is available. Even the list of passengers is not complete. Many have registered with the government website in Manipur but not in Goa. There is confusion about where one has to register. Some are not sure whether they will have to pay for the ticket. On the news, there are reports people are being charged for the train tickets.

There is also confusion about whether they should leave or stay. Some, who want to leave, want to sell some of their assets before going. Married couples disagree on the wisdom of leaving; they quarrel over the future of their children.

Thursday, 20 May

The list of 996 persons in Goa who want to leave for Manipur includes Nagas, Kuki, Zomi, Meiteis and Meitei Muslims. No one knew that there were so many people from Manipur in Goa. Here in Goa, as in Manipur, they lived largely separate lives.

It has been rumoured that the train will leave tomorrow from Karmali. They need to know so that they can make arrangements for transport—or will the government provide them with a bus? Everyone has packed and is waiting. The uncertainty feels lethal. Nobody knows what arrangements are being made for food. My husband and I offer to buy water but who will sell us a thousand bottles of water and how do we carry the bottles to the station? Deputy Collector Mamu Hage tells the migrants that food and water have been arranged for. They are reassured. After all, she is from Arunachal Pradesh.

At nine at night, the migrants from Manipur get a message: the Shramik special train is scheduled for tomorrow, Thursday, from Madgaon at 16.00 hours. Arrival is at Sunday at 5 am at Jiribam. It will carry 914 Manipuris and 75 Arunachali. The passengers from

Arunachal will deboard in Guwahati. The rest will be taken to Jiribam in Manipur.

The last paragraph states: 'Request the representatives to give an advisory to carry all the essentials including some food/snacks, water and take other safety measures throughout the three days.'

So food and water are not to be given! Those living in the hostel in Mapusa requisitioned for the North East migrants have no way of buying anything—they have neither the transport to go out and buy provisions nor the money.

Thursday, 21 May

The migrants living in rented rooms in the northern beaches like Calangute make their own arrangements to get to the station. Those at the Mapusa hostel leave in a bus provided by the administration. Most leave without eating anything and arrive by 1 pm at the Madgaon railway station where there will be a lengthy check-in process. This includes registering and a medical examination.

At 3 pm, they are given some fried rice and a bottle of water. They board the train at 4 pm. They will be home after three nights. My husband and I, along with some leaders from the community, heave a collective sigh of relief.

Two hours later we start getting calls: the train has not left. They do not have water to drink. Many are hungry and they do not know why there is a delay. The nightmare has begun.

I phone Puneet Goel, the IAS officer who had helped me when we were looking for shelter for North Eastern migrant workers in Goa. Goel gets back to say the train left a few minutes ago. It had been delayed because some people from Tripura had got left behind. He could not help with the food and water; but the next stop was Bhopal so they would get food and water there. Bhopal seems a long way away but this train is supposed to be super-fast and they are to reach Jiribam on 24 May.

We start getting frantic calls from the train. They have reached Pune but they have not been given any food or water. The train has been stopping every 15 minutes. Everyone is scared that if they stay long in Maharashtra they may catch the deadly virus.

From now on, it is Edwin who is going to be giving us the details of the journey. Edwin says the train has arrived at Chalisgaon. He has no idea where that is. They have been given two bananas and water but no meal. Edwin hands the phone to a railway man on the platform and I talk to him in Hindi and ask why these delays. He says there is a shortage of staff and there is traffic congestion.

Edwin is not too worried because he tells me he is in touch with a fellow Tangkhul and Wormila, an officer in the Railways. He forwards her message: 'I am an officer with Indian Railways so if you all need any help pl feel free to contact me. In case I don't pick up kindly drop a message and I will get back.' I ask Edwin whether we should organise a meal and water but he says no, Wormila has promised to do so. He forwards another of her messages: 'For now IRCTC will provide food at Bhusawal station. Edwin you will have to wait till Bhusawal.' No meal arrived at Bhusawal. Edwin is now getting really worried. Apart not having had a meal, they do not have water and the heat is punishing.

We are getting frantic calls in Goa from friends and family members who have people on the train.

Friday, 22 May

Sebastian and I decide to organise food and water for the migrants on the train. But I do not know the route and I do not have the train number. Edwin sends us a photo of his ticket but it has no number or the stops.

If the next stop is Bhopal, I feel I can tap into old contacts from the time of the Bhopal Gas tragedy and get a meal served. I ask a friend and she says I must first find out the number of the train so they can track it. Sebastian phones Wormila to ask whether she can tell us how we can get the train number. She is obviously harassed but she says she has been doing everything. She doesn't give us the train number.

If we are to get a meal to them at Bhopal, we must hurry. I phone an old trustworthy friend and comrade in Kolkata, Dilipda. He gives me the number of a Fellow of the Ashoka Foundation. The person is in Ahmedabad but he will find a person who will help us. I do a quick Google check to discover that Ashoka is the world's largest network of leading social entrepreneurs. I need to ask Dilipda something but he is not answering. After a little while he rings back. He apologises for not answering but they had been hit by the cyclone and there is no light or water in their home.

The friend in Ahmedabad puts me in touch with Prateek Sharma. He was a banker who had left his lucrative job to help farmers a few years ago. I ask whether he can organise food and water, at least five litres each for 1,000 people on the train that should be arriving in Bhopal the next day. He asks, can I give him the train number. I can't.

He asks for names of the passengers—at least five so he can keep close touch. We finalise the items to be given to the passengers. No one has spoken about who will pay for it all. We are two strangers talking to each other but he does not even ask that question. Sharma informs me that he is actually not in Bhopal but reassures me that the food will reach the train the next morning. Dilipda phones to say I should also contact Ramesh Sharma, a Gandhian activist. But, he too is travelling. I wonder how all these people are travelling in the midst of the lockdown. All the same, Ramesh Sharma is very calm and assures me that he will do all he can.

Since 3 pm on 21 May, the people in the train have had only two litres of water and two bananas. This is now the third day since they left Goa.

Sunday, 23 May

I am woken up at 7 am by Prateek Sharma. He has arrived at Bhopal station with *puris, achaar* and five litres of water for each person on the train but is not being allowed to enter. He has started unloading the truck so he can rush to the train. But now, he has been told that the train will not be stopping at Bhopal but at Habibgunj, which is before Bhopal. He needs to reload and rush to Habibgunj. The train must be delayed or else he will not be able to get the food and water to the passengers. By some miracle, he has discovered the train number: 01650. I phone Ramesh Sharma. He says I should not panic.

Despite his advice, I do panic. I phone another reliable ally, my cousin Sanat Kaul. It was he who had introduced me to the North East when he was posted in the newly created state of Arunachal Pradesh. Sanat says it is just too early to call the Chief Minister's Office but can I send him a message with the train number and details of the problem? Kaul forwards my message to Vineet Narain, the prominent journalist who had exposed the hawala scam in the early 1990s. Narain says he will try to get the message to Piyush Goyal, the Railway Minister.

Edwin announces that the train has arrived at Habibgunj. An hour later, it turns out that Vineet Narain has managed to reach someone in the minister's office. The train was delayed and the Gandhian volunteers, the police and his own friends managed to unload and distribute the food and water. We are all congratulating ourselves but by the evening Edwin calls again to say the bathrooms on the train no longer have any water and the toilets are clogged. The water we had provided is now being used for toilet purposes.

By 9 pm, the train reaches Satna in Madhya Pradesh, where they are given seven *puris* each and a bottle of water but the toilets still have no water. It is already past ten at night. Now Edwin's tone, usually calm, is desperate.

The train is already late by 32 hours.

It is nearly 11 pm when I remember Somi. Somi is Samuel Zimik, retired Additional Chief Security Commissioner and Railway Protection Force. Miraculously, he answers my call. It is a miracle because he is in Ukhrul in Manipur and the town is fast asleep by 8 pm and the connectivity is usually very bad. Somi says he will contact the Railway Protection Force to get the toilets cleaned but we will have to wait till the train reaches Bihar, where he knows the officers currently in service. But the train is still only in Madhya Pradesh.

Sunday, 24 May

The train was scheduled to reach Jiribam at 5 am today but it has only reached Uttar Pradesh.

Edwin has posted a video of the state of the toilet; a passenger from Arunachal Pradesh texts a friend in Goa that she feels she will die on the train.

There is no food or water to drink again. Temperatures are running at 45 degrees. Edwin informs us that officials have said food would be provided at Mughalsarai, now called Deen Dayal Upadhyaya station. The food does not materialise. I post the video of the toilet on a Goa-based WhatsApp group and they start to tweet. I send it to my niece Mahima Kaul, head of Twitter Public policy. She too tweets about the condition of the toilet in train number 01650. The Railways responds and asks her where the train is at the moment.

Should the Railways not know where a train is? We have even supplied the train number. But we soon discover this is a ploy the

Railways is using to distract people from demanding information. They ask you to provide the train number and location but there is no way to track the train because they keep changing the stops.

I phone Somi again. He says Edwin has phoned to say, please do not allow the train to stop in Bihar because people from the North East have been attacked there. Who was attacking the trains and why? I phone Edwin to ask him to please allow Somi to organise a stop at Barauni for food, water and so that the toilets may be cleaned; the Railway Protection Force would be there to look after their security.

By this time, I am also feeling desperate and I again send a message to Vineet Narain and tell him of the situation on the train. I also forward the video of the toilet. He forwards it all to the Minister. It is evening by now. A friend who had been active in this area tells me that the work of *safai karamcharis* has been privatised so there are cleaners only at the junctions and we have to wait for the train to reach Barauni.

At 8.30 pm, I receive a picture forwarded by Edwin of two sharp stones. The train has stopped just outside Barauni and they have been attacked. He has been hit by a stone in the stomach. Everyone else in the train quickly closes their windows, making the situation inside even more unbearable.

I make more calls and within half an hour, Edwin calls to say they are at Barauni station. The toilets are being cleaned; they have been given two big buns, packets of khatta-meetha and the ubiquitous banana. The train moves again but they have not filled water in the bathrooms.

Somi says we must wait till they reach Katihar, where he has spoken to the Railway Protection Force to organise water. It is just two hours away. I go to sleep at 3 am, by which time the train had not reached Katihar. No water in the bathrooms, so once again the drinking water was being used for toilet purposes.

Monday, 25 May

Sebastian wakes me up. Edwin is calling. The train has stopped outside Katihar station and they are being attacked again. He sends videos of shattered glass. I desperately try calling Somi; he is not responding. Who else can I call?

This is when I feel a sudden surge of anger. Why has the Member of Parliament not done anything at all to help these migrants? I send him all the videos and leave him missed calls, but unsurprisingly get no response, either to the messages or the calls. I call a former Member of Parliament from Outer Manipur, Mani Charenamei, who is able to get the present MP, Lorho S. Pfoze, to call me. I know him from the time I was fighting legal cases in Manipur.

I tell the MP of the situation and tell him he should take responsibility and he is a doctor he should....he cuts me short and says I should not get personal. He puts down the phone and writes me a message about how I should behave. I write apologising for even thinking of contacting him and that I was not being personal; I was addressing a representative of the people.

Sebastian's cousin in Ukhrul reaches Somi and tells him of the situation. He calls the Railway Police. Edwin calls to say water is being filled and they have been given something to eat.

I write thank you messages to the journalist Vineet Narain but cannot help wondering that in an era of Swachh Bharat where cleanliness was at the top of the government's agenda, we needed the intervention of the railway minister's office to get toilets cleaned.

I am exhausted. Once they are across the Chicken's Neck, the 22 km corridor that connects the North East region with the rest of India, I feel the local people should take responsibility. Former MP Charenamei agrees to help organise food for the migrants at Siliguri in West Bengal.

He contacts local church leaders and when the migrants reach Siliguri they get hot fried rice, chillies and salad. It is the first proper rice meal they have eaten since they left Goa.

My thoughts are with the Pangals, the Meitei Muslims. It is Eid and I wish I could have somehow acknowledged this.

Tuesday, 26 May

I ask Edwin if he knew who were the people who attacked them in Barauni and Katihar. He said that they were migrants who had been walking home and felt angry at the 'privileged ones' who were travelling by train.

Finally at around 3 pm, Edwin calls to tell me that they have reached Jiribam.

My mobile rings again. It is a man called Angkyajai Mog from Tripura. He says he was supposed to have been on the train that left on 21 May but they were told it would leave on 22 May so they missed the train. Could I help them?

Notes

1 Haskar, N. (2020, May 25). 'Covid-19 lockdown: For North East workers in Goa, a struggle for dignity and dreams of home'. *Scroll.in*. Accessed 19 May 2021. https://scroll.in/article/962761/covid-19-lockdown-for-north-east-workers-in-goa-a-struggle-for-dignity-and-dreams-of-home

6

When Shelter Homes Became 'Prisons' for Migrants

RADHIKA BORDIA

New Delhi: On 25 March 2020, the Indian prime minister Narendra Modi, imposed a strict three-week-long total lockdown, with little warning.

Soon after the lockdown began, the first visuals of thousands of migrants walking, hungry, fatigued, trying to return to their villages gave way to others, as stark, of the surge at the border, fighting for a place on the buses or trains headed home.

Among them were many who had tried before but were caught and sent to live in temporary shelters across Delhi. This is the story of some of them, of the conditions they were forced to live in thanks to a lockdown enforced with haste and a lack of planning which never factored them in. Many of them have only now managed to leave the shelters, but others, mostly from Uttar Pradesh continue to remain there as a fresh set of migrants passing through Delhi joins them.

The SDMC Primary School in Sarai Kale Khan II in Southeast Delhi is located at the end of a narrow lane, just wide enough to let a car in. Since 18 April 2020, the Delhi government has turned it into a 'shelter camp' for migrant labourers and others, the homeless who are the more permanent residents of the streets of Delhi. More than a hundred such school-shelters have been set up across Delhi's 11 districts which at the peak of the crisis housed more than 25,000 people.

Pushpendra from Bulandshahar used to work as a driver at a taxi stand in Delhi. Left with no means to support himself when the lockdown was imposed and his taxi stand shut down, he decided to walk home. 'As I got closer to the Delhi border, I saw hundreds of others walking, some were going to Bihar, I considered myself lucky that I had only a 100 km to go.'

He did not make it; with the central government's order not to allow migrants on the road in force, the police caught him and brought him to the Sarai Kale Khan shelter. He found himself locked in with about a hundred others, some with families and small children. 'None of us were allowed to leave, sometimes not even allowed out for fresh air but no one was able to tell us under what law they were holding us captive [*qaid keeya* was the term he used].'

When he spoke to us on 11 May 2020, days before the lockdown was eased, he had already spent 45 days at the shelter, or as he termed it, a detention centre. He said he couldn't even begin to describe how he had spent these days, 'For 20 years I have put in sweat and toil in the city to ensure my daughter Prachi gets a good education, and that my wife and I are able to build a small home for our family.' A home he found himself unable to return to, under laws that were never explained to him. On 17 May he again left for his village, and this time called back to say that the police had finally let him through; his imprisonment had at last ended.

Imprisonment has been the term I have heard repeatedly over the past two weeks as I accompanied my friend Nidhi Jalan, a health activist who has been distributing supplies at many of the shelters. Like Pushpendra, each one of the 'detainees' of the Sarai Kale Khan shelter had a story of their own.

'For 45 days now, I have been living like a *qaidi* (criminal) for no fault of mine. I beg you to let me go home,' pleaded Nand Ram Ahirwal from Lalitpur in Uttar Pradesh. His wife Leela held on to their four-year-old daughter Radhika as he spoke. The couple was working on a construction site when the lockdown left them without any food. They were picked up by the police close to the Uttar Pradesh border and brought to the school.

'Please take a look at the place where we go to get drinking water and then see the condition of the bathroom next to it,' said Leela before she was rebuked by a policeman who had been hovering around us, ostensibly to ensure we maintain social distancing. 'These people are never satisfied with what they're given, it's in their nature so don't take them seriously,' he told us.

As the policeman walked off, Leela felt confident to talk to us. 'On the rare day when we have a soap to bathe with, we don't have one to wash our clothes, but on most days we have neither. We've lost jobs, we've run out of all our money but the hardest thing is to be stripped of our dignity, to be made to feel like beggars, to be treated like prisoners,' she said before breaking into tears.

At the DAV Senior Secondary School, Jangpura, Komal from Mauranipur in Jhansi said in a voice laced with anguish and anger, 'You think we are poor so we are dirty, why bother giving us soap, toothpaste and shampoo. The truth is we don't have big bathrooms like the ones we build for your homes, but even in the winter we make sure we bathe with cold water.'

It was almost as if she felt the need to remind us that she was human in the face of a lockdown that had sought to strip her, and others like her, of this humanity.

Ironically, when we spoke to the principals, who are in charge of the coordination of their respective centres, they said they were facing a shortage of supplies. One of the principals, candid about the acute shortage, asked us if we could bring soap, sanitisers and milk for the children.

Soap was being treated as a luxury but it was of concern to almost every person we met. Uma Shankar from Pursuri village in Azamgarh, Khaleel Ahmad from Badayun and Virender from Moradabad, echoed each other as they detailed the humiliation they faced each time they asked for an essential item. 'We ran out of bathing soap five days ago; we had just one bar between seven people. When we asked them for more, we were told we should be grateful we're being fed.'

We were joined by Trivendra from Shahjahanapur, who spoke in greater detail about how they were being treated. Each time they tried coming out of the shelter, he said, sometimes just for a breath of fresh air, the police would hit them with *lathis*, ordering them inside. 'This feels like an endless prison term but I'm told I should be grateful as it's for our safety. I'd rather die of a virus than tolerate the abuses I get here.'

The Aam Aadmi Party's work on overhauling the physical structure of these schools has meant that most of the buildings and their roofs and windows, unlike in other states in northern India, are in far better condition. But the conditions inside are a different story. In most places, the quality of the food was poor, and hygiene was a problem.

The situation has been made worse by the attitudes of those with any authority; these include the police deployed in each school, the school's own security personnel and the school staff tasked with managing the shelters.

At the Jangpura Co-Ed primary school, one of the supervisors took us to meet a group of men sitting at the school reception. 'Sit up straight, put your feet together and talk properly,' he told the men.

As he said this, one of the men in the group picked up a *lathi* lying next to a table, held it out and told him, 'Go on, why don't you just beat us like you usually do, show her your usual behaviour.'

On several occasion across schools, the migrants spoke of the ease with which the authorities used the *lathi*. The supervisors denied the occurrence of any violence but added that occasionally the police, or even they themselves, had to use the *lathi* to keep the people 'safe'.

But even more than the physical violence, it was the taunts and abuses they received that had left them shaken them to the core. '*Modiji toh apne aap ko chaiwallah batatey hain, unko toh pata hona chahiye ki ek dum se chai kee dukaan band kar dein toh kya beetegee,*' (Modiji says he worked in a chai shop, he should know what it would be like if a chai shop was shut down suddenly) said Mukesh from Jhansi. He is in his mid-20s, and ran a chai shop at the Patiala House court. His parents worked at a shop nearby. They were walking back to Jhansi after the lockdown was announced when they were caught at the Badarpur border.

Apart from the migrants, the shelters also house others who had been living on the streets of the capital well before the lockdown. Raju Salve, from Mankhurd in Mumbai, had come to Delhi for medical treatment. He eventually ran out of money and had been living for several months under the Nizamuddin flyover. As one of Delhi's 'homeless', Salve was finely attuned to how the hierarchies of poverty were playing out in the shelters, 'There are two types of people here. Most of the people are *mazdoors* (labourers) or even some who were salaried once, and then there are people like myself, *beghar* (homeless). We are used to living off alms, accustomed to taunts, to the *lathi*, of being treated like we were junglees. The other lot are not. So, they are angry and they fight for better treatment. I am grateful to them for that.'

What we saw was commonplace. Others who have been taking relief material to these centres have much the same stories to tell. Avani Gupta, a data scientist, who has formed a small group distributing rations and supplies to those in need, related some of what she had seen: 'At the Sarojini Bharat Ghar, the food was inedible, the *rotis* were like rock, the dal like water, the rice uncooked. The staff was openly abusing the migrants, calling them '*bhookey nangey*' (a description that came up several times). They asked us not to distribute toothpaste as the migrants would eat it up.' One man was so incensed by the treatment he faced that he went on a hunger fast for four days before being shifted to another shelter.

The school-shelters that worked were inevitably the ones with more compassionate staff. For instance, the Peshwa Road School had supervisors who were empathetic and knew the needs of each person there. Similarly, at one school, Ankita, a security personnel, came up to Nidhi, asking us if we could get sanitary napkins for the women. Her one act of kindness mattered a great deal to the women, a reminder that so much that is wrong with these centres has to do with attitudes.

Much of this could easily be remedied with some hands-on intervention by those in power. But none of the departments of the Delhi government were willing to field questions on the shelters. The Delhi Shelter Improvement Board said they are not in charge of the school shelters, only the night shelters. The schools were set up by a notice of the Delhi Disaster Management Authority but its CEO messaged to say that it is the district magistrates who are responsible for the schools in their area.

The Delhi government did make a bid to involve civil society in the running of the camps, but as Indu Prakash, known for his work on homeless shelters and a member of the advisory panel formed by the Delhi government to oversee the centres, said, 'The suddenness and the magnitude of the problem left everyone unprepared; we were short of staff, and were not able to monitor things as closely as we would have liked.'

On 17 May 2020, as the lockdown eased, a large number of those we met were finally able to leave the shelters. This does not mean that the conditions at the shelters no longer matter; a huge number of migrants remained in transit through Delhi and the rush at the borders meant that many of them were still being brought to these shelters. For instance, on 20 May, just at the Kashmere Gate centre alone, 120 people arrived fatigued, hungry and traumatised by their interrupted journey to their villages. If the government does not intervene to improve things, the stories they carry back will be no different from the ones recounted to us.

7

Lockdown and the Urban Poor

ANJALI BHARDWAJ AND AMRITA JOHRI

Rajesh from Bijnor in Uttar Pradesh moved to Delhi in 2002 and lives in Lal Gumbad Camp slum *basti* with his wife, Sushila and two children Deepanshu and Ashwin, aged 8 and 4 respectively. Tucked away behind Sadhna Enclave, one of Delhi's most expensive residential areas, Lal Gumbad Camp is home to about 2,500 residents. The *jhuggis* are located along an open drain and residents rely on one common toilet complex as there are no individual sewage connections. Before the lockdown was imposed, Rajesh worked in a paper mill in Okhla earning Rs 11,000 per month. Of this, nearly a third went towards rent for their *jhuggi* and he sent some money for his elderly mother who lives alone in the village. During the months of the lockdown, he earned nothing. In June 2020, the paper mill owner indicated that he does not require Rajesh to work full-time and offered him Rs 4,000 a month, which he accepted in the absence of any alternative employment opportunity. Meanwhile, Sushila started doing part-time domestic work in a house in the adjoining colony, which pays her Rs 1,500 a month. They have accumulated a debt of

Rs 12,000 in the last three months. Rajesh has not been able to send any money to his mother since the lockdown and has not paid rent. The family has reduced their food intake and even as they struggle to make two ends meet in the city, they live in constant fear of being evicted from their *jhuggi*.

Rajesh is not alone. The devastating impact of the lockdown on the economy has thrown the lives of most unorganised sector workers into turmoil.

The COVID-19 crisis has exposed the underbelly of our development paradigm which has completely dispossessed the working poor who toil to build and run the country's economy. Nearly 70 per cent of Delhi's population works in the unorganised sector and lives in slums or slum-like conditions. Hidden in the crevices of high rise buildings and plush colonies, a majority of the poor live in shanty towns and *bastis*, bereft of basic infrastructure and services. Lack of sewerage facilities, water supply and sanitation, coupled with extremely high population density, make these settlements highly vulnerable to disease and disaster.

According to government estimates, there are more than 10 crore inter-state migrant workers in the country. Often the poorest from the villages migrate to cities like Delhi in search of livelihoods. Not only do they have to fend for family members living with them but also send money home to support those left behind. Despite being the lifeline of the city's economy—working as construction labour, domestic help, drivers, security guards, plumbers, electricians, rickshaw pullers and hawkers—they struggle to earn minimum wages. Most are left out of the porous social security net, since they do not possess the requisite documents to apply for government programmes and schemes. Despite the exclusions and injustices, they work resiliently to sustain themselves and their families with dignity.

The lockdown imposed to combat the COVID-19 pandemic pushed the poor in Delhi over the brink. It meant an instant cessation of all income-generating opportunities and hurled the poor into total destitution. The little savings they had ran out in no time, leaving them unable to afford even two square meals a day. Forced to queue up for hours to get a meagre cooked meal, the working poor endured indignity and hunger thrust upon them by biased and faulty state policy. Lack of social infrastructure in the city, coupled with recurring expenses —the average rental for a *jhuggi* in Delhi is around Rs 3000—made it unviable for most of them to continue living in the city without any proper source of income. Heart-wrenching images of families carrying their young on their backs, walking towards villages hundreds of miles away, bore testimony to their economic fragility. While the plight and struggle of those migrating back to their villages was extensively covered by the media, forcing even the Supreme Court of India to take *suo motu* cognisance of the issue, the challenges faced by those left behind in low-income settlements remained largely invisible and missing from public discourse.

Pallu, a welder living in Delhi's Jagdamba Camp slum, used to share his tiny 10 by 10 feet dwelling with rickshaw pullers, Hansraj and Sri Kishan. The densely populated Jagdamba Camp, home to around 7,000 people, is settled along the *nallah* connected to one of Delhi's main outfall sewers, next to a cremation ground. Over the years, people have built on top of existing *jhuggis*—dwellings precariously going up to three storeys. Pallu and his roommates hail from Azamgarh district of Uttar Pradesh, where they left their families several years ago when they shifted to Delhi in search of work. Pallu used to find work through a network of contractors and managed to earn about Rs 500 a day while Hansraj and Kishan earned Rs 300. All of them sent money home for their families. Hansraj, who supported a large family in the village, including four children, sent Rs 2,000 every month. None of them were covered under the Public Distribution System (PDS) or any other social security scheme of the government. When the lockdown was imposed, they were hurled into absolute destitution and became completely dependent on a local civil society group for the supply of basic rations for their survival. Finding it impossible to get work even after the lockdown was lifted, they have been forced to go back to their villages.

What the working poor in the city needed was immediate income support and measures to ensure food security to tide over the crisis induced by the pandemic. Unfortunately, the economic relief packages announced by the central government in the form of the Pradhan Mantri Gareeb Kalyan Yojana (PMGKY) and the grandiose 20 lakh crore *Atma Nirbhar* scheme, have failed to adequately address the needs of the millions in distress due to the crisis. For instance, as part of the PMGKY, the government provided additional foodgrains for three months to those covered by the PDS under the National Food Security Act. This did nothing to address the food security needs of people like Rajesh, Hansraj and Shri Kishan, who do not possess a ration card and are excluded from the food security net due to complicated identification criteria requiring people to produce multiple documents and mandatory linking with Aadhaar. Further, lack of inter-state portability of ration cards means that even if migrants have ration cards back home, they cannot be used in the state they migrate to.

The Delhi government's policy response of providing foodgrains to those without ration cards also did not take into account the ground realities of the poor. The government set up a mechanism of e-coupons, which required people to possess a smart phone and have access to the internet to upload the necessary documents and photographs. It was only through the intervention of the High Court that physical help-desks were finally set up.

Children in low-income settlements have fared no better. A very large number of Delhi's children are no strangers to hunger. The post-mortem of three sisters aged two, four and eight, who died in East Delhi two years ago, revealed that they succumbed to starvation;

there was zero gram of fat on their little bodies. At a time of a looming food crisis among the poor, instead of augmenting and increasing the provision of food for children, the Delhi government completely stopped the mid-day meals provided in government schools. For many, it was the only proper meal they had in a day.

In their hour of desperate need, the city's poor were let down by the employers and the state alike. Across low-income settlements, people reported not being paid a single paisa during the lockdown by their employers. A survey[1] with about 1,400 residents of slum settlements in Delhi found that 85 per cent earned no wages during the lockdown.

Apart from being a moral obligation, payment of full wages was also mandated through an order issued by the Ministry of Home Affairs (MHA) under the Disaster Management Act. Though criticised for ignoring the plight of the self-employed, it did direct state governments to ensure that all employers—industries, shops and commercial establishments—pay wages to workers without any deduction during the lockdown. Even the inadequate MHA order was flouted by most establishments and the government did nothing to ensure compliance, resulting in workers being left penniless to cope with the crisis. Unfortunately, instead of ensuring that workers get their dues, the Supreme Court, on petitions by companies, diluted the MHA directive. In its interim order, the SC ruled that the issue of wages should be resolved through negotiations between the employers and their employee, completely ignoring the skewed power equation and the economic distress of workers which leaves them no choice but to accept the terms offered. Even the few income support schemes, like the one-time relief of Rs 5,000 announced by the Delhi government for construction workers, eluded most as they did not fulfil eligibility conditions set forth by the state.

Rajjak Hussain, from Dakshin Dinajpur in West Bengal, falls in this category. He and his wife, Jasnoor, migrated to Delhi in search of work leaving behind their two children in the village with his sister. Rajjak earned around Rs 12,000 per month working on construction sites, from which he paid rent and sent money home for the schooling and upkeep of his children. Even before the lockdown, he had been finding it difficult to get work since construction activity was temporarily suspended in Delhi in the winters of 2019 due to high pollution levels. To supplement the household income, his wife had taken up work as a domestic help. Neither earned a single rupee for the duration of the lockdown. Even after the easing of restrictions in the lockdown, Rajjak has been struggling to find work. He is anxious about the welfare of their children for whom they haven't been able to send any money for months. The couple had attempted to apply for a ration card under the Public Distribution System but couldn't afford to pay the bribe demanded. The family is living on the brink like most construction workers in the city, who remain unregistered and bereft of rights and entitlements that accrue to them thanks to the cumbersome registration processes. Registration under the Delhi Building and Other Construction Workers' Welfare Board has to be renewed annually upon payment of an application fee. In addition, a certificate of employment from the employer to show 90 days of work done during the preceding 12 months is required, which is virtually impossible to obtain.

The grim reality that they are left with virtually no money has become a cause for tremendous stress and anxiety among residents of low-income communities. Workers like Rajesh, Pallu and Rajjak are painfully conscious of the fact that with all their savings gone, they have nothing to rely on in case of any sickness or unforeseen expense. The recurring refrain in the narrow lanes of *bastis* is that hunger will kill them before the virus.

The lockdown has fallen like a rock wrecking the lives of the working poor who, in the true spirit of *atma nirbharta,* had created their fragile ecosystem without the least bit of state support. The lives they had built for themselves have been destroyed by blatantly biased policies that have served to protect the haves—those who can afford 'social distancing' in the comfort of their well-equipped homes. The poor have been left to deal with hunger, destitution and mounting debt.

The pandemic has thrown the country into a state of unprecedented chaos. Implementation of a lockdown in a city like Delhi was never going to be anything short of a Herculean task. Lack of proper planning and prompt implementation of requisite relief measures has hurled the national capital into an economic and health abyss.

It is imperative that without unduly worrying about fiscal deficit, employment in public works be guaranteed to people. For those who cannot get work, basic income support must be provided to enable them to survive with dignity. Universal coverage of the Public Distribution System can ensure basic food security for everyone and prevent hunger and starvation. There surely cannot be a better time than this to utilise the stock of nearly 80 million metric tons of foodgrains lying in the godowns of the Food Corporation of India. After all, society cannot abdicate its responsibility towards the vulnerable and destitute in this hour of crisis.

Notes

1 Afridi, F., Dhillon, A. & Roy, S. (2020, May 11). 'Lockdown Survey: 85% of Respondents Among Delhi's Poor Earned Zero Wages From Main Job'. *The Wire*. Accessed 24 May 2021. https://thewire.in/rights/urban-poor-lockdown-phone-survey

8

Falling through the 'Safety Net'

Stories of People with Multiple Vulnerabilities

ABDUL KALAM AZAD AND KAZI SHAROWAR HUSSAIN

On 11 April, one of our young colleagues at the Karwan-e-Mohabbat visited his village in Dhanbanda, in Assam's Barpeta district, to distribute coupons that would enable vulnerable families to buy essential items from grocery stores. To maintain physical distancing and lockdown rules, our colleagues have deployed this strategy across Assam.

The colleague in question went to meet Shajahan Ali at his rented house surrounded by green paddy fields, where he lives with his wife and their 13-year-old daughter. Shajahan wasn't home.

His wife Mafida, who was pregnant at the time, said they had faced a lot of difficulties over the previous week. 'We have no option,' she said. 'I pick green chillies from the fields, dig up garlic, mash them together and eat it with rice. We are barely keeping ourselves alive.'

Shortly after, she gave birth to a son, who died within a week.

No Social Security

Shajahan works as a mason in Barpeta. His income allows him to pay the house rent, pay his daughter's school fees, buy medicines and food for the family. However, the Covid-19 pandemic and the sudden lockdown came as a rude shock. The contractor could not pay his wage for a month due to the lockdown. 'No one can go out on the streets,' said Mafida. 'The police beat people up.'

According to an advisory issued by the Union Minister of State Santosh Kumar Gangwar, Shajahan should have received Rs 1,000 through the Building and Other Construction Workers Welfare Board. In Assam there are an estimated 10 lakh construction workers, of whom approximately 7 per cent are registered with the board.

To avail of the benefits, workers need to send their registration card and bank details to the authorities. Shajahan is not registered with the board. However, Barpeta-based labour rights activist Faruk Ahmed said that many registered construction workers had not been able to avail of the benefits either. Another activist Faruk Khan added that there were more than 50,000 construction workers in the district out of which hardly 1,000 to 15,000 workers had received the money.

Over the years, the Assam Building and Construction Workers Welfare Board has collected a cess of Rs 454 crore and spent only Rs 7 crore on the welfare of workers. News reports allege that the board's top officials siphoned off Rs 121 crore.

A Life of Struggles

Shajahan Ali originally belongs to Dharmapur *Char*, a river island on the Brahmaputra in Southern Barpeta. In Assam, there are more than 2,200 *char* villages, which accommodate nearly 10 per cent of Assam's total population. These are temporary land masses formed out of sand, silt and debris, carried by the flood water and susceptible to erosion in the perennial floods.

Shajahan's parents were prosperous farmers here; they grew rice, jute, pulses and vegetables. He spent part of his childhood herding cattle in the *char*, until his home and 30 *bighas* (around four hectares) of agricultural land were submerged by a flood. This is a common occurrence in the region, affecting millions of people, especially Bengal-origin Assamese Muslims, who hardly get any sympathy from the state's ruling dispensation.

Shajahan's family took shelter in a place nearby from where he was trafficked to Dimapur in Nagaland and engaged in a brick kiln. As a teenager, he worked in the brick kiln and at other hazardous sites as a bonded labourer for five years. He fled to Barpeta 14 years ago, where he became a helper on a construction site. He then started working as a mason, married Mafida and started living in a rented house.

No Place Called Home

On paper, Shajahan's address is still listed as the submerged land in Dharmapur. This includes his name in the National Register of Citizens and the electoral list. However, when he tried to get a ration card on that address, he could not do so.

He has no idea when the submerged land will re-emerge, but continues to pay revenue on it. 'If I don't pay the revenue, the government will take my land rights,' he said to me over the phone. Meanwhile, the government is yet to announce any compensation or protective measures for victims of river bank erosion and other internally displaced persons.

Mafida too is registered as a voter as per her parents' address. She was denied a ration card as well, owing to discrepancies in the photographs. 'We do not have our own ration card,' she said. 'We buy rations throughout the year. If we can buy ration, we eat. If not, we don't eat.' Though she has a bank account and heard that the government will deposit Rs 500, her account is lying dormant. 'I have an account,' she said. 'I couldn't keep it active because I didn't have money to save. So no money has entered my account.'

Mafida also alleged that while others received benefits under the Prime Minister Awas Yojna, Swachh Bharat Mission and flood relief measures, they got nothing. Since Shajahan is only a tenant and cannot vote in the village, the panchayat representative does not pay heed to their challenges. The panchayat has distributed Rs 1,000 among few poor families who do not have ration cards, but they have not been the beneficiaries of this relief effort 'I could have [had] provisions for some days if I were chosen,' she says wistfully.

Counting Down the Days

Amid the lockdown, Mafida gave birth to a baby boy at the Fakhruddin Ali Ahmed Medical College and Hospital. After the birth of their daughter, she had previously given birth to two sons, who had both died within a week of being born. The couple had told the doctor about her history. But they were told that their new-born son was fine and released from the hospital the next day.

However, the baby soon fell ill. '[On the] first two days, the baby was fine. However, from the third day onwards, the baby was crying and [started having seizures].' Due to the lockdown, the couple could not even think of admitting the baby in a hospital. On the fourth day, he died.

Over the phone, Shajahan told us that Mafida is traumatised and ill. He had managed to get her some medicines from the village quack. He said he cannot fathom why such terrible things are happening to his family and how they will survive the lockdown.

9

On Yamuna's Dirty Banks

The Brotherhood of the Dispossessed Gathers in the Only Place they Know as Home

HARSH MANDER

On a scorching summer afternoon in Delhi, amid the second extension of the nationwide lockdown to prevent the COVID-19 spread, I met a group of around 15 men living in a depression on the banks of the river Yamuna. The spot was strategically chosen, as it was hidden from view from the main road. The Hume pipes in which the men were living contained their only belongings—a pair of new clothes, a *gamcha*, a bucket and some vessels to cook and eat in.

Finding food is a challenge every day, they told me: they have no savings and employment is out of the question. But even amidst these hardships, the Hume pipes have become a haven as the police cannot spot them there. They know, from years of experience, that being invisible to the state is their best bet for survival.

Over many decades, a population of 4,000 to 6,000—some of the poorest in the capital—have settled on the western embankment of the river, Yamuna Pushta. In my work with homeless people over two decades, I have learnt that a majority of the men at Pushta have broken bonds with their families. For some, it was the shame of being unable to provide for their families in the village, while others had abusive and alcoholic fathers. Some had abandoned their families, while others had been abandoned at birth. It is a brotherhood of the dispossessed.

The air in Pushta is always laden with smoke from human bodies burning in the adjacent Nigambodh Ghat. They subsist in the crannies of the banks of the now-shrunken feculent river, under the noisy canopies of the river bridge, on the rocky ground under trees, in the shelters that the government has set up after being ordered by the Supreme Court or under the smoggy open sky.

In the summer months, they sleep close to the highway because the vehicle fumes drive away the mosquitoes; sometimes, they are run over by drunken drivers. On winter nights, they sleep in the tin shelters built by the Delhi government on the embankment. Others squat around modest bonfires of twigs to keep warm, or cluster in makeshift video parlours in halls made with plastic sheets and old saris, showing films the whole night, charging a few rupees for a ticket—with companionship, the warmth of the crowded gathering, and a few hours of sleep thrown in free.

Work is hard to come by. They gather at labour *addas* most mornings, offering their services for dirt-cheap wages. The men often work 36-hour stretches at wedding parties, as casual cooks in *dhabas* or daily wagers. Others push carts or pull cycle rickshaws. Still others sort waste.

On days that they find work; they share their earnings with the group of men with whom they live in informal collectives. If work runs out, their last resort is food at the *gurudwaras, dargahs* or temples. A Sikh man, who insists on remaining anonymous, has been visiting each morning for 15 years to feed those who live here.

A month into the countrywide lockdown, this rough informal commune, this brotherhood of the disinherited, is broken. The banks of the Yamuna are deserted for the first time in decades.

Livelihoods Disrupted

Within hours of Prime Minister Narendra Modi's televised announcement on 24 March of the lockdown to slow the spread of the Coronavirus, these men knew that the frail strings that held their lives together had been snapped. With weddings, eateries, wholesale markets, construction and public transport shut down, all pathways to employment were blocked. Their last refuge, the *gurudwaras* and other shrines, were also shut.

By the second day of the lockdown, the number of hungry men in Pushta swelled to over 10,000, as homeless men who earlier lived in smaller clusters and migrant workers stranded in the city converged here. They went hungry for the first few days, until volunteer groups stepped in. These efforts, however, were insufficient to plug the swirling, swelling hunger that rapidly enveloped Pushta.

Men squatted in lines longer than the eye could see, pressed against each other, waiting for hours for someone to arrive and give them food. If word went around—a whisper, a rumour, a shout—that someone had arrived with food, the lines would shatter, as men ran desperately, often falling over each other in near-stampedes.

It took a few days for the state government to organise cooked food, through NGOs, at Pushta. For inscrutable reasons, the government prohibited private charities including the Sikh man earlier mentioned from supplying food in the area. Residents of Pushta learnt that he had shifted his *langar* to Chandni Chowk. Some old-timers risked *lathi* beatings from the police to stealthily make their way to Chandni Chowk each day for this reason.

In Pushta, tempers began to fray because lines for meals were interminable and the men complained testily that the food was monotonous and tasteless. The food sometimes ran out before the lines ended. The heat and overcrowding did not help, nor did the surge of strangers.

In my years of work there, I have known these men to be peaceable, even passive, despite the many profound deprivations and provocations of their hard and bare lives. However, into the third week of the lockdown, something snapped. On 11 April, enraged homeless residents of Pushta set on fire three homeless shelters. Pushta had never known such violence.

Violence Breaks Out

As can be expected, there exist two contrasting versions of what transpired, depending on who you ask. The homeless men I spoke to and my colleagues who work with them report that government had deployed civil defence personnel to police the men as they waited their turn for food. These guards were often rude and disrespectful—roughing up men, hitting them with batons if they found them unruly and shouting abuses—as were some of the shelter organisers.

On 11 April, it is not clear whether food ran out or some men quarrelled about its quality. The civil defence constables beat the men with their batons. Tempers flared and the men fought back. The police was brought in after the scuffle, and they grabbed some men who they believed to be the ringleaders of the discontent. Some of the men ran towards the river and four of them jumped in.

The next afternoon, a decomposed body surfaced from the river. A few homeless men spotted the body, and a restive crowd quickly gathered. Some men said they recognised the body to be of Suraj, a young man from Varanasi in his 20s.

The provoked men spoke of Suraj as their brother and demanded action against the authorities responsible for his death. Acting out of rage, they rushed to the shelters and set them on fire. Smoke billowed high until fire tenders rushed there to quell the conflagration. By then, three homeless shelters had been gutted. No one was harmed, but all the men's belongings were reduced to ashes.

The official version was entirely different. A spokesperson of the Delhi government, Bipin Rai, who has a favourable record of work with homeless people before he joined the government, told reporters of *Asiaville* that many Pushta residents are drug addicts and were experiencing high stress levels since the lockdown was imposed.

'They don't have any earning sources now and the cost of drugs or liquor has shot up due to the lockdown,' Rai said. 'Hence, the addicts cannot afford it,' he added, suggesting that they might have resorted to violence due to their anxiety from substance withdrawal.

Rai also denied the claim that some Pushta residents had jumped into the river or that any dead body was recovered on the banks. 'A dead body was found from the Yamuna near Burari [kilometres away from Kashmere Gate] and rumours spread that the body has been found at Pushta site,' he said.

However, *Asiaville* reports that Rai's claims were contradicted by Delhi Police's Public Relations Officer Anil Mittal, who said, 'Four to five people jumped into the Yamuna River. They came out of the river after a while but one of them didn't return.'

He further added that the body recovered by the residents was sent for a post-mortem. Rai also argued that, 'Even if the body was recovered from the said site and we are to believe that it was one of the homeless people who had jumped in, it is impossible for the body to travel in the opposite direction of the water flow.'

Unwarranted Crackdown

After the fire, the police, wielding their batons, evicted thousands of men from Pushta. Migrants and homeless men from other parts of the city fled to unknown corners of the metropolis. The 4,000-plus original residents of Pushta moved further down the bank.

The government also immediately stopped all food supply at Pushta and police personnel even prevented food charities from operating in the area. There was no moral rationale to punish the entire homeless population for the violence that had occurred, that too without a thorough and unbiased investigation. Moreover, no action was taken against civil defence or NGO personnel involved in the scuffle. Many of us intervened and requested the officials that the provisions must recommence. But three days passed and food supplies were not restored.

The route from the highway to where the thousands of homeless men were now assembled was forcefully blocked by a large police picket. My colleagues discovered a circuitous rear pathway to the banks and organised food for 800 people. The devoted Sikh man also found his way to the men and fed as many as he could. But the numbers were far larger than what any private food charity could cater to. We found the men in despairing hunger. Someone sent in a large clump of overripe bananas and videos circulated of the men falling upon these to quell the craving in their bellies.

As criticism of the state government mounted in some sections of the media, three nights after the fire, a fleet of buses lined up on the highway parallel to the riverbank. The policemen surrounded the men, pushed them into the buses and caned them into submission if they resisted. Only a few escaped. One of the young men I met in the open pipes later said that he had climbed a tree, and stayed there for many hours until the police left.

Confined against Will

The Pushta residents were driven to and dispersed in schools in various corners of the city. At the schools, the men were first checked for fever. One of the men I met at Pushta, from Jalpaiguri district of Bengal, was unfortunate enough to be found with both fever and a cough. He was shifted to a local government hospital, where the hospital staff took his samples for testing. They told him that the test results would be known only after four days. Until then, he would have to stay in the hospital.

He reported to us that in the hospital, two patients were made to share one bed. He was made to lie next to corpses. When COVID-19 patients needed physical handling, people awaiting test results were tasked with touching them, without any protective gear.

Fortunately, at the end of four days, he tested negative. That night, he quietly slipped out of the hospital and walked all the way to Pushta. Here, he met other friends who were hiding in the pipes and joined them. I have no way to verify if the horrors of his experience in the hospital are true. I report what he told me.

The government designated the schools in which these men were housed as shelters, and claimed that the men had been moved there to ensure their safety during the lockdown. The men in the schools saw these not as shelters but jails, where they were confined against their will. The men I met weeks later had escaped from there and stealthily found their way back to Pushta. Some said that officials allowed restive residents to leave after a week of confinement. In Pushta, they hid in pipes and crags and depressions on the river bank, where police patrolling the highway would not see them.

They complained to me about the food served in the school shelters. They were doled half-cooked rice and watery dal twice a day. Many from North India were not rice-eaters. The rest of the day, they could do nothing except lie on their mats. The schools were hot and crowded, and in many there were already several men confined before they were accommodated there. If physical distancing was the aim of the government, the open skies and sprawling confines of the riverbank surely afforded these destitute homeless men far better chances of escaping the contagion than the close human contact inescapable in the school shelters.

However, the main reason the men ran away was that they were desperately lonely, longing for rough-hewn brotherhood and the familiar stretches of the Pushta—unsanitary, inhospitable, strewn with excreta and waste, smoky from the burning corpses of the city's largest cremation ground, and yet the only place in the world that they knew as home.

10

'Her hands may be infected'

Domestic Workers in the World's Strictest Lockdown

MIHIKA CHANCHANI

Twenty days into the strictest lockdown in the world following the COVID 19 pandemic, Manish[1] had been walking up and down the street in one of Bengaluru's extremely affluent areas in search of someone who could help, when I first met him. He approached me tentatively, asking 'kuch kaam hai?' (do you have any work?). He didn't ask for food, nor money. With hardly any entitlements or a safety net to fall back on, he relied on the only thing he could, his labour. And that is precisely what the lockdown took away—work.

When asked what had happened, Manish explained that he and his wife had been living and working as domestic workers at the house of a lawyer in Bengaluru's Abshott Layout for the past month and a half. They had now been laid off.

Originally from Jharkhand's Ghaghra village in Gumla district, Manish had left the village in search of work five years ago. The small patch of land his family owned in Ghaghra wasn't yielding much for many years due to drought conditions and erratic rainfall in the area. Being the sole breadwinner for a family of six, including his wife, elderly mother, younger brother, two sisters and their families, Manish had no option but to migrate to the city in search of work. Before moving to Bengaluru, Manish had been working at the cafeteria of a large private hospital in Hyderabad since 2015, while his wife Rani was in the village. In January 2020, Manish and Rani were able to find work in a home through a 'broker'[2] and move to Bengaluru. This seemed like a better option for them since they could live and work together.

Sitting at the entrance of a nearby building, Manish (21) and Rani (19), recounted their story. Ever since they started cleaning and cooking at the house, harassment of one form or another had been an everyday affair—verbal abuse, insults and slurs. Being routinely overworked, they often had no respite till late hours in the night.

Their experience is not uncommon for the estimated 4 million domestic workers in India, most of whom are women.[3] Even under 'normal' circumstances, stories of exploitation and harassment are rampant but barely make the news. There are widespread reports of domestic workers being underpaid, overworked and abused by their employers. Incidents range from withholding of wages, starvation, not allowing time for sleep or rest, beatings, torture and sexual abuse. They are often asked about their caste and religion when they are looking for work. Whatever be the appearance in public, the middle-class private home remains a den of Brahmanical purity-pollution.

After a month and a half of facing abuse, the last straw for Manish was when his pregnant wife was not being given enough food.

'Aur sab mein seh leta, lekin sabse bura laga jab woh unko accha se khaana nahi detey the.'

(I could bear anything, but the worst was when they wouldn't feed my wife properly), he said indicating towards Rani who was quiet and looked nervous.

Manish told me that he had had an argument with his employers the day before when he demanded more food for Rani. Heated words were exchanged, and he admits that in his anger he said that he didn't want to work at their house any longer and would leave. At this point, his employer shouted, *'Jaao, tu kutta hai aur road par police ki dandi khhayega'* (leave, you are a dog and will get beat up by the police on the road!).

There was no staying after that. They packed their things, were given one month's pay and left to fend for themselves in the midst of a global pandemic. Even though I kept asking her questions, Rani didn't say much. She sat still, looking down at her feet, fiddling with the end of her dupatta. I could only attempt to imagine what she must be going through, pregnant at 19, in an alien city, and now without shelter and with no means of going back home to the village due to the lockdown.

Employing a domestic worker has become very common among India's fast-growing middle class who depend on them for almost all of their household chores. The deep-seated class, caste and gender biases that are embedded in the interactions between employer and workers has only been exacerbated during the lockdown.

Domestic workers from across the country reported that they had not received any pay during the lockdown period putting them in extreme distress,[4] with some reporting that they had been calling former employers 8–10 times a day for their dues.[5] In Noida, Bengaluru and Kolkata, relief workers reported that they have been receiving distress calls from domestic workers who claim their employers are not feeding them. In fact, it is often the employers themselves who have given numbers of relief providers to domestic workers claiming that they could not feed them, even as they continued to work in their homes, so they should make alternative arrangements for food. This included standing in long lines in the sweltering heat to be fed by one of the many relief efforts across different cities. In Jaipur, workers reported facing harassment from their landlords who threatened to evict them, rendering them homeless if rent wasn't paid for the months of lockdown. With employers withholding wages, domestic workers resorted to taking loans from friends, family or local lenders going deeper into debt.[6] The ever-growing Indian middle-class cared little for their own domestic workers, on whom they depend to take care of their own homes.

With the lifting of some restrictions, domestic workers and others re-entered the lives of the middle and upper classes. While the virus and pandemic remain a threat to us all, it has only served to further expose the fault-lines that cleave our society. A major point of concern for many Residents Welfare Associations (RWAs), for instance, revolved around 'allowing' domestic workers, drivers, gardeners, etc., to return to work. The derogatory, discriminatory and apathetic manner in which many gated communities in affluent neighbourhoods placed guidelines for the return of domestic workers clearly demonstrated the class and caste biases at play. Unitech Fresco, residential apartments in Gurgaon, directed residents to accompany domestic workers from the tower lobby to their flats 'so that the maid doesn't touch the lift buttons'. In Gurgaon's DLF colonies a circular to residents claimed that 'all maids, drivers, gardeners, basement laundrymen and car cleaners will have to undergo the basic CBC blood test before starting work as per doctor's advice'. The cost of this would be borne by employers even though it was later clarified by medical professionals that there is no connection between CBC blood tests and the novel Coronavirus. Furthermore, many RWA guidelines restricted work times of all support staff so as to avoid 'spending unnecessary time in common spaces'.[7] Women from Jaipur even reported being forced to bathe and change their clothes in order to be allowed entry into employers' homes.[8] These biases are so deep-rooted and normalised that Kent RO Systems, a popular water purification company, posted an ad on Instagram with the catchphrase 'Are you allowing your maid to knead dough by hand? Her hands may be infected'.[9] Kent later apologised for the ad after much backlash from civil society.

The nationwide lockdown has exposed the deep fault-lines in a system that was already broken. Manish and Rani are one among millions who were going through similar experiences of abuse but are trapped with no place to go. Manish is certain that if not for the lockdown they would have left the job earlier and returned to Jharkhand. Instead, when we met them, he had spent hours walking up and down the street asking anyone who passed by for any help as they hadn't eaten anything all day.

> *'Itni door se aayen hai kaam karne ke liye. Humne socha yaahan aayengey, khushi se kaam karengey, paisa kamayenge. Lekin har din woh hamey chidhate the. Isse behetar hum Jharkhand mein hi rehtey.'*
>
> (We have come from so far to work. We thought we will work happily and earn some money. But they used to harass us every day. We were better off staying in Jharkhand.)

When I asked them if they wanted to pursue legal action against their employers for harassment, Manish declined saying, *'Hum jaisey logon ko kaun sunega'* (Who will listen to people like us?).

This is unsurprising given the lack of coherent legal protections for domestic workers. Few attempts to provide legal protections have failed[10] leaving their work precarious and dependent on the goodness (or not) of their employers.[11] There is no formal register or record maintained by the government that enumerates domestic workers; an absence that is characteristic of our informalised workforce which rendered them even more vulnerable in times of crisis like this.

As I sat with Manish and Rani, a network of volunteers who had come together on Facebook helped in locating a shelter for stranded workers in the outskirts of Bengaluru. About three hours later, a volunteer arrived to pick them up to take them to the shelter where they would be able to stay until travel restrictions were lifted. As they gathered their belongings, just two small backpacks that contained everything they owned, Rani looked at me for the first time since we met. She said, visibly relieved,

> *'Agar hum aapko nahi miltey, pata nahi humara kya hota.'*
>
> (I don't know what would have happened to us if we had not met you.)

The lockdown lasted almost 60 days. When I spoke to Manish and Rani a few days later, their whole demeanour had changed. On a video call, Manish smiled as he told me he was doing well and helping maintain a small community garden, and Rani smiled widely as she helped prepare the evening meal for the other stranded workers staying at the shelter. They seemed like completely different people from the ones I had encountered on the street a few days prior. It struck me, what difference living without constant harassment and fear, with dignity and a sense of community, can make. For those few days, Manish and Rani said they were able to breathe and relax for the first time in months, a luxury that would soon be taken away when they would be allowed to go back to the village to face the many challenges that the lockdown had brought on.

By mid-June, when travel restrictions eased slightly, Manish and Rani, along with thousands of stranded workers across the country, embarked on the somewhat dangerous journey back home in the Shramik Special Trains[12] organised by the government. Upon arriving in Ranchi, they were sent to a government quarantine centre. Manish called me one morning in distress recounting the horrible conditions of the quarantine centre. Heavy rain had caused flooding in the building and the little bedding offered for residents had become damp and unusable. Rani, who was pregnant, was again not being given enough food and faced verbal abuse from officials when she asked for more. Manish recounted that the large room where the residents were supposed to sleep was never cleaned, had rats and that mosquitos were a menace.

By early August, after enduring two months of abusive working conditions and six months of lockdown, they had finally returned home safely. Manish began working as a daily wage labourer earning Rs 250 per day driving a tractor. When I spoke to them again two months later in October, Rani seemed content, back in the village with her family to assist with the pregnancy. She said she felt safe. However, to my surprise, Manish said he was considering returning to Bengaluru after Diwali to work as a domestic worker. When I asked him how he felt about this given his recent experience, he said,

> *'Aur kya karein, gaon ka paisa ghar mein hi khatam ho jata hai. Apne liye kuch nahi bachta. Baccha bhi thodi der me paida hoga, uske liye vapas shehr jakey kamana padhega.'*
>
> (What else can I do, the little money I earn in the village finishes in household expenses. There is nothing left for ourselves. To take care of my child who will come soon I need to go back to the city to earn.)

The cycle continues.... For the thousands of domestic workers who are trapped in abusive employment, facing slurs and discrimination from RWAs of gated communities as they try to go back to work or without work at all, the lockdown has been a microscope from hell, bringing the many challenges they already faced to the fore. The most heart-breaking tragedy of this situation is that years of broken and exploitative systems have left workers without any option but to return to abusive conditions to survive. It is evident from the experiences of domestic workers that class, caste, gender, informality and privilege have shaped how each Indian experiences the pandemic.

Notes

1 Name changed.

2 **Brokers:** Domestic workers are often exploited at the hands of brokers or so-called placement agencies who lure workers from rural areas to cities, promising them a lucrative salary, lifestyle and benefits. A significant number of women migrate from states like Jharkhand, Bihar, Bengal and Orissa in this way. Most come from vulnerable communities, lower caste or ethnic minority communities. As per broad estimates, there are over 800–1000 placement agencies in the capital city of Delhi itself. There is no record of the individual 'brokers' who facilitate jobs for domestic workers.

Placement agencies also take commissions, amounting to Rs 10,000, from employers promising to place skilled workers. Most agencies do not share the information regarding the negotiated wages with the workers. Some adjust a considerable proportion of domestic workers' salaries of the initial months as brokerage expenses, transportation cost, etc. There are many tales of employers who have failed to get the promised placement of workers, and the agents have also become untraceable. Many times, an employer pays the workers' salaries to the agent believing the wages are being paid to the workers, but in actual reality the wages are kept by the agents. This situation clearly poses a 'lose-lose' situation for both workers and employers, yet placement agencies remain firmly embedded in the dynamics of supply and demand because of the highly informal nature of the domestic work sector, which enables this kind of exploitation to go unregulated.

International Labour Organisation, Accessed 24 November 2020, http://www.ilo.org/newdelhi/areasofwork/WCMS_141187/lang--en/index.htm.

3 **Number of Domestic Workers**: According to official sources there are around 4 crore domestic workers in India; however, organisations put the estimate at 50 crores. According to the National Domestic Workers Union, girls and women make up the significant majority of domestic workers. Between 2000 and 2010, women accounted for 75 per cent of the increase in the total number of domestic workers in India. In 2009–10 more than two-thirds of all domestic workers in India were employed in urban areas. National Domestic Workers Union, Accessed 24 November 2020, http://ndwm.org/domestic-workers/.

4 Loiwal, M. (2020, May 5). 'Domestic Workers Go without Salaries, Work during Lockdown'. *India Today*. Accessed 24 November 2020. https://www.indiatoday.in/india/story/domestic-workers-salaries-lockdown-coronavirus-1674475-2020-05-05.

5 Butani, A. (2020, May 29). 'Domestic Helps at Noida Societies Cut off by Employers, Some Forced to Beg'. *The Indian Express*. Accessed 24 November 2020. https://indianexpress.com/article/cities/delhi/domestic-helps-at-noida-societies-cut-off-by-employers-some-forced-to-beg-6432229/

6 Reported by domestic workers from Jaipur during Centre for Equity Studies' webinar series *Conversations with India's Margins-Domestic Workers*, held on 12 September 2020.

7 Dayal, S. (2020, May 20). 'Among Gurgaon RWA rules: "Domestic Helps shouldn't Touch Lift Buttons"'. *The Indian Express*. Accessed 24 November 2020. https://indianexpress.com/article/cities/delhi/

among-gurgaon-rwa-rules-domestic-helps-shouldnt-touch-lift-buttons-6418360/

8 Reported by domestic workers from Jaipur during Centre for Equity Studies' webinar series *Conversations with India's Margins-Domestic Workers*, held on 12 September 2020.

9 The Wire Staff (2020, May 27). 'Kent RO Issues Apology After "Infected" Maid Advert Sparks Social Media Backlash'. *The Wire*. Accessed 24 November 2020. https://thewire.in/labour/kent-ro-advert-social-media)

10 EPW Engage (2018, November 2). 'Where are the Laws to Protect the Rights of Domestic Workers in India?' Accessed 24 November 2020. https://www.epw.in/engage/article/domestic-workers-rights

11 Vishwanth, K (2020, May 27). 'It Is Time to Stop Seeing Domestic Workers as COVID-19 "Carriers"'. *The Wire*. Accessed 24 November 2020. https://thewire.in/labour/covid-19-lockdown-domestic-workers

12 The Wire Staff (2020, May 30). 'Almost 80 Persons Have Died on Board Shramik Special Trains'. *The Wire*. Accessed 24 November 2020. https://thewire.in/government/almost-80-persons-have-died-on-board-shramik-special-trains

11

'Who Cares about Care Workers?'

MADHURIMA MAJUMDER

Some days I am not so sure I will be able to leave this place alive if I keep working. But I can't leave my job, because then I am certain I will be responsible for the death of my patients.

These were the parting words of a head nurse. She works in the COVID-19 ward at a government hospital in Nadia district of West Bengal. Our telephone conversation had started on a very different note. I stated that I was trying to make sense of how the COVID-19 crisis affected care workers. She said she did not have much time as she would have to resume work in a few hours. But nonetheless started categorically listing the details of how the nature of her duty has changed and the protocols that she as a head nurse has to follow. She then told me about how she is privileged enough to leave her children in the care of her husband and in-laws and take up temporary residency in an apartment she owns. She travels by her own car unlike many of the other staff who still have to go live with their families in small spaces and depend on favours to travel to the hospital they work in. If they can manage, how can she even complain? She reserved all her complaints for the long waiting period required to get approval for testing even when someone is showing symptoms. Everyone with fever and cough is being admitted as a suspected COVID-19 patient. This is creating complications in treating other patients. Without much prompting from my end, the conversation went on for nearly an hour. Feeling guilty by now, I apologised for wasting her precious time and wished her well. It is at this point that a distinct note of anxiety replaced her previous calm. She confessed she is disturbed by the disease that has no cure and she is scared for herself and her colleagues. But above all she was scared that the system did not care about them.

Most of the chapters in this book discuss how the pandemic and the subsequent lockdown meant loss of work among different groups of people, in effect making them more vulnerable to the disease. However, the effect it has on health care workers is the opposite. Most of their workload has been increasing exponentially post the lockdown and they have been working round the clock with very few breaks. Needless to say, all care workers run a high risk of getting infected working on the frontlines. Nurses are being forced to work continuous shifts and their leave requests are being turned down. Even when there are visible symptoms, they are not getting tested. As a result, when they fall sick, they either have to exhaust their sick leave or take a loss of pay.

Primary health care staff such as ASHA[1] and Anganwadi workers are in a far more precarious position than nurses and ANMs[2]. Since they are considered 'volunteer workers', they have no access to social security such as health benefits, leave, etc. However, they have been tasked with the vital and mammoth job of conducting door-to-door surveys in the middle of the pandemic that goes a long way in identifying containment zones. They keep a close watch on community spread. They in fact, are the strongest link in India's approach to tackling the pandemic through the method of trace, test and contain. Yet, they have been allotted the 'least-risk' category for protective gear distribution. However, this is just a fraction of the issues that they have to deal with at present. The current crisis has exposed the blatant fault lines that have existed all along in the health care work industry.

Pre-existing Problems

Life even before the lockdown was extremely taxing for health care workers. They have chronically been overburdened due to understaffing. Occupational health risks have always been high for them. A large number of health care workers suffer from back problems and anxiety. Several nurses have reported varicose veins due to long hours of standing and having to lift heavy loads. Many fall sick after being exposed to contagion or harmful chemicals at work. Nurses working on a contract basis are particularly vulnerable to abuse and wage exploitation.

When asked about the biggest problem the workers faced, Yasim, the state leader for ASHA Workers Union in West Bengal said that it was the utter lack of any social security. ASHA workers have no days off and are expected to work 7 days a week. Since they are the primary contact person for health-related issues for their communities, they end up working round the clock. Wednesdays are designated as the day they have to be available for consultation in the respective sub-centre. Yasmin painfully recollects how her husband had died on a Wednesday and they cut her salary for going home. Even when they fall sick due to their job, they get no compensation or leave. The Chief Minister of West Bengal had promised all ASHA workers on COVID-19 duty Rs 10 lakh insurance coverage. However, Yasmin points out that no governmental order has been issued so far to this effect. She quickly added that even if it were to come after the

Union intervenes, it would still not solve their problems. To avail of the insurance, they would have to go through endless bureaucratic hurdles while maintaining their job that does not allow them to have any days off.

Differential Treatment

'I don't think they realise we are humans. We, just like them, can get thirsty and want to sit under a shade.' Rubina[3] (ASHA worker in South 24 Parganas, West Bengal) and her colleagues are made to sit outside the health sub-centre[4] for hours under the unforgiving afternoon summer sun. ASHA workers have to report to the centre on a regular basis. However, when the centre wanted to adopt rules for social distancing, they saw it fit to make the ASHA workers sit outside without making any arrangements for their comfort. Since the lockdown ASHA workers are also discouraged from using the washroom and the water dispenser at the centre. While social distancing is imperative, these rules are nothing less than inhuman, considering Rubina leaves for her fieldwork in the morning and runs out of water before noon.

Rati[5] is a nurse at a government hospital in Delhi and has been working in a COVID-19 ward since March. She will not be able to see her family for the next 30 days. She has to work 12-hour shifts for 15 days at a stretch and then quarantine for another 15 days. The 15-day shift is long and stressful as there are only two of them in a ward. She hardly gets time to sit, drink water or use the toilet. Backache, anxiety and stress migraines are a constant. But this is nothing new. It is her absolute dependence on the hospital for her accommodation, food and transport during duty as well as the quarantine period that bothers her the most. To make matters worse, the food that she gets is of low nutritional value and is delivered to her with no fixed schedule.

She knows from first-hand experience that she is considered dispensable. In the initial days of her COVID-19 duty, nurses and para-medical staff were asked to stay in a special wing inside the hospital that was far from being fit for residence. The bathrooms were unsanitary and the rooms were very crowded with no space for storage. When they demanded transportation, they were carpooled in un-sanitised ambulances. Meanwhile, the Delhi government arranged single rooms for doctors at the five-star Lalit Hotel; doctors were also assigned cars. It took three weeks of agitating for the nurses to get hotel accommodation. However, due to paucity of space in certain cases, double bedrooms are being shared by several nurses. To add insult to injury, people in Rati's neighbourhood avoid making eye contact with her or talking to her even though she gets tested before going home.

Policies don't Talk to their Reality

Governmental plans are oblivious to the realities of care workers despite them being tasked with vital roles. Most health care workers, immaterial of how far they live from their work, have not been provided with transportation facilities. They are being forced to commute at odd hours on deserted roads, sometimes on foot. Polly,[6] a nurse working in a private hospital in Kolkata, often skips her meals. She has been working continuous shifts without any break. This barely leaves her time to cook. Moreover, eateries around the hospitals are shut due to the lockdown.

Rehana[7] works as a nurse under the Municipal Corporation of Delhi. She was assigned the duty of screening COVID-19 patients at the international airport. She was asked to travel all the way to the airport in the middle of the lockdown with just one day's notice. She was assured that food would be provided during her 12-hour shift as the canteens at the airport would remain closed. The next day, however, she was handed a small packet of juice and two dry biscuits. But what disturbed her the most was that when she was relieved from duty and it was time for her to rejoin her usual place of work, she was refused access to the dispensary until she got herself checked for COVID-19. However, due to government orders, all government testing centres refused her the test as she was 'asymptomatic'. As if she were a protagonist in a Kafkaesque plot, she could neither join work nor get tested. Meanwhile, it was noted as 'absence from work'. At a certain point she even feared that she might lose her job. These bizarre and sometimes impossible protocol-based situations make the nurses' already challenging tasks even more risky.

Shoma,[8] an ASHA worker from West Bengal tells us that these days she leaves her house at 7:30 in the morning only to come back at 8 in the night. ASHAs have to visit those in quarantine every day, do a routine check-up of anyone with fever, record their travel history or any pre-existing condition. They have to do these additional duties along with their regular surveys, check-ups and then report to their sub-centres. Shoma's sub-centre is far from her field and she has to walk three kilometres on an empty highway under the scorching sun as there is no public transport. Primary health workers have also not been issued travel passes. This not only affects their ability to do their job but also exposes them to police violence (Prasad, 2020).[9] A blatant governmental oversight? 'No, apathy,' Shoma responds.

Governmental Apathy

When asked about PPE, Yasmin laughed and narrated.

They gave us 4 disposable masks, a pair of gloves and half a bottle of sanitiser in the beginning of March. So I made a shrine of them at home and pray before I leave for my field. Clearly, they don't want us to actually use it. Then they would have given more and better quality PPE. And remember I am a Union leader and have a big mouth. I am sure other workers have not even received this token PPE.

Several health care workers have fallen sick and even lost their lives owing to the lack of PPE.[10] Several nurses in smaller hospitals, especially those who are not posted in COVID-19 wards, still don't have proper PPE. The story gets bleaker when it comes to primary health care workers who are told a dupatta is all they need for their protection. In fact there are YouTube tutorials available on the said subject now. In fact, all health workers, given they interact with a large number of people every day, run a high risk of infection.

The strongest case for government apathy can perhaps be made when it comes to the procurement of PPE. On 31 January 2020, a day after the first COVID-19 case was reported in India, the Directorate General of foreign trade imposed a ban on the export of all medical protective gear. But this was only a temporary measure since the government relaxed the order on 8 February allowing the export of surgical masks and gloves to re-start. This ban was further relaxed on 25 February allowing the export of eight more items. It should be noted that on 25 February, 80,828 people were already infected with COVID-19 and 2,763 deaths had been reported globally. Needless to say, the WHO guideline on 27 February to stockpile on PPE fell on deaf ears (WHO, 2020).[11] India continued to export medical protective equipment as late as 29 March. This would have been understandable if it was done for humanitarian reasons. However, it was not. Rather, the PPE was being sold for profit. What is even more bizarre was that the Minister of Textiles, Smriti Irani, while acknowledging the shortage of PPE insisted on centralising the procurement of PPE through one government-owned company. Despite being contacted by several PPE manufacturers in February, the government did nothing until 21 March. This set our PPE manufacturing capacity back by five weeks. Even without reading too much into the situation, it seems rather counterintuitive (Krishnan, 2020).[12]

In order to mitigate the damages of their erroneous actions, the Ministry of Health and Family Welfare issued a press release by 30

March which said that 11 domestic manufacturers are going to be making PPE kits. Most of them are producing PPE kits to their full capacity. The Ministry of External Affairs has been sourcing PPE kits from other countries. However, this news is far from reassuring for multiple reasons. First, there have been several reports of corruption and low-quality PPE. Second, it is far too inadequate. Third, the safety needs of nurses and primary health workers are often not being prioritised in the usage of these kits.

Invisible Workforce

As the popular narrative heralds them, health care workers are indeed our frontline warriors. Out of all health workers, a sizable section (nearly 30%) consists of nurses and midwives (Rao, 2011).[13] This figure excludes the nearly 1 million primary health workers working through various schemes like the Integrated Child Development Scheme and National Health Mission. Figures 1 and 2 show the division of labour in this sector.

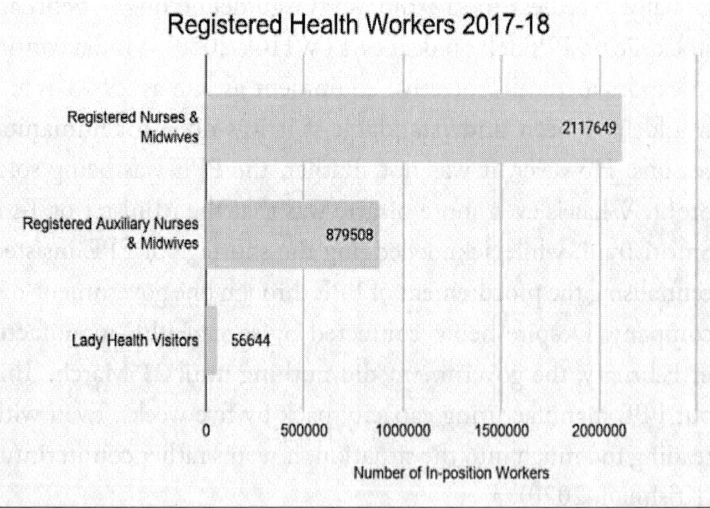

Figure 1 Source: Indian Nursing Council Annual Report, 2017–18

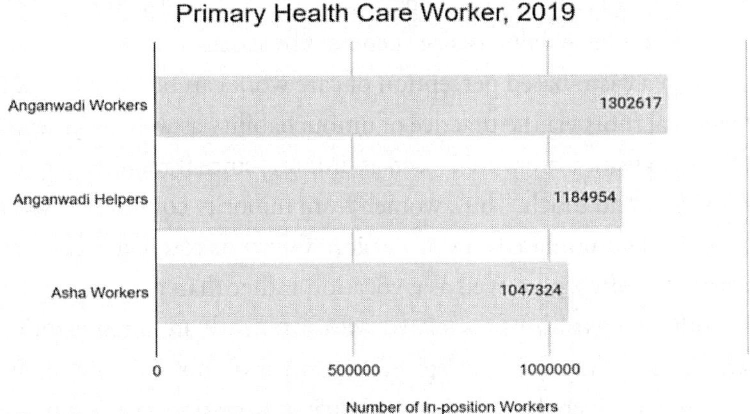

Figure 2 Source: Ministry of Women and Child, Press Release & Ministry of Health and Family Welfare, 2019 Report.

Despite being a sizable portion of the health profession, care workers have been made invisible from the conversations on or by health care professionals. They have either been celebrated as sacrificial heroes or been serenaded with grand but empty gestures of thali beating or petal showering. Very few resources have actually been spent on meaningfully addressing the issues that they face. This is perhaps reflective of the fact that care workers are rarely made part of the decision-making process.

The Baggage of History

Unsurprisingly, India's COVID-19 task force has no representation of care workers. The real reason for this lies in the history of this profession. Care work has been dominated by women globally, perhaps a result of the traditional binary which associates women with care (nursing) and men with cure (doctors). This has led to the devaluation and feminisation of care work. Even though it is intellectually, physically and emotionally demanding, it is perceived as unskilled labour. Within the Indian context, apart from gender, this difference in value is also mediated by caste.

Such a caste-based perception of care work can be traced back to historical roots via the practice of untouchability as well as the legacy of colonialism. Care work is seen as 'impure' since it requires physical proximity and touch. Thus, women from minority communities have historically dominated this profession. Given its roots in missionary work, it is often perceived as a vocation rather than a profession. As a result, the hardships associated with care work are often valorised which takes away from the legitimacy of their claims to labour dignity and rights. Overall, there is an implicit expectation of docility and deference from care workers.

With the rise of global demand for nurses, there has been a moderate increase in women joining the profession from more dominant communities. This coincides with a further widening of wages; however, there is no standardisation of wages across the board. Some nurses make less than Rs 4000 working in private healthcare facilities, whereas the in-hand salary for a staff nurse with a basic GNM degree working in a government hospital located in a tier-1 city would start at Rs 64,000. There have been several protests and legal petitions by nurses, therefore, to standardise wages.

In contrast, ASHA workers get an honorarium of Rs 2000–4000 per month which varies from state to state (Ministry of Health and Family Welfare, 2020).[14] Despite such a meagre salary, the onus to pay for travel and stationery is on them. Anganwadi workers earn between Rs 2,250 and Rs 4,500 and Anganwadi helpers between Rs 1,500 and Rs 2,250 per month (Ministry of Women and Child Development, 2019).[15] They have organised several protests in this regard and were assured of a raise by the government in 2018. However, this promise is yet to materialise; in fact, many have not received their wage for several months during the lockdown. To make matters worse, nursing is categorised among the 'essential services' as per the Essential Services Maintenance Act, 1968. This Act gives the government the power to prohibit strikes in the sectors deemed as essential services.

A Moment of Reckoning

It is important to keep in mind that India's total health care spending was 3.6 per cent of the GDP, out of which public healthcare spending was only at 1.29 per cent for the fiscal year 2020 (Mehra, P. 2020).[16] This is the lowest among the BRICS countries.

Care work was already in a state of crisis before the pandemic as evidenced by several protests to increase and standardise wages. Since the pandemic has clearly demonstrated how central care work is to the functioning of our society, it is imperative that the state invest massively in healthcare, in order to remedy the perilous working conditions and paltry wages of our nurses. It also needs to strengthen the legal framework for Occupational Health and Safety and by extension make PPE a right of health care providers. Additionally, higher investment is also required to increase the health care to worker ratio. Apart from this, care workers should be involved in the decision-making process. After all, the only silver lining to this looming crisis can be the lessons we glean from it for the future. It must be clearly understood that devaluing care work hurts us all.

Notes

1 Accredited Social Health Activist
2 Auxiliary Nurse and Midwife
3 Name has been changed.
4 Health sub-centres are the most peripheral units available at the village level to take care of the health needs of the community. They are equipped to deal with basic maternal and child care, communicable diseases surveillance, health education, checking of births and deaths registration, etc.
5 Name has been changed.

6 Name has been changed.
7 Name has been changed.
8 Name has been changed.
9 Prasad, P. (2020, April 18). 'ASHAs: Fighting a Pandemic with no Protection'. *People's Archive of Rural India (PARI).* Accessed 17 May 2021. https://ruralindiaonline.org/articles/ashas-fighting-a-pandemic-with-no-protection/
10 Personal Protective Equipment
11 World Health Organization. (2020) *Rational use of personal protective equipment for coronavirus disease 2019 (COVID-19).* Accessed 17 May 2021. *https://apps.who.int/iris/bitstream/handle/10665/331215/WHO-2019-nCov-IPCPPE_use-2020.1-eng.pdf?sequence=1&isAllowed=*
12 Krishnan, V. (2020, 22 March) 'India did not stockpile COVID protective equipment for health workers despite clear WHO guidelines', *Caravan*. Accessed 17 May 2021. https://caravanmagazine.in/health/india-did-not-stockpile-covid-protective-equipment-health-workers-despite-clear-who-guidelines
13 Rao, K. D. (2011) *Situation Analysis of the Health Workforce in India.* Public Health Foundation of India. Accessed 17 May 2021. http://uhc-india.org/uploads/SituationAnalysisoftheHealthWorkforceinIndia.pdf
14 Ministry of Health and Family Welfare (2020) *ASHA Workers.* Delhi: Press Information Bureau. https://pib.gov.in/PressReleasePage.aspx?PRID=1606212
15 Ministry of Women and Child Development (2019) *Anganwadi Sevikas.* Delhi: Press Information Bureau. https://pib.gov.in/PressReleasePage.aspx?PRID=1578557
16 Mehra, P. (2020, 08 April) 'India's economy needs big dose of health spending', *Mint*. Accessed 17 May 2021. https://www.livemint.com/news/india/india-s-economy-needs-big-dose-of-health-spending-11586365603651.html

12

Shamsher Ali & Sons

Unpacking the Cumulative Tragedy of the COVID-induced Lockdown

SAZID ALI AND ANIRBAN BHATTACHARYA

The coming generations are going to remember the COVID 19 pandemic of 2019–20 as one that stretched the entire humanity to its brink and brought in its wake untold miseries. Like any crisis, it also split open the existing fissures in our society, of class, caste, community and so on. The depth of a crisis at any given time can only be measured as a cumulative process of several layers of precarity, insecurity and prejudice.

Here we engage in an exercise of peeling these layers for just one Muslim family, that of Shamsher Ali in Kairana, Uttar Pradesh. What we find is that for them, the pandemic and the subsequent lockdown was one of several realities they were exposed to, and each of the other realities had a bearing on their experience of the lockdown.

Footloose Migrants

The town of Kairana, located 100 km north of India's capital, falls within the sugarcane belt of western Uttar Pradesh (UP) which is largely dominated by landed peasantry—Gujjar, Jat, Tyagi and Rajput communities—from among both Hindus and Muslims. Shamsher, however, comes from a caste that is largely landless, economically poor and educationally deprived. Hence, he and his sons, like others in his basti are either engaged in agricultural labour, or are part of the millions on the move doing odd jobs, much like what Jan Breman calls the hunters and gatherers of jobs.[1]

Shamsher's eldest son Afroz is 28 years old and in his nearly 12 years of work life he has already travelled across Maharashtra, Telangana, Andhra Pradesh, Rajasthan, Gujarat and Madhya Pradesh. He has largely been a *feriwala* (street vendor) selling saris and salwar-kameez on foot in villages and small towns, retaining a thin margin over what he has to pay the *thekedar*. When we called in early April, Afroz was stranded at Wardha. He used to earn an average Rs 500–600 per day and had been able to send home about Rs 25,000 in the last four months. He shared a room with five others paying Rs 500 (per head) for rent. He thus had hardly any cash left to sustain himself when suddenly faced with the lockdown. 'For the first seven days or so, a local community elder fed us, but then that too stopped. With no support coming from the government, we had nearly finished even what we had borrowed.... The *thekedar* had promised to send money, but he is not picking up our calls and the landlord has said that we can skip the rent, but we would have to clear the electricity bill,' said Afroz.

The lockdown by then had already been extended beyond the first 21 days. He said, 'Even if the lockdown ends sooner than later, hawkers like me would not have any income for months.' The general customer base for hawkers consists of lower middle class and poor households. 'With no income for weeks, they would be in no position to spend on clothes,' explains Afroz. He added that he was looking at months of nearly no income. Given a chance, he was eager to head home.

He took his chance on the morning of 17 May, the day the third phase of lockdown was scheduled to end. He and one of his fellow *feriwalas* first took a rickshaw to the nearest highway where they joined a stream of migrants all headed home in UP. They were all taken to a camp where they went through a process of registration and medical checkups for COVID-19 clearances. A bus was arranged to take them to the Maharashtra-MP border.

The endless streams of migrants crossing state borders on foot in the course of the lockdown have been reminiscent of the streams of humanity during partition as they travelled with their children and elderly, meagre belongings and even pets. Only this time, the divide was not between nations, but between the rich and the poor. Braving the virus, the summer heat, police brutality, hunger, the endless wait and state apathy, they walked or travelled like cattle huddled into buses or trucks making a mockery of social distancing. The political disputes and bureaucratic insensitivities between states over the crossing of migrant laborers added to their suffering.

Afroz got a bus from the Maharashtra-MP border that took him to Hanumana, Reva (MP) which shares a border with Allahabad district of UP. He felt cheated when he found that instead of taking him close to Agra, as was promised, he had reached the eastern part of UP which was still far from his home. Now they hopped on to a loaded truck that again took 5–6 hours to cover a 50–60 km distance to Allahabad. From Allahabad he was asked to go to Kanpur to catch a bus to Muzaffarnagar. From Kanpur he was sent to Lucknow on yet another bus. At Lucknow he was told that a bus could be arranged only if there were enough people going in the same direction. This took hours to materialise and finally he reached Muzaffarnagar town/

city. The remaining 50 km distance to Kairana, he covered on foot. The whole journey took more than 60 hours. The very next morning after reaching Kairana, Afroz went to the nearby hospital to inform the authorities of his arrival and the doctors asked him to stay in self-isolation for 14 days. However, given the meagre square feet that his residence offers, isolation was out of question.

Amjad, Afroz's younger brother, was in Alwar district of Rajasthan when the lockdown was announced. His work entailed making pillows through the night with the material provided by the *thekedar* and then selling them through the day by going around in the villages. On an average he earned about Rs 300–400 a day. But as the uncertainties of the lockdown became overwhelming, he, along with other work mates, scampered back to the village riding their two-wheelers through the night. 'One of us who was riding his bike with his wife sitting behind dozed off from exhaustion and met with an accident midway,' he said. Nonetheless, they consider themselves lucky to have made it back home. As the mayhem unfolded, hundreds could not make it back alive.

Communal Carnage

The COVID-19 lockdown came too close on the heels of the worst communal violence that the national capital had witnessed in decades. The densest district in the country, home to lakhs of informal workers, NE Delhi burnt for three days leaving 52 people dead, thousands displaced and livelihoods adversely affected for many; one of them was Shamsher's second son, Jamal.

Like Afroz, Jamal too started working at a very young age. Having worked as a *feriwala* like his brothers for many years in Maharashtra and Haryana, he wanted to venture into something a tad more stable. Four years ago, he started working as an apprentice under an *ustaad* in Delhi near Mustafabad. For about two years or more, the arrangement entailed an erratic *kharcha paani* of Rs 1500–2000 a month while he lived with the *ustaad* at his house. After Jamal's marriage, the amount grew to Rs 4000 a month. He was planning a step up to having his own mechanic's garage when the violence broke out in February 2020.

Jamal happened to be in Loni when the violence erupted on 24 February and somehow managed to may his way to the village. 'I heard from my *ustaad* over the phone that while several shops owned by the Muslims were burnt in the vicinity, our garage was spared as a Hindu acquaintance intervened,' said Jamal. Just when he was contemplating his return to Delhi as things calmed a bit, the lockdown was announced. Following that, he had no regular work for months.

When we spoke to him in May, the ustaad had called him back to work and he was contemplating returning to Delhi right after Eid. The *jhagda* (violence in NE Delhi) and the subsequent lockdown had meant that he had exhausted all his savings and was left in debt. His dream of having a garage of his own, therefore, has been postponed indefinitely.

Exposed to Hate that is Viral

The nature of their work, as *feriwalas*, exposes these hawkers to a range of threats and vulnerabilities. Hatred for Muslims has become more rampant in recent years, said Afroz. 'Earlier people used to feed us when we went on our rounds as salesmen, but now people don't even offer us water,' he said. In Burhanpur (MP) about a year and a half back, he recalled how he was stopped in his tracks while he was hawking and was threatened for having a Muslim name. A Hindu woman intervened and asked him to scoot. On another occasion a woman asked him to leave the moment she came to know his name. 'Leave before my husband comes home,' she said. Months back in

Nagpur, he was charged Rs 500 for a Rs 20 auto-ride and when he protested, the driver said, *'Yeh tum logon ka area nahi hai'* (This is not *your* area). Afroz protested, but when the driver threatened to gather people, he thought it best to pay up. *'Kaam ke liye ghumna toh padhta hai, lekin aajkal dar lagta hai,'* he said (We have to move around given our kind of work, but these days fear follows us). Amjad, the brother who worked in Rajasthan, said that the viral videos of lynching had led to a deep-seated fear (*ghabrahat*) in his mind. There was an occasion when he even had to hide his name in apprehension.

'Feri to feri hoti hai, koe bhi kuch bhi bol deta hai. Ye jo mahol hai, agar daadi hai, topi hai to dar ki bhavna rahti hai,' said their father, Shamsher, who has also been a *feriwala* for many years. (In this line of work anyone ends up telling us anything they please. In the situation today, if one has a skull cap or has a beard, one has to live with fear.)

After trying his hands on a range of odd jobs amidst the lockdown in Kairana, Jamal had no option left but to take to street-vending selling children's diapers. Sales were, however, lower than in other times. He would leave at 4 am in the morning, buy the stock and roam through 4–6 villages selling it. During the second week, he was confronted by a few locals in a Hindu area. The virulent communalisation of the pandemic in the media after several attendees in a Tablighi Jamaat event in Delhi were found COVID-positive,[2] had led to an atmosphere where Muslims in general were viewed as contagion. The TV and social media had popularised the terms 'corona jihad' and 'super-spreaders'. Jamal was forced to reveal his religion to the men who surrounded him. They said '*Tum logon ke chalte virus phail raha hai*' (It is because of *your kind* that the virus is spreading). He was strictly asked not to come near Hindu areas. Since this incident, he would only go to sell his stock in Muslim areas, but this naturally meant even lower sales than before and far lower income.

Slowing Economy, Surplus Labour and Shrinking Pay in Villages

The lockdown has led to a sudden increase in the reserve pool of labourers desperately looking for work, any work. This has drastically depressed the already low wages in the agrarian economy of villages- and small towns, adding to the woes of the distressed. Jamal and Amjad are both looking for work in their village. Under the lockdown, since there were such few options, one among them went to work in local Gujjars' fields for the Ravi harvest. But they found no work for the longest time as there were too many hands and too little pay. Their neighbours, who had been working in the fields earlier, were, in fact, asked to leave as the owner found cheaper labour because of increased supply. This is an aspect of exploitation that is defined more by land, power and caste than by religion per se, as Gujjar landowners, Hindus and Muslims alike, are making use of cheaper hands.

As Shamsher's family ran out of cash and the grain received under the PDS depleted, his youngest son Ramzan, who had just appeared for his senior secondary education, had to go around in search of work as well. First, he went to a nearby brick kiln where after a lot of pleading he managed to get some work for 3–4 days. Since the work was laborious, he and his brother Jamal worked in shifts for a single person's wage: a meagre Rs 300 per day for nearly 10 hours of hard labour. Before lockdown the rate used to be at least Rs 450. When we spoke last in May 2020, Ramzan had been working in the fields with his father for a few days and also in construction sites (*chinaai ka kaam*) with his brothers, both at slashed wage rates.

Ramzan took his board examinations on 29 February 2020. But the future seems uncertain. '*Padhaai shayad nahi ho paaygi,*' he said (Don't think education is on the cards for me). 'Have to earn now.' He had planned to go to Delhi and live with his brother Jamal once the latter had his own garage. Ramzan wanted to help Jamal in his work and also do '*taiyaari*' (preparation)on the side for a government job. He wanted a '*belt ki naukri*', a policeman's job. But now all of that suddenly seems like a distant possibility.

Uprooted Survivors of Communal Violence

This brings us to their other cardinal reality. The whole family is now housed in a congested basti in Kairana. The basti was set up to house those displaced in the Muzaffarnagar violence in 2013.

Most of those inhabiting this basti are poor, uprooted people who largely belong to the lower strata, i.e., Teli, Darzi, Dhobi, Naai, Ansari and Sheikh Sarvari in the Muslim community. Most of them work in the informal sector—as agricultural labourers, construction workers, mechanics or *feriwalas*. A large proportion of them are migrants like Amjad, Jamal and Afroz.

'We lived in that village for generations,' said Shamsher, 'I spent my childhood there. But no one stopped the looting. No one even asked us to stay back.' His wife even had a small sewing enterprise in the village. He had put his life's savings to build a house of his own in the village just four years before the communal violence. And in one stroke, they were uprooted from a 900 square feet house to two 50 square feet *kamras* in a shelter. Like many others when the 2013 violence hit villages, he had no option but to undertake a distress sale of his house at less than half its market price.

So, whatever follows in their present, can never be fully fathomed without due acknowledgment of this past reality of displacement, betrayal and impoverishment.

A Cumulative Tragedy

The economic slump India witnessed again in the second quarter of the year (July–September 2020) has now officially been recognised as a recession. The cheers around a reduced percentile of shrinkage or a marginal value addition in certain sectors (like manufacturing), one must not forget, has been achieved 'not by selling more, but by ruthlessly getting rid of employees'.[3] This will only add to the already alarming rate of joblessness the country is witnessing, and will make the situation even more dire by further dwindling demand.

Recalling Afroz's anxiety, there is still no hope of a demand-induced recovery, given the reduced purchasing power, particularly for non-essentials. In his instance, the clothes he used to ferry. Private consumption expenditure, the biggest driver of GDP, continued to shrink in the second quarter of 2020 'reflecting both consumer wariness to spend amid the pandemic and the impact of lost jobs and reduced incomes'.[4] These are outcomes, not of the virus per se, but the absolute mindlessness in the way the government chose to respond to it: by imposing the strictest lockdown in the world, that was not just scientifically unsound, but also apathetic to the miseries it would unleash on the unprotected, informal and migrant workforce. The effects and aftershocks of this crisis are more than likely to linger for much longer, perhaps even having intergenerational consequences, despite all exhortations by the government to 'move on' or attempts to distract. With regard to the latter, of course, the best means of distraction it has is of using the time-tested tool of communal polarisation.

What sailed with the vicious propaganda of 'Corona Jihad' in March-April reached the shores of the bogey of 'Love Jihad' by the end of 2020. In between there has been the criminalisation, media trials and arrests of equal citizenship protestors (largely Muslim youth) after being falsely accused for the February violence in Delhi. Not to forget the *bhumipujan* at Ayodhya in the middle of the raging pandemic.

So, while the pandemic and the heavy-handed lockdown spelt doom for millions, the socio-economic trajectory of a community, the history of communal prejudice and the political climate all combine to create a crisis which was akin to a cumulative tragedy with several overlapping layers of vulnerability.

In the first half of the year, there were several incidents across UP of Tablighi Jamaat members being picked up by the police after tracing their links to the Tablighi Jamaat Markaz incident in Delhi.[5] Given that there was surplus labour in the rural economy, COVID-19 added another layer to the already communalised space. For instance, in a nearby village, Muslim men were asked by Hindu landowners to first go get their COVID-19 test done before working in their field. Hate has been harnessed to exclude the Muslims from already scarce opportunities of work. Simultaneously the countryside seems to be rife with rumours in the wake of the communalisation of the virus, so much so that Amjad had to stay up for three consecutive nights keeping vigil apprehending attacks.

Displacement, insecure jobs, hard labour, circular migration, hate, fear, violence all come together to inform the extent of the vulnerability of a family under lockdown. Their fate also demonstrates how communalism further pushes the minority to the margins of an economy affecting their livelihood, education and social mobility. In any case a much larger share of Muslims (50%) are in self-employment than Hindus (32.9%), while their share in regular wage earning is abysmally low (27.7%) as compared to Hindus (43.9%) in urban areas.[6] The repeated and relentless jolts of violence in Muzaffarnagar, lynching, CAA, NRC, the violence in NE Delhi and the hate being brewed in the name of 'Corona Jihad' in the middle of the lockdown has further added to their woes.

Notes

1 Breman, J. (1994). *Wage Hunters and Gatherers: Search for Work in the Urban and Rural Economy of South Gujarat*. Delhi: Oxford University Press.

2 The Mumbai High Court in October acquitted all foreign nationals belonging to the Tablighi Jamaat saying there was not an iota of evidence against them. 'A political government tries to find a scapegoat when there is pandemic or calamity and the circumstances show that there is probability that these foreigners were chosen to make them scapegoats,' the Aurangabad bench of the Bombay high court observed.
The Wire Staff. (2020, October 20) '"No Iota of Evidence": Mumbai Court Acquits 20 Foreign Tablighi Jamaat Members'. *The Wire*. Accessed 17 May 2021. https://thewire.in/law/tablighi-jamaat-foreigners-mumbai-court-acquits-20-covid-19-coronavirus

3 Misra, U. (2020, December 1). 'Five Main Takeaways from India's Q2 GDP Data'. *The Indian Express*. Accessed 17 May 2021. https://indianexpress.com/article/explained/india-q2-july-september-gdp-takeaways-economy-7073526/

4 *The Hindu*. (2020, November 30). 'Historic Recession: On India's GDP slump'. Accessed 17 May 2021. https://www.thehindu.com/opinion/editorial/historic-recession-the-hindu-editorial-on-indias-gdp-slump/article33207269.ece

5 Press Trust of India. (2020, May 4). 'Muzaffarnagar: 15 Tablighi Jamaat Members sent to 14-day Judicial Custody'. *The Economic Times*. Accessed 17 May 2021. https://economictimes.indiatimes.com/news/politics-and-nation/muzaffarnagar-15-tablighi-jamaat-members-sent-to-14-day-judicial-custody/articleshow/75534015.cms?utm_source=contentofinterest&utm_medium=text&utm_campaign=cppst

6 Ministry of Statistics and Programme Implementation, National Sample Survey Office (2016). *Employment and Unemployment Situation Among Major Religious Groups in India NSS 68th Round (JULY 2011 – JUNE 2012)*. New Delhi: Government of India. Retrieved from http://mospi.nic.in/sites/default/files/publication_reports/nss_report_568_19feb16.pdf

13

Locked Down in a Country Not One's Own

The Rohingyas at Nuh

AMITANSHU VERMA

'*Burma mein humnein apne haathon se zakat diya haai, aur yahan khaane peene ke liye majboor ho gaye* (In Burma, we used to distribute alms as zakat, and here we are unable to manage food for ourselves),' says Noorullah,[1] barely concealing the dismay in his voice as we talk over the phone.

Not expecting a sudden rush of nostalgia, I am taken by surprise. After all we had barely begun talking. Two complete strangers distanced by lockdown discussing life in the refugee camps during the pandemic.

'*Burma mein khetibaadi tha bohot achchi tarah zindagi guzaar kar aaye hain. Sab kuch chala gaya*' (We owned land in Burma that used to yield a decent income. We were content and comfortable in our lives till we lost everything). Noorullah remembers a good life in Myanmar before persecution by the Buddhist majority state forced millions of minority Rohingya Muslims to flee the country. He was saved from getting caught in the deteriorating situation in Myanmar as he had already moved to India in 2009 to study at a madrasa, an Islamic school, in Muzaffarnagar.

Rohingya communities have been settled in camps in Haryana, Jammu, Delhi, Rajasthan, Hyderabad and Tamil Nadu. There are approximately 14,000 registered Rohingya refugees in India according to the United Nations High Commission for Refugees (UNHCR), although some estimates put the actual number at 40,000. The UNHCR has issued registration cards to refugees and attempts to look after their interests. This is only a small portion of millions of Rohingya refugees settled in West and South East Asia. Most of them have been sheltered by Bangladesh. Noorullah's relatives are scattered in Bangladesh and Myanmar.

With no citizenship and rights, the Rohingyas in India are also daunted by a global scenario where Muslim refugees are unwelcome in most countries, including India. In India, they often find themselves as targets of vilification by politicians and the media. Members of the ruling Bharatiya Janta Party (BJP) have regularly threatened the Rohingya refugee population with violence and deportation, labelling them a threat to national security. Social media has been rife with accusations of cannibalism, prostitution and murder against Rohingyas. In October 2018, seven Rohingya refugees were deported to Myanmar by the Indian government, drawing widespread condemnation.[2]

In India, the Rohingya community in India remains perpetually anxious about its future, and has not dared to voice minimum demands about their living conditions. Life for them is a lonely struggle to secure bare essentials like food, clothes, water and a roof over one's head. Stigmatised, marginalised and allowed to fall through the cracks of our apathy, their lives are a struggle even in regular times. Unsurprisingly, the lockdown has pushed them further into distress and despair.

Noorullah voiced this resignation when he said, *Hum kya maang sakte hain, agar insaniyat ke naate de dein toh bahut meherbaani hogi*' (How can we ask for anything, we can only be grateful if they provide us something out of humanitarian concern).

Since the interview was facilitated by members of Karwan-e-Mohabbat who had supplied ration to the refugee camps, I expected Noorullah to talk about the lockdown-induced hunger.

'The initial days of the lockdown were tough and we were worried about how we would manage. But gradually with the help of friendly neighbours and NGOs who distributed food and rations in the camps we were able to survive and at least for now hunger is taken care of,' Noorullah tried to assure me.

I asked whether the United Nations had provided any relief to the refugee settlements. Noorullah responded that twice during the lockdown food aid had been sent by the UN which comprised 10 kg packets of rice and flour for every family. There had been no help from the government, he iterated. In the refugee camp, Shahpur Nagli 1, where Noorullah resides, there are approximately 78 more families. This is only one of the seven refugee camps in Nuh district, formerly known as Mewat. There are more than 1,500 refugees, locally known as *Burma waale,* in these camps. The United Nations-affiliated NGO Action Aid as well as several others have been involved in distributing rations to the refugee population here. With no arrangement by the government for providing food to the refugee population, the camps are in the throes of intense apprehension and uncertainty.

Cutting short the conversation on hunger Noorullah points out, 'The real difficulty right now is of water.'

'*Yahan koi intezaam nahi hai, na sarkaar ki taraf se aur na koi hand pump hai yahan*' (There is no arrangement of water here, nothing from the government, no hand pump).

Explaining further he says, 'We have a big *hauz* [tank] in our camp to store water. We would collect *chanda* [donation] from everyone and buy water to fill that *hauz.* With the lockdown all of us have lost work, our savings are over and we can no longer buy water.'

'The *hauz,'* he says 'was built by funding from Delhi-based NGOs.'

'What work do people at the refugee camp do otherwise?' I ask.

'All sorts of work. Most men do *beldari* [manual labour] work,' he says.

'A majority of men,' he says, 'work as daily wagers at construction sites and factories in Nuh and neighbourhood districts of Delhi and Panipat. A lot of men also work as builders of bamboo structures. They build huts and other structures out of bamboo for roadside eateries, shops and resorts, and are acknowledged for their expertise.'

With no entitlements to speak of, the Rohingyas had only their hard labour to depend on for their living. The acute shortage of food and water affecting the refugee camps was engendered mainly because the Rohingya had lost work owing to the sudden lockdown. When their savings ran out there was no way to procure either food or water. As non-citizens they are not entitled to food aid provided by the Indian government. The centre as well as the states have issued several orders, since the lockdown was enforced, to the effect that no person should go hungry or without shelter during the period of the national quarantine. Such orders, it turns out, are not intended for the relief of refugees. The lockdown has left the refugee settlements entirely dependent on NGOs and community organisations.

And then he adds, '*Ab toh sab ghar par baithe hain*' (now they are all sitting at home whiling away their time).

'What about your family? How are they coping with the lockdown?' I ask.

'What about them? They are all whiling away their time at home. Playing all the time. Schools are shut, I fear my children will lose an academic year,' says Noorullah, a father of three.

'The madrasas too have been shut.' Being an *ustad* [teacher] at the local madrasa this issue is close to his heart.

'None of us have been paid for months,' he says.

Education is a tricky affair for the refugee children, as I learn from the interviews. Noorullah teaches at a madrasa which attracts students from Delhi, Faridabad and Mathura apart from the local *Burma waale* students. With a mix of Indian and Rohingya instructors, the institution imparts training in Hindi, Urdu, Arabic, Religion and Computers. Although the madrasa remains closed in lockdown times, the state of education for the refugees remains uncertain even during 'normal' times. As foreigners, Rohingya kids are not permitted to enrol or take exams in government schools, though they are allowed to attend classes. Noorullah is part of a team of seven *ustads* who teach at the local madrasa, which is run on collections received from the refugee community and donations from others. The lockdown deepened the financial troubles for the school. Noorullah and other teachers, who are paid Rs 6000 a month, had not been paid for three months at the time of our meeting. Being the only wage earner in his family, with a wife and three children, Noorullah found himself under additional stress. His eldest son, aged 6, is one of the very few children from the refugee settlement who study at a nearby private school, as a result of the intervention of Delhi-based activists. Although a little better off than his fellow residents who were daily wagers, after the prolonged lockdown, Noorullah found himself in the same boat as them. 'If my children don't get educated they will suffer the same fate as us,' says a visibly worried Noorullah, voicing the anxiety of most families at the camp.

Noorullah was pained about another section of the refugee community. 'The widows and their children are having the worst of it. Women in our community do not work. We used to support our widows collectively, but now everyone has run out of money.'

'If possible try and arrange clothes for them and their children, after all Eid is around the corner,' he requests me as our interview comes to a close.

The situation is far worse in the Rohingya refugee settlement at Punhana block which is 40 km from Nuh city headquarters. Azhar,[3] a teacher at the local madrasa which he helped establish after they set up camp there in 2016, tells us, '*Pados mein jo mewati saathi hain humara haalat dekh kar aata tel aur chawal de dete hain*' (The Mewati people in the neighbourhood provide us with flour, rice and oil considering our impoverished situation). Owing to its far-off location from the city centre, the Punhana settlement does not receive as much attention from NGOs as the camps at Nuh city headquarters. An NGO provided 10 kg of rice and wheat twice during the hard lockdown months. But those supplies proved insufficient and the refugee families have had to rely on the goodwill of local Mewatis.

The prospects of finding work at Punhana, Azhar told me, were better than at Nuh, largely owing to the fact that there were only 28 families at the refugee camp here, while Nuh city block had several camps with hundreds of families, which made it a far more competitive place. Everyone at the camp was looking forward to the time when lockdown would be lifted and they would be able to earn their daily bread.

'Eid is coming but how can we think about getting new clothes, we are barely managing rations,' said Azhar, echoing the concerns which I had encountered in my interaction with Noorullah.

As a *hafiz,* Azhar is a religious instructor at the local madrasa. His earnings support a family of seven comprising his wife and five children, all of whom are very young with the eldest being seven years of age. It is their future which worries him the most. He said that they did not get to study properly. Here too, the Rohingya children are allowed to attend school but cannot enrol or take examinations. Azhar bemoans that the instructor who taught Hindi and Urdu at the local madrasa left because he was not paid his salary. A better future for his children requires proper arrangements for their education now.

Unlike other camps, which are exclusively inhabited by the refugees, the Punhana settlement has a mixed population. The refugees built their dwellings wherever the plot was available in between the houses of locals.

'*Hum toh yahan khauf se reh raha hai*' (we live here in fear), says Azhar referring to the fact that they are often asked by the landowners to vacate the land.

He says that the UN ought to make permanent arrangements for them.

'*Humein pahad ya kahin aur jagah de do*' (Give us some land even in the mountains), says Azhar, underscoring the significance of possessing a plot of land of one's own and the peace of mind it enables.

I also asked how he and other refugees took the constant vilification campaigns against them in the Indian media and whether they faced hostility at the local level owing to such propaganda. Azhar replied that at the local level they shared extremely cordial relations with Indians, often offering *namaaz* together and holding *daawats* (community dinners). In addition, Azhar said that they exhorted everyone in the camp to follow the rules of the country.

During the lockdown, the refugee population was asked by the administration to not venture out. Being non-citizens and dependent on the 'goodwill' of locals and 'kindness' of the government, the refugees felt obliged to follow what they had been told and maintain good relations with everyone. Azhar is emphatic that his Indian neighbours liked the refugees, and that he exhorts people of his community to be polite to the locals.

The Labouring Refugee

The Indian government, by its own admission, sees the Rohingya population as 'illegal immigrants' regardless of their registration by UNHCR, and thus offers no protection or rights to them.[4] Thus, thousands of Rohingya refugees in India have been made dependent on charity extended by individuals and NGOs during the lockdown. In contrast to the image of the 'illegal infiltrator' who is a drain on national resources which is often conjured by the politician and his media, what one comes across is a figure of the 'refugee labour' willing to sell her services at minimum remuneration, unprotected by labour laws and the police, entirely at the mercy of her employers and compelled to have cordial relations with everyone around. In my interactions over the phone with Noorullah, Azhar and several others, it became fairly evident that neither did the government make any arrangements for rations, nor did the Rohingyas expect anything from it. Instead, one came across statements from Noorullah and Azhar like '*Hum log bahar se hain, humein sambhal kar rehna chahiye*' (We are outsiders we should stay cautious) and '*Madad se pet nahi bharta hai, apne haath se kaam karna padega*'– (Charity cannot fill our stomachs forever, we will have work ourselves).

Far from the myth of a 'security threat' that drains national resources and despite the apathy of the government, the Rohingya refugees in India are attempting to build their lives as well as contribute to the local community by building educational institutions like madrasas. As labourers they are contributing to the local economy and infrastructure development. Even the land where the camps have been set up is of uncertain status with leases having expired and no clarification from the government. In contrast to the migrant labour though, whose heartrending stories of hunger and hardship filled the lockdown days, the fact that the Rohingya refugees had places to stay saved them from extreme suffering. Fortunately, despite no medical aid from the government, the camps did not report a mass COVID-19 outbreak.

Despite this, India's lack of a refugee policy becomes all too glaring in the light of the hardship being faced by the Rohingyas during the lockdown.[5]

Beyond the socio-economic value that the refugees are adding as demonstrated above, it is after all a moral, humanitarian and civilisational necessity that we accrue rights to them. Particularly at a time when the ruling regime is talking about granting citizenship rights *only* to non-Muslim refugees, it is even more imperative that we demand a secular refugee policy whereby rights and entitlements are not linked to one's identity or religion.

Finally, the lockdown has shown that the stuff of life is a lot more than food and shelter; it is about a home rather than a shelter, and it is about being with people one can call one's own. It may not be possible for the refugees to return or regain what they have lost at their homeland, but at least an attempt can be made to make them feel a little more at home and not at anyone's 'mercy'.

Notes

1 Name changed.
2 Mander, H. (2018, October 9). 'India's deportation of seven Rohingya men to Myanmar is a profound failure of public compassion'. *Scroll.in*. Accessed 14 December 2020. https://scroll.in/article/897478/indias-deportation-of-seven-rohingya-men-to-myanmar-is-a-profound-failure-of-public-compassion
3 Name changed.

4 Miglani, S. & Das, K.N. (2017, August 14). 'India says to deport all Rohingya regardless of U.N. registration'. *Reuters*. Accessed 14 December 2020. https://www.reuters.com/article/myanmar-rohingya-india-idINKCN1AU0U2?edition-redirect=in

5 Lalwani, V. & Chakravarty, I. (2019, December 9). 'No law for refugees in India – and the Citizenship Bill does not fill the gap'. *Scroll.in*. Accessed 14 December 2020. https://scroll.in/article/946220/no-law-for-refugees-in-india-and-the-citizenship-bill-does-not-fill-the-gap

14

Dikkat, *Majboori* and Survival

for Home-Based Sex Workers During the COVID-19 Pandemic and Lockdown

SHIRIN CHOUDHARY

When I called Sudha[1] at 4 pm in the afternoon, she had to go out into the balcony of her home in the intense summer heat to talk to me. 'I have to come outside to talk, my children are at home, they don't know about my work,' she explained. It wasn't a usual day in her life. Because of the COVID-19 pandemic and lockdown in Delhi, she was spending more time in her two-room flat with her three children. On a usual day, Sudha would be getting phone calls from clients and going to meet them. She would also be going to the NGO office where she works to bring more HIV awareness amongst sex workers and transgender people in her area in Northwest Delhi. Her 13-year-old daughter and 16-year-old son would be in school and her 20-year-old daughter would be in Lucknow attempting entrance exams for higher education. That was what Sudha had planned for them. But the pandemic and lockdown meant all her plans were completely thrown to the winds and left her struggling to even feed herself and her family.

'Yahaan koi kaam nahi hai....Ham sab ghar pe hai. Kuch logon ko toh ration bhi nahi mil raha hai. Hamare kaam ke liye hi hamein logon se milna hota hai. Abhi toh nahi ho payega kaam.' (There is no work here....We are all at home. Some people are not even getting ration. We have to meet people for our work only. That's not possible right now.)

The COVID-19 pandemic for working people across the world meant a loss of jobs and opportunities to create self-employment, especially for those in the least paying and most thankless jobs. 'Social distancing' as a tool of controlling the spread of the virus was disastrous for those whose daily sustenance depends on daily wages. As an increasing number of countries went into lockdown from March 2020, unemployment rose in swathes (The Hindu, 2020).[2] This was not just a crisis of the pandemic, but the loss of work increased financial pressure and a lack of public safety nets which pushed lakhs of people into a corner.

One of the most vulnerable groups in India who lost their work and livelihood because of the lockdown are sex workers. Their work, which is marred by stigma and prejudice, is not even accepted as work by either the law or in common public understanding. Largely slipping through the cracks of India's meagre social security net, they only have their work to rely on for their earnings. And that is precisely what was taken away by the lockdown. In Delhi, according to a Joint Stakeholders Submission to the UN, there are over 5,000 sex workers, who are either home-based or work from the brothels of GB Road (as per 2016 figures).[3] Many, like Sudha, live with their families who are not aware of the nature of their work.

Over the period of the lockdown, I reached out to a few women who have been working as home-based sex workers in Delhi for several years. Many of Delhi's home-based sex workers live in

Northwest Delhi. Though perhaps plagued by the limits of 'social distancing', our conversations over the phone over a span of one month became more engaged and less awkward with time. The irony of me being a complete stranger, asking them for intimate details about their lives during the lockdown on the phone was not lost on me. But slowly and with some apprehension in the beginning, they shared their fears about the virus, about losing their work, their experience of being home with their families, their own struggle and those of other sex workers to support their households. As my voice over the phone became more familiar to them, the narrative became more and more revealing.

Sudha lives in Northwest Delhi in the Rani Bagh area, with her three children. She is a single mother, separated from her husband years ago. She has been living in Delhi for 17 years, but still lives in a rented flat. She runs her household and ensures that her children go to school and college supported by her earnings as a home-based sex worker. I called her and asked her how she was managing in the ongoing lockdown, how it had been for her. 'It was difficult in the beginning, because my daughter was stuck in Lucknow,' she said. Her daughter had left to take her exams in Lucknow, and there was no way of ensuring her return till restrictions on travel were lifted in mid-May. Like any mother, she was worried about her daughter's safety; her 18-year-old daughter was staying in her grandparents' house but with little supervision. 'I asked her not to go out anywhere. She is there alone. It was only after I became a sex worker that I realised how unsafe it is.' When the restrictions were lifted, she went with her son to Lucknow to bring her daughter home: 'Only then did I feel better, when she was back home. Till then, throughout the lockdown, I was feeling restless.'

I also spoke to Meena,[4] in her 40s, who lives with her two daughters, her elderly parents and her brother in Shakurpur. Her young daughters are 18 and 22; one of them was writing her board exams before they were suspended due to the lockdown, and the older one is in the final year of her BA programme. On the phone, Meena told me how she was worried about her daughters' studies during the lockdown. While the middle class was busy fetishising 'online learning', they were barely managing their coursework. 'We have one smartphone in the house. If one uses it, the other one can't. I can't even buy them a new phone right now when my work is stopped.' Being a single mother, she does not have any support in raising her daughters. Her husband left years ago and remarried. 'He does not even call us now,' she said.

For both Sudha and Meena, this life of precarity did not begin with the pandemic and would surely outlast it. 'Sex work is like a game of gambling,' Meena says in the middle of our conversation, 'Some days you get less and some days you get more.' They have endured ill-treatment from the police, low payments, abuse from clients and the shame and stigma associated with their profession for years. But losing their income, whatever little savings they have managed and being left with no support from the state and community was something they had never before experienced.

The 'Relief' Package: A Mirage in an Arid Desert

The added hardship of losing work during the lockdown was only compounded by the fact that the central and state governments' relief packages were hardly adequate or accessible for sex workers in the country.

The Finance Minister's 1.7 lakh crore relief package announced on 26 March hardly gave much relief to most of Delhi's sex workers (*Al Jazeera* 2020).[5] Their work is unrecognised and criminalised. Without ration cards, many of them are unable to access most of the schemes under the package. Sudha does not have a ration card either, despite having lived in Delhi for 17 years. Though she had tried making a Jan Dhan Account earlier, she was unsuccessful because of the complicated process and her unfamiliarity with technology. Only a few of her acquaintances received money in their Jan Dhan Accounts.

In Shakurpur, where she lives, there was a government school where one could get cooked meals twice a day. 'People have to stand there from 10 in the morning to get only one scoop of rice and dal at 1 in the afternoon,' she said, 'I have three children. How can I make them stand in line with me? Or take such little food for them?' Seeing this situation, Sudha began relying on ration kits from NGOs and borrowing from the ration shop nearby. But borrowing from the shopkeeper often came with the condition of sexual favours later. She feared this, 'What if, someday, he asks me for something in return? I don't have a husband. I don't want to be in that situation, but I have no other source of ration or support.'

Like Sudha, Meena too did not receive any support from the government. She does not have a ration card and could not get an e-pass because of the complicated process of signing up with her Aadhar card details online. From Shakurpur, Meena walked 8 kilometres to Sultanpuri to collect ration from Kusum, President of the All India Network of Sex Workers. But it was difficult to get ration from such a distance as she had to carry it back on foot. 'There were police barricades everywhere, and they would stop me at every point on the way. I had to tell them, sahib, I don't have food at home, that's the only reason I am out. I am not doing anything wrong.'

Sudha's friend live in Prem Nagar, where the closest government school (serving 2000 residents) is 6 km away and the road is not fit for cars or scooters. People can only reach the school on foot, not even by cycle rickshaw. 'In such a situation,' she recounted almost wearily, 'I would rather continue borrowing ration and preparing food at home. At least I have been living here for years, I know the people around here, and they can help me when I need it.'

Restrictions Eased, Unease Amplified

The loss of work and income because of the lockdown pushed Sudha and Meena in different directions, depending also on their own personal networks and relative positions. It was not as if things got better with time, from Lockdown 1.0 to 4.0. Indeed, as the virus spread further through the city, it became riskier for sex workers to return to their normal lives. When I called them again in mid-May, there was not much change in their voices or their situation. Both had reached a point of helplessness as never experienced before. Sudha's stock of ration borrowed or acquired through NGOs was running low again.

She had to resume working, despite the risk to her and her children's health. There was less work than before, she said, but she did as much as she could. There were only a handful of clients calling, and she had to be careful to only meet those whom she trusted, nobody new. Aware of the risk of exposure to the virus, she said it was *majboori* (compulsion) to take the risk so as to at least feed herself and her family.

After more than two months of unemployment, Meena, living close to a COVID-19 quarantine centre, accepted a part-time job in the hospital canteen. While her earnings of a few thousand rupees were not even close to what she could earn before as a sex worker, she had to make do with it. It was not only 'social distancing' that forced her out of sex work for this duration, but the fact that many clients from her area who were migrant workers themselves had left the city. Moreover, after the Janta Curfew, Meena had moved with her children to her parents' house, expecting there to be a lockdown. This meant that sex work was out of the question, as she could not go very far from there and therefore, she could not even meet the old clients who called her.

Sudha and Meena both said that their earnings even after resuming some form of work was not enough to sustain them and their families. They still had to borrow money and rations. Meena borrowed from an old client, and though he didn't ask for anything in return she suspected it was not for free. Sudha continued to borrow from the shopkeeper near her home despite having no safety net or assurance of how she would pay him back. She was also contacted by an old client who offered to let her borrow some money. About this, she said, 'I didn't want to borrow money from him at this time, who knows later he might ask me to do something or the other which I don't want. I would rather not take his money.'

Facing Abuse and Violence on Multiple Fronts

Despite the hardships, the near-empty bank accounts and a loss in the mobility that financial independence had earlier made possible for her, Meena felt that her situation was still better than many others she knew. Living with her family, she had their emotional and mental support. But for many others the loss of income translated into a loss of bargaining power in the household and disempowerment in their relationships. Meena relayed her friend's situation, who was facing abuse from her husband on a regular basis: 'Late at night when she is sleeping, around 2 am, he would wake her up and beat her. He tells her, "bring me money". She is stuck there.... You tell me, when everything is closed from factories to shops, how will the poor woman alone bring him anything?'

In the public sphere too, violence and harassment are not unknown to sex workers in Delhi and did not stop with the lockdown either. Before the COVID-19 crisis sex workers would have to regularly pay off the police ('*hafta*') in order to continue working. According to Sudha, it is like a negotiation or agreement. 'When we want something from them, we also have to give something. We cooperate a little so they cooperate a little. So we do it.' Since their work stopped, the regular payments had to stop as well. But these same police officers who used to extort from them threatened them with jail if they tried to work during the lockdown. Sudha was told by the police officers that if anyone went to meet her, she would be sent straight to jail. These threats made it harder for her to find work, even after the lockdown restrictions were partially lifted.

The lockdown brought on unprecedented difficulty for sex workers around the country. Facing the catch-22 situation of choosing between exposure to the virus or going without food, many would have risked their health to survive and feed themselves at the time.

Most women sex workers, managed to earn Rs 500 or Rs 1000 in a day before the COVID-19 lockdown. Most clients would not pay more than a few hundred rupees at any rate. It was unlikely, therefore, that they had enough savings to sustain themselves and their families for months without any earnings. Nor would they be able to resume their work even after restrictions were lifted as the threat of the Coronavirus would continue to loom over their heads. But despite the efforts of sex workers' groups like AINSW to appeal to the state government and the targeted interventions staff of the National Aids Control Organisation to support sex workers through the lockdown, very little was done for them. Health services, money and livelihood aside, even their basic need of food for sustenance was ignored.

Solidarities and Sisterhood

During my conversations with Sudha and Meena, they kept talking of their sex-worker friends and acquaintances, and the difficulties *(dikkatein)* they were facing. Despite the adversities they faced through the lockdown months, they continued to reach out with support to others in their community who they felt were suffering even more than themselves. Meena took pains to ensure that her HIV-positive friend received her prescribed antiretroviral therapy despite hospital services not working fully because of the lockdown. Sudha continued to be part of the local ration distribution efforts despite not knowing sometimes where her children's next meals would come from. She said, 'Today I am able to eat, I am still able to feed my children. So when I see another woman and she is feeding her babies roti and salt, I give her my grain.' It wasn't just that she *wanted* to help the others; she didn't see the choice not to. Nor did she hesitate to criticise the government which had abandoned the people in her neighbourhood whom she saw making do with a meagre ration supply for months.

The depth of crisis faced by sex workers during the lockdown could have been avoided. If their work had been recognised as work, and not criminalised. If the government had created policies to reach out to sex workers and ensured their access to essential identity documents and ration cards. If they had been assured by the government that their loss of income during the lockdown would be supplanted by an allowance or free ration without bureaucratic hurdles. Sex workers have been struggling against this invisibilisation of their labour in the mainstream and trade unions organisations for decades. Sex workers' collectives and networks around the country have time and again pointed out that this lack of recognition of sex work as regular work has led to their complete marginalisation. But despite this, the government left them to fend for themselves in the face of the crisis caused by the pandemic and lockdown.

The stories of Sudha and Meena are not just those of difficulty or resilience in the face of it, but important narratives of solidarity that marginalised communities extend to one another in the face of crushing public apathy. It was in these neighbourhoods of Northwest Delhi where sex workers, transgender women, disabled persons, people living with HIV, widowed women, the elderly and daily wage workers formed networks of support for one another. Sudha and Meena fostered these networks of support in their own neighbourhoods. And on the other end of the phone line, I was privileged to be witness to it.

Notes

1 Name changed.
2 Press Trust of India. (2020, May 5) 'India's Unemployment Rate Rises to 27.11% amid COVID-19 crisis: CMIE'. *The Hindu*. Accessed 30 November 2020. https://www.thehindu.com/business/indias-unemployment-rate-rises-to-2711-amid-covid-19-crisis-cmie/article31511006.ece
3 Joint Stakeholders Commission. (2016). *Violations faced by Sex Workers in India*. Accessed 30 November 2020. https://www.upr-info.org/sites/default/files/document/india/session_27_-_may_2017/js9_upr27_ind_e_main.pdf
4 Name changed.
5 Tatke, S. (2020, April 13). 'India's sex workers fight for survival amid coronavirus lockdown'. *Al Jazeera*. Accessed 30 November 2020. https://www.aljazeera.com/news/2020/04/13/indias-sex-workers-fight-for-survival-amid-coronavirus-lockdown/

15

Cobweb of Restrictions

Migrant Workers and the Lockdowns in Kashmir

MISBAH RASHID

'Pehle Article 370 pe lockdown hua to hum ko Kashmir chhodna pada. Ab Corona ka lockdown hai to socha hai nahi jayenge. Iss lockdown se sirf Kashmir mein mazdooron ko nahi balki poore desh ke mazdooron ko bhugatna pad raha hai, lekin hamare liye to kuch naya nahi hai.'

(First it was the lockdown that followed the revocation of Article 370 due to which we had to leave Kashmir. Now it is the lockdown due to Corona, but we have decided to stay put. This lockdown is a challenge not only for the labourers in Kashmir but for all the labourers of India, yet lockdowns are not new to us)

—Ram, a daily wage labourer from Bihar.[1]

The former state of Jammu and Kashmir (J&K) has been the abode of survival for Karimullah and his 16 other co-workers for over a decade. As circular migrant workers for almost 12 years, they have witnessed cycles of lockdowns and curfews in this haven, unseen or or even unheard of in their native place, Bijnor, Uttar Pradesh. Karimullah belongs to the large section of the Indian workforce referred to as its 'informal sector' made up of an estimated 100 million internal migrants (Chatterjee, 2020).[2] The local economy of the country rests on the shoulders of this million-strong migrant worker population from the northern and eastern states of India and Nepal.

Migrant labourers are an integral part of the local economy of J&K. They are mostly masons, carpenters, labourers, barbers, embroiderers and workers in gold ornament shops. Migrant labourers are estimated to make up 80 per cent of the Valley's construction workforce. The number of seasonal migrants in Kashmir varies between two to five lakh and as per the 2011 Census data, around 28 lakh migrants from other parts of India visit Kashmir (Turrey, 2019, p. 2).[3]

In comparison to any other part of India from where migrant labourers originate and to where they migrate, Kashmir has many more security and safety concerns with frequent encounters and Cordon and Search Operations (CASO) being an everyday reality. Despite this, thousands of migrant workers travel to various parts of Kashmir in search of livelihood. Every year, migrant workers start arriving from February onwards after the harsh winter abates. In 2020, the migration started just before the World Health Organisation declared a worldwide COVID-19 pandemic and the Government of India announced a complete lockdown in the country starting from 25 March 2020. As soon as the government declared a nationwide lockdown, a phenomenon of reverse migration from cities to native villages kicked off across the country. Left with no employment in cities, stranded migrant workers felt compelled to return to their native villages. However, in Kashmir, labourers who had already arrived in February 2020 were still stuck in the valley, bereft of work in the first phase of unprecedented lockdown.

Pre-Corona: Working in a Conflict Area

Among Karimullah's 16-member team, a few had been able to get work in Kashmir through contractors while the others had arrived via a network of other migrant workers. Karimullah had first come to Kashmir in 2008. Since then, Kashmir has been his home despite its volatile political situation. Karimullah describes his first encounter with security forces in Kashmir thus: 'When I first saw the army bunkers covered with sand bags from sides and corrugated tin sheets on the top and army personnel on all sides peeping out with their guns through small gaps made in between the sand bags, the sight was fascinating as well as terrifying. Fascinating because I had not seen anything like this in any city I have worked in before. But having lived here for years I could say, I live here without fear.' '*Yahaan darr ka mahaul nahi hai,'* he adds, alluding to the growing intolerance and recent acts of violence against minorities in India.

'I earn about ₹750/800 per day as wage for my skilled labour whereas my unskilled co-workers make about ₹600 per day, all of which has ceased due to lockdown. I live in a rented accommodation of two rooms and a kitchen, which I share with my 16 co-workers. The rent of ₹6000 per month is shared between us,' explains Karimullah. One of the primary reasons why migrant labourers prefer that their wives and children remain in their native villages is the volatile political condition of Kashmir. Outbursts of violence and skirmishes between civilians and the police are a common occurrence here. Curfews and *bandhs* have become an integral part of the everyday lives of people in the Valley. Despite this, they say that work is not hampered. They walk to work even during curfews and *hartals*. And if the workplace is far away then the contractor provides accommodation to those who get work through him. 'We have gone through hardships before and have worked even in curfews and *hartals*. But this lockdown is a different challenge,' says Karimullah.

In August 2019, the Government of India revoked two constitutional provisions—Article 370 and Article 35-A—which took away a host of special rights bestowed upon the erstwhile state of J&K (ET, 2019).[4] Fearing a worsened political situation, Karimullah and others had left for home, only to come back a few days later on the request of their contractor and resume their 'business as usual'. However, this was not the case for several others like Sunil* and his village mates who worked as carpenters in the valley. Originally from Punjab, they left after curfew was imposed in August 2019 and returned only in February 2020 to resume their work and earn something after a gap of six months. On being asked who would take care of their daily needs, Sunil, alluding to the loss of work days, said in a firm voice, '*Khana peena contractor dega aur kon dega, usne bheja hai hamein yahan to usi ko dena padega*' (The contractor will provide for our food because he has sent us here).

This is not the first time that the economy of the valley has got bulldozed. Due to the political unrest since the 1990s, and the regular civil uprisings of 2008–2010 and 2016, its fragile market economy has faced regular disruptions. According to the Loss Assessment Report by the Kashmir Chamber of Commerce and Industries, the devastating floods in 2014 resulted in a loss of ₹40,000–1,00,000 crores for the J&K economy. The post-Burhan Wani crisis[5] and new economic policies like demonetisation and implementation of the Goods and Service Tax (GST) has caused further stress to the Kashmiri economy. The report also gives an estimate of the decline in various sectors since the August 2019 lockdown (KCCI, 2019).[6] Table 1 gives an idea of the cumulative loss suffered by various industries as well as job losses is Kashmir.

Sl.	Sector	Loss Per Day (in₹)	Loss in 120 Days (in₹)	Job Losses
1	General Trade	264,833,334	31,780,000,080	120,000
2	Tourism	88,027,200	10,563,264,000	74,500
3	Handicrafts/Kashmiri Carpets	60,081,667	7,209,800,040	70,000
4	Industry	210,000,000	25,200,000,000	70,000
5	Service Sector	58,100,000	6,972,000,000	66,000
6	Transport	134,300,000	16,116,000,000	60,000
7	Contractors & Infrastructural Construction & Power Projects etc.	133,333,334	16,000,000,080	20,000
8	Horticulture/Floriculture/ Agriculture/Sericulture	166,666,667	20,000,000,040	12,000
9	Medical & Healthcare	4,500,000	540,000,000	2,500
10	Finance Sector	67,500,000	8,100,000,000	1,000
11	Education Sector	4,000,000	480,000,000	0
Total Amount		**1,191,342,202**	**142,961,064,240**	**496,000**

Source: https://im.rediff.com/news/2020/jan/21kashmir.pdf

The general trade and tourism sector suffered the greatest losses after the abrogation of Article 370. As per the Economic Survey 2019–20, 58 per cent of the former state Gross Domestic Product (GDP) comes from the services sector (GOI, 2019, p. 256).[7] According to the estimates, 'The cumulative figures for the August to December 2019 period stand at 43,059. This is a fall of 86 per cent vis-à-vis the same period in 2018 (3,16,424 arrivals) and a fall of 93 per cent vis-à-vis 2017 (6,11,354 arrivals)' (Bhat and Choudhury, 2020).[8] Artisans and weavers have been left jobless due to the spiralling effect of the clampdown on various sectors of economy. The direct bearing of the August 2019 shutdown was on the transport sector and the communication blackout resulted in losses for the education and medical sectors.

Migrant workers are part of some of the major industries in Kashmir. With the August 2019 lockdown, the workers engaged in various sectors like fruit picking, construction work and other activities were not able to find work (Barauh, 2019).[9] Many fled the region due to fear of uncertainties. The exodus of migrant workers just before the harvesting season emerged as a major challenge for the farmers of Kashmir. The apple trade also suffered due to the non-availability of migrant labourers and drivers. 'Despite a bumper harvest, only a truck or two are at the loading docks, and thousands of boxes of apples are lying around. Truck drivers—both local Kashmiris and non-locals—are refusing to go to villages to pick up the fruit, and growers are forced to hire vehicles to bring them to the big *mandis*, eating into their profits' (Ehsan, Jyoti and Ramachandran, 2019 and Majid, 2019).[10]

From One Lockdown to the Other

When India declared the COVID-19 lockdown, Kashmir was still calculating the losses caused by the previous lockdown. The new lockdown caused a loss of ₹270 crores per day as per the estimates in the first phase itself. This grew to a loss of ₹8,500 by May 2020. Till 12 May, the loss in J&K GSDP was about 17 per cent which is a cumulative loss of ₹31,200 crore (Ayoub, 2020).[11] According to the preliminary report of the Kashmir Economic Alliance as cited by Junaid Nabi Bazaz (2020)[12],

> The industrial sector suffered losses of ₹1,248 crore, followed by the transport sector, of ₹1,140 crore, while Real Estate and Housing took a hit of ₹900 crore, livestock and constructions of ₹882 crore and ₹874.2 crore, respectively.
>
> Tourism and hospitality, a sector that has trickledown effect on other sectors too, recorded losses of ₹810 crore in the two months of coronavirus lockdown, so far. Tourism has been suffering losses right since the government itself asked tourists to leave Kashmir in early August last year. Any hopes of revival this year were dashed by the coronavirus pandemic.
>
> One of the backbones of the Kashmir economy, handicrafts, suffered losses of ₹300 crore in the last two months. The services sector suffered ₹240 crore losses. Education sector lost at least ₹30 crore in the 60-day lockdown period.

After the March 2020 lockdown was announced, a large number of migrants were compelled to remain in mega cities like Mumbai and New Delhi even though they were desperate to go back to their native homes; many embarked on a long and arduous journey on foot to villages located hundreds of miles away. It brought back memories of the mass migration when the country was partitioned following the British exit in 1947. These days, however, what is of primary importance is that the divide is largely between those with money and those who live on daily wages.

The official estimates revealed that more than 56,000 migrant workers were in Kashmir when the lockdown was announced. Sensing the exigency of the situation, the High Court of J&K on 16 April 2020 directed the Divisional Commissioners of J&K to submit a report on the conditions of migrant labourers (*Daily Excelsior*, 2020).[13] In May 2020, the government devised a strategy to engage migrant workers in economic activities which could temporarily solve their livelihood issues while a safe plan was being devised to send them home. Industrial units were set up across J&K, 'out of which 4,829 are operational and have engaged about 41,386 workers, as per official figures. Nearly 2,645 units are operational in Jammu, engaging 29,122 workers, while 2,184 units are operational in the Valley 12,264 workers' (Irfan, 2020).[14]

Karimullah and his co-workers, however, consider themselves very lucky that they are in their rented accommodations rather than the government relief camps set up in various parts of Kashmir. The circulation of Whatsapp videos showing awful conditions at government relief camps had made them reluctant to seek shelter there. None of these labourers have agonising stories of fleeing on foot from cities as may be seen among migrants in the rest of India. Most of them have come to Kashmir with the mediation of contractors and are taken care of by them during the lockdown. Some have also managed to get their basic necessities from past savings as well as credit from shopkeepers and landlords. Some labourers have also been given verbal assurances for leniency in rent payments.

The contract-labourer relationship, according to them, is one of '*lein-dein*' (give and take), which in lockdown conditions (which are quite common in Kashmir), works well for them. The contractor takes the responsibility of the care of workers during curfews and *hartals* in Kashmir in any case; the lockdown conditions are therefore nothing new. Unlike in the other interviews in this book, what they talked of to us was not the perils of losing their livelihood; on the contrary they explained to us how it had become the responsibility of their contractor to take care of them during these unusual times.

However, not all migrants were in the same situation and others had a different story to tell. A group of self-employed and daily wage labourers stuck in North Kashmir and working as brick kiln workers had decided to go back to their native places instead of being stuck in the valley with no work. Ram* and five of his co-workers originally belonged to Betiya village of Bihar. They worked on piece rates and earned not more than ₹ 600/700 per day. They left the valley during August lockdown and did not return here till February. For them their seasonal work of six months was to start now. But with no work and no wages, despite the hardships that travelling on foot would pose, they preferred to go back to their villages. The uncertainty of their future loomed large on them as they had had no work from August 2019 onwards, and hence no savings to help them during the COVID lockdown. The local administration had reached out to them with relief packages, masks and gloves, and they were instructed to reach the nearest police station for the next batch of supplies. '*Makaan malik ne hamara kiraya maaf kar diya hai lekin aise nai reh sakte hum yahan. Lockdown khulte hi hum nikal jayenge ghar k liye*' (The landlord has waived our rent, but we can't live here like this. When this lockdown lifts, we will prefer to go back to our homes).

Access to Government Schemes

While the Ministry of Home Affairs (MHA) had issued an order in March 2020 'which stopped landlords from demanding rent from students, workers and migrant labourers for a month,' (Dubey, 2020)[15] these labourers were oblivious of any such order or any other scheme flagged off by the government for them in the lockdown. The NITI Aayog had sought the contribution of Civil Society Organisations (CSOs) to address the problem of migrant labourers amid the COVID-19 pandemic in J&K. It had appealed to the CSOs to assist and support the local administration in setting up community kitchens particularly for migrants (Sharma, 2020).[16] Besides, there were other central schemes that had been launched by the government for the lockdown. A ₹1.7 trillion relief package was rolled out by the government to help the marginalised and tackle the loss of livelihood by millions of poor. The relief package, under a newly framed Prime Minister Garib Kalyan Yojana, aims at alleviating the financial pain faced by migrant workers, farmers, urban and rural poor and women (Mishra, 2020).[17] The Union Labour Minister, Santosh Gangwar, had reportedly asked states to transfer funds to construction workers via the Direct Benefits Transfer (DBT) mode from its declared Building and Construction Workers (BOCW) fund (*The Week*, 2020).[18] Cabinet Secretary Rajiv Gauba had further asked state governments to ensure 'safety, shelter and food security of migrant labourers' stranded in various cities due to the lockdown. The Centre also directed district administrations to undertake a comprehensive enumeration of migrant labourers and stranded persons and make all necessary arrangements for providing food and shelter to them (Srivastava, 2020).[19] But even after months, no concrete steps were made to implement these orders.

In J&K, Lt Governor G. C. Murmu had announced a relief package of '₹1,000 to each of the 3.50 lakh workers registered with BOCW Welfare Board for purchase of rations during the 21-day lockdown. It also included provision of two months ration under PDS, one month's advance ration under mid-day meal, ration packets for slum dwellers and destitutes' (cited in Bhat, 2020).[20] Sadly though, none of our respondents knew about these new schemes or the relief packages announced for them. And without the portability of ration cards, these seasonal workers were not even able to avail PDS facilities. The lack of information about relief measures announced by the government, a general lack of valid identification documents, lack of an Aadhar card linked with the ration card or an employment card (like BOCW card) and inactive bank accounts, meant that these migrant workers were unable to access the benefits of the relief efforts made by the government. All of the workers we spoke to had ration cards, Aadhar cards, PAN cards, etc. and the access to basic government schemes only in their native villages. '*Mera raashan card ka toh Bihar ka hai. Srinagar mein nahi chalta. Kya karoon!* (My ration card is registered in Bihar. It is of no use in Srinagar. What do I do!),' said Ram remorsefully. Migrating seasonally without their families makes it difficult for them to carry their ration cards.

The government started the inter-state portability of ration cards w.e.f April 2018 under the Integrated Management of Public Distribution System (IM-PDS), but its implementation in all states is still pending even though it was supposed to be finalized by July 2020. The digitised portable PDS (E-PDS) for the beneficiaries of the National Food Security Act is particularly for migrants so that they can purchase subsidized food items outside their native states as well; but this programme has also been tried only in selected clusters. Without portability, the likes of Karimullah, Sunil and the 100 million circular migrants in India remain excluded from access to these entitlements outside their native states.

On 19 April 2020 in a nationwide radio address, Prime Minister (PM) Narendra Modi said, 'I had to take certain decisions which have put you in lots of difficulty, especially when I look at my poor brothers and sisters. They must be thinking what kind of a PM is this who placed us in this difficulty. I seek their forgiveness.'

Ram complained, 'Modiji declared a lockdown of 1.3 billion people for 21 days, with a notice of less than four hours. We would have been happier had Modiji kept us in mind before declaring the lockdown. What difference will his apologies make now?' He added, 'While the government was planning the lockdown, I wonder if we were anywhere on his mind!'

Notes

1 All the names in the chapter have been changed.
2 Chatterjee, P. (2020, April 12). 'The Pandemic Exposes India's Apathy Toward Migrant Workers'. *The Atlantic*. Accessed 3 May 2020. https://www.theatlantic.com/ideas/archive/2020/04/the-pandemic-exposes-indias-two-worlds/609838/.
3 Turrey, A. A. (2019). Economic profile of in-migrants workers in Kashmir Valley. *Indian Journal of Economics and Development 7 (11)*, 1–7. Accessed 30 March 2020. https://www.researchgate.net/publication/337257384_Economic_profile_of_in-migrant_workers_in_Kashmir_Valley.
4 ET online. (2019, August 5). 'Article 370 and 35 (A) revoked: How it would change the face of Kashmir'. *The Economic Times*. Accessed 15 August 2020. https://economictimes.indiatimes.com/news/politics-and-nation/article-370-and-35a-revoked-how-it-would-change-the-face-of-kashmir/articleshow/70531959.cms.
5 Burhan Wani was the rebel commander of Hizbul Mujahideen who was killed in an encounter in July 2016. His killing led to the various incidences of stone pelting and killing of civilians. There was a communication blockade and the valley was under curfew for approximately four months. *PTI*. (2016, 15 October) 'Wani's killing: Curfew lifted across Kashmir after 99 Days of Unrest', *India Today*. Accessed 1 August 2020. https://www.indiatoday.in/india/jammu-and-kashmir/story/kashmir-unrest-curfew-across-kashmir-lifted-burhan-wani-346696-2016-10-15.
6 The Kashmir Chamber of Commerce and Industry. (2019). *Preliminary Economic Loss Assessment Report*. Srinagar: KCCI.
7 Government of India. (2019). *Economic Survey 2018-19*. New Delhi: Ministry of Finance.
8 Bhat, M. & Choudhury, C. (2020, January 26). 'Number of tourists in Kashmir down by 86% in August-December 2019: RTI'. *The*

Wire. Accessed 30 August 2020. https://thewire.in/government/kashmir-tourism-article-370-rti.

9 Baruah, A. (2019, November 3). 'Fear, cold and lack of work prod migrant workers to leave Kashmir'. *The Hindu*. Accessed 30 May 2020. https://www.thehindu.com/news/national/fear-cold-and-lack-of-work-prod-migrant-workers-to-leave-kashmir/article29869790.ece.

10 Ehsan, M, Jyoti, D and Ramachandran, S. K. (2019, November 3). 'Fear looms over the economy driven by migrants, traders in Kashmir'. *Hindustan Times*. Accessed 15 July 2020. https://www.hindustantimes.com/india-news/fear-looms-over-economy-driven-by-migrants-traders-in-kashmir/story-0POc6qRr8mxR2cMzifUm8K.html

11 Ayoub, E. (2020, May 27). 'With one lockdown after another, J&K's economy is shuttered and shattered'. *The Wire*. Accessed 12 September 2020. https://thewire.in/economy/with-one-lockdown-after-another-jks-economy-is-shuttered-and-shattered.

12 Bazaz, J. N. (2020, May 18). 'Sinking Kashmir economy loses Rs 8,500 crore in Covid lockdown, so far'. *Kashmir Reader*. Accessed 30 June 2020. https://kashmirreader.com/2020/05/18/sinking-kashmir-economy-loses-rs-8500-crore-in-covid-lockdown-so-far/.

13 Excelsior Correspondent. (2020, April 18). 'HC seeks report from Div Coms on people stranded in J&K'. *Daily Excelsior*. Accessed 1 July 2020. https://www.dailyexcelsior.com/hc-seeks-report-from-div-coms-on-people-stranded-in-jk/.

14 Irfan, H. (2020, May 16). 'J&K engages 41,000 labourers, mostly migrants, in 4,800 industrial units'. *The Economic Times*. Accessed 16 June 2020. https://economictimes.indiatimes.com/news/politics-and-nation/jk-engages-41000-labourers-mostly-migrants-in-4800-units/articleshow/75766104.cms?from=mdr.

15 Dubey, V. (2020, March 29). 'Coronavirus Crisis: Landlords can't ask rent from students, workers for 1 month'. *Business Today*.

Accessed 29 March 2020. https://www.businesstoday.in/current/economy-politics/coronavirus-crisis-landlords-can-not-ask-rent-from-students-workers-for-1-month/story/399551.html

16 Sharma, V. (2020, April 15). 'Coronavirus: NITI Aayog seeks civil society bodies to help address migrant labour problems in J&K'. *The Tribune*. Accessed 30 April 2020. https://www.tribuneindia.com/news/j-k/coronavirus-niti-aayog-seeks-civil-society-bodies-to-help-address-migrant-labour-problems-in-jk-71532.

17 Mishra, A. R. (2020, March 27). 'Sitharaman announces ₹1.7 trillion package for the poor hit by the lockdown'. *Mint*. Accessed 2 April 2020. https://www.livemint.com/news/india/covid-19-centre-announces-rs-1-7-trillion-package-for-migrant-workers-poor-11585207289279.html.

18 Web Desk. (2020, March 24). 'Disburse fund to labourers using DBT: Labour Ministry to states'. *The Week*. Accessed 30 March 2020. https://www.theweek.in/news/biz-tech/2020/03/24/disburse-fund-to-labourers-using-dbt-labour-ministry-to-states.html.

19 Srivastava, A. (2020, April 17). 'Ensure safety, shelter, food to migrant labourers: Cabinet Secretary to state govts'. *India Today*. Accessed 17 July 2020. https://www.indiatoday.in/india/story/ensure-safety-shelter-food-stranded-migrant-labourers-cabinet-secretary-state-governments-1667839-2020-04-17.

20 Bhat, T. (2020, March 26). 'Coronavirus lockdown: J&K govt okays relief measures for 35 lakh people'. *The Week*. Accessed 26 August 2020. https://www.theweek.in/news/india/2020/03/26/coronavirus-lockdown-jammu-kashmir-govt-okays-relief-measures-for-35-lakh-people.html.

16

Disability Lockdown

RADHIKA ALKAZI

The many silent crises that play out in different communities, within groups of people at all times often get dwarfed, their sharpness dulled, by everyday existence and the demands of the majorities, those more powerful than others, as well as the resistance to structural changes.

The country is often unaware of these silent emergencies—for instance, the emergency of a child from a very poor home becoming disabled after an attack of Encephalitis in the Terai region of eastern Uttar Pradesh, followed by long hospitalisations and ICU stints; recurrent fits and changes in behaviour and other impairments leading to all kinds of exclusions, as a result of which they join the ranks of thousands of other children with disabilities who have been excluded from school. Or the young wheelchair user who cannot get on the bus to get to their preferred job or place of work and therefore has to settle for far less. The person with blindness living in a remote village in the hills who has never been given the skills to move about and become more independent in order to live their own life, and is now stuck in their home without any meaningful education or occupation. Or a person living with schizophrenia who wanders away from their home and is picked up and put into an institution from where she is never able to get out for the rest of her life. Or someone living with depression in their home, condemned to a life of nothingness because there is no countrywide provisioning or programming that is able to pick up their distress and reach out with support in time. Or the family living in the village (even those living in class-2 cities), that gives up its home to travel to the city and live in a congested urban slum in a large metropolitan city just so that they can be close to medical systems. They do so with the hope that at least in the city, there will be an explanation about what has happened to their child and what might be a remedy for the condition.

Then comes a big crisis, a public health calamity, one that shakes the whole world and makes people sit up and rethink societies, its structures and our mortality. The effects of this pandemic on children and persons with disabilities cannot be understood in isolation. The pandemic arrives and settles on systems that are already part of the country, on the silent emergencies that were already taking place unseen and often unheard rendering children and persons with disabilities even more vulnerable. It is the same additional vulnerability that might arise out of manmade crises like conflicts or wards, or natural calamities such as earthquakes, tsunamis, or indeed, a major public health crisis, like the COVID-19 pandemic.

Some of the major reasons for this include: the close links between disability and poverty; the attitudes of society that do not see the child and person as an equal citizen; systems and institutions of society that are not designed to cater to diversity and the lack of inclusion; and the political insignificance of this group of people as compared to others. Because of their underlying impairments and barriers to participation, people and children with disabilities are particularly susceptible in a public health crisis such as COVID 19. They are often unable to protect themselves during the crisis or properly seek care once a crisis has passed.

It must also be kept in mind that humanitarian disasters such as earthquakes, tsunamis, wars and conflict result in more people and children becoming disabled as do public health crises. The long drawn polio epidemic, still fresh in our memory, for example, became known as the largest cause of childhood disability in India and elsewhere in the world. The more recent Ebola pandemic is now said to be leading to long-term disabilities.[1]

The links between disability and COVID-19 are yet to be unearthed but we have enough evidence from the past to know that our response and planning must take cognizance of the child and person with disability. Yet, in our planning for a disaster and in our implementation of relief and later redevelopment, children and persons with disabilities are rarely factored in. Also rarely factored in are the huge mental health fallout and disabilities that will occur in the aftermath.

In India, according to the 2011 census, persons with disabilities account for 2.21 per cent of the population. Since then, the 2016 Rights of Persons with Disabilities Act has added more categories to the acknowledged 21 groups as persons with disabilities. According to disability groups, persons with disabilities would now account for at least 5 per cent of the population of the country.

Firdaus is a 12-year-old with cerebral palsy who has been living for the last six years in a one-room tenement in the mazdoor camp locality of Okhla Industrial Area in Delhi, with his father, mother and older brother. Like many other parents, his too travelled from their village in Bihar to Delhi because they were told that the big hospitals in the capital could help their child. They felt they would earn better here as well and have help for their child.

For Firdaus, having cerebral palsy and no support of rehabilitation strategies and information has meant spending his early days lying down and not being able to sit up on his own. It has also meant no speech and therefore difficulty in expressing his thoughts and ideas to others. Because of the tightness in his limbs and no therapy, Firdaus is not able to use his hands either, making him entirely dependent on his mother and older brother for all activities of daily living. Living on the second floor of the slum tenements with a precarious iron staircase leading to the ground level, it has been impossible for Firdaus to step out of his home for the six years that they have lived in the city.

The big hospital doctor told the parents that Firdaus cannot be cured and that he needed therapy. They told the parents to bring Firdaus to the hospital regularly for sessions. But Firdaus's mother found it impossible to navigate the big city roads and make her way to the hospital, changing two buses while carrying her child in her arms and then waiting for his turn when they reached their destination. For the last six years, therefore, Firdaus has been at home, very rarely going beyond its four walls.

Firdaus's father, a daily wage earner, is the only earning member of the family and often away from home for long periods. Both parents dote on their son and have struggled to provide for him as well as they can.

It took a whole year for Firdaus's parents to be convinced that their younger son could become more independent and that he could be educated. Their first step was to find a small rented room on the ground floor so that Firduas could be taken outside. As he started attending a Centre nearby, his educators and therapist realised that Firdaus was actually quite bright and could lift his hand slowly and point to pictures.

The world was just beginning to open up for Firdaus when the pandemic struck.

On 24 March, the Prime Minister gave the nation four hours' notice before it went into what was supposed to be a three-week-long lockdown. In that one moment Firdaus's father realised that he would no longer be earning; they had hardly any savings to begin with. They would have food stocks for a week but none after that. Their first thought was to try and walk back to their home town as thousands had begun to do. But it was impossible to walk carrying Firdaus. There was no option but to wait but food was running out.

When the Delhi government announced that it would be to distributing cooked meals twice a day at 500 designated schools, Firdaus's parents and older brother decided to walk to the nearest one to avail of this amenity. At the school, as thousands jostled for food, it was difficult for them to ask for an extra plate for their son who was alone at home. As all parents would do, they ate half the meal and took the rest back for their son.

Like Firdaus, there are thousands of others, young and old, who could not come out of their homes because of a disability to gain access to the food that was being distributed. Some were with their families while some others were all alone. From all over the country, there were reports of people with vision impairment totally left to themselves, with no one to orient them about where to get food. Suddenly, the known places for food had changed and without being guided to these new destinations, it was impossible for them to gain access. It was even more difficult for people with vision impairment to observe the 'social [physical] distancing' in these times, as they needed someone to guide them physically. Many were left desperately seeking a way to charge their phones, their only link to the outside world. As new orders and advisories kept being announced, people with hearing impairment spoke of having no access to information about where to go and what to do. For those with mobility impairments, like Reena, walking to the school for food was a long, difficult and exhausting exercise. For many others, it was impossible. Those who did manage to get there found it difficult to jostle with others for their share. After all, the unsaid devaluation of lives that are vulnerable and discriminated against in so-called normal times, will play out even more aggressively in situations of crisis, unless it is anticipated and planned for. Reena, and many others like her, decided that they would have to do with one meal a day till help came.

Like Firdaus's family, large numbers of children and persons with disabilities living in urban slum localities like the Okhla Industrial Area have migrated from states such as Bihar and Uttar Pradesh. According to (Centre for the Study of Developing Societies) CSDS, 40 per cent of Delhi's population is comprised of migrants. Among them, 48 per cent are from UP and 18 per cent from Bihar, and a large proportion of these migrants are daily wage earners engaged in unskilled work, in unorganized sectors or providing labour to the industrial units in and around Delhi and residing in the urban slums of Delhi.[2]

At a time like this, having a disability certificate, disability pensions and ration cards for food could have provided a safety net for children and people with disabilities. On 20 March the Government of Delhi announced that 'all the recipients of monthly financial assistance under the government pension scheme will get an additional amount equivalent to one month's annuity. The government has also decided to double the pension under the widow, old age and disability pension scheme.'[3] For children and persons with disabilities in Delhi, this meant that Rs 5000 would be put into the bank accounts of those who were already receiving a pension for the months of April and May. However, the required paperwork and documents are such that large numbers of people who have migrated from other states are unable to produce them and are therefore excluded from these entitlements. Firdaus's family, for instance, lives in rented accommodation and is unable to show five years of domicile in Delhi as required for the disability certificate.

Meanwhile on 26 March, the Union Finance Minister too announced an ex-gratia one time amount of Rs 1000 for poor pensioners, widows and people with disabilities. This was to be given in instalments over three months.[4] However, as the months went by, disability groups in different states realised that this announcement was not for all people with disabilities. Instead, the disbursement would benefit only 7.6 per cent of working age persons with disabilities—those who are beneficiaries of the Indira Gandhi Disability Pension (NSAP).[5] Unaware of this, lakhs of disabled citizens kept complaining of the non-transfer of the declared amount to their bank accounts.

In the months of April and May, ASTHA, an organisation that works in the urban slums of Delhi with children and people with disabilities reached out to 250 families of children with disabilities it works directly with, as well as over a thousand other people with disabilities, and families of very young and school-going children with disabilities, all over the city who needed food urgently. In a bid to proactively reach out to children and persons with disabilities in a planned manner, the organisation accessed lists of school-going children and worked through the DCPCR to reach out to Anganwadi workers and get lists from them of children and persons with disabilities who were in need in their areas. Members of the organisation spoke with each family and every person with disability to understand whether they had disability certificates, were getting pensions, had access to ration cards and the means to get to the food that was being distributed. The aim was to enable people to access government support wherever possible, to give them relevant information, and to provide the much-needed ration when this was not possible. Sources of income were checked and people gave details of the work they did and the situation that their family was in at present.

The picture that emerged was an alarming one, of large numbers of persons with disabilities and families of children with disabilities stuck without work and money, without rations cards and other entitlements. Children and adults with disabilities were not part of the social security net. While ASTHA decided to focus its support on families with no work, no disability certificate, pension and ration card, it soon realised that without any source of income, even families with ration cards and pensions were in distress due to different reasons.

The nature of state entitlements and social security support is often so small that it is impossible for families to survive on just that. The amount given as pension varies across states in the country, with Delhi being one of the highest: at Rs 2500 per month. The questions that needs to be asked is whether in unusual situations like the humanitarian crisis brought on by the pandemic, does the state need to think beyond the specific entitlements already present and support one and all more generously?

Very few persons with disabilities have the disability certificate and receive the disability pension and there are many hurdles in every state in gaining access to these—such issues have festered in the disability sector for decades. The vexed issues of those who migrate from one city to another and cannot use their disability certificates or produce adequate documents continue to be a big barrier. According to the NSSO, 2018, only 28.8 per cent of persons with disabilities in the sample had disability certificates.[6]

Given the large-scale interstate migration of people in the country, the disability sector has long been asking for universal identity cards to be used throughout the country for all eligible children and persons with disabilities rather than just within a state. However, this long-standing demand of more than a decade is yet to bear fruition. At present there seems to be no official data on households with children and persons with disabilities and their participation in food security nets. Such omissions and delays in tackling long-term issues are taking their toll as large numbers of families of children and persons with disabilities became supplicants in one go in the present crisis.

Not everyone is born with a disability. Many people acquire disabilities later in life. For instance, Basu a truck driver, had a serious accident when he was 28 and was confined to his bed. Even as he recovered, it was clear that he would not be able to go back to his earlier occupation. Slowly and arduously, over a period of time, he set up a small shop in his house to earn money to support his family. There were many other changes in the family. He could not afford the private school fee for his children anymore and had to put them in a government school. His wife had to go to work now and also look after his needs. Basu was making much less than he had made earlier as a truck driver but he had more medical bills now, as pressure sores and other difficulties needed continuous intervention. With the pandemic and the lockdown, the small shop had to be closed. Basu's source of income was once again snatched away. Without support from the state or his community, it would be impossible for Basu to rebuild his life. Data from the 2018 NSSO on persons with disabilities tells us that like Basu, 57.2 per cent of people with disabilities who were working previously, lost their work after the onset of disability. Sixteen per cent had a change of work after onset of disability and only 26.9 per cent had no change or loss of work.[7]

Given the dismal participation of children and persons with disabilities in education, and the very low literacy rates (52.2%), [8] it is not surprising that a majority of them are engaged in uncertain and informal work. According to the 2018 NSSO, only 15 per cent of people with disabilities are wage or salaried workers. The larger percentage of people are either self-employed (59.7%) or involved in casual labour (25.3%).[9] People with disabilities are very much part of India's large informal economy. In a virtual meeting of disability organisations to discuss the fallout of COVID-19 on persons with disabilities, a member from Bihar spoke about how so many highly qualified blind people were already having to work in petty jobs because of lack of access to more suitable employment. As a result of the lockdown, even these sources of income had dried up.

It is also likely that in all the job losses that are taking place, disabled persons will be amongst the first to lose their jobs. With employers already stretched, the accommodations and changes and support required for people with disabilities to do their work may not be provided any longer.

Pandemics such as the COVID-19 place a big strain on the health systems of the country. World over, people with long-term health issues have faced a huge crisis as hospitals and other health facilities became engaged primarily in COVID-19 care. A significant number of children and persons with disabilities have pre-existing health conditions that make them more susceptible to contracting the virus and experiencing more severe symptoms upon infection, which might lead to possible elevated levels of death. People requiring personal assistance for daily tasks, long term medication or regular medical intervention are at risk among others.

For example, children and people living with thalassemia were recently added as an acknowledged disability group by the 2016 Rights of Persons with Disabilities Act, as were children and people with other blood disorders, such as sickle cell anemia and hemophilia. Before COVID-19 hit India, children with thalassemia would come from the adjoining states of Haryana, Himachal Pradesh, Uttar Pradesh and others to Delhi every 10 to 15 days depending on their need for medical attention. They would travel to hospitals in capitals when they needed blood transfusions. There was a system in place which ensured that the blood required for children was arranged through regular blood camps. They would visit the National

Thalassemia Welfare Society for other medication and social support as well.

Not having required services closer to their homes, children and persons with disabilities often have to spend much more out of their pockets and go to long lengths in order to avail of rehabilitation services. With the lockdown, in one go, everything stopped: blood camps, and the ability to travel interstate for blood transfusions and medication. As the lockdown later eased and cases of Coronavirus increased, hospitals that earlier served children and persons with Thalassemia were designated as COVID-19 hospitals and these prior services ceased or redirected elsewhere. For children and people with Thalassemia travelling from all over the country for these services, the disruption of regular transfusions 'can lead to severe anemia, making them highly prone to infections which is disastrous during the COVID pandemic,'[10] warned Dr J. S. Arora, the General Secretary of the Thalassemia Welfare Society.

Equally difficult is the situation of large numbers of people in the country who live with mental illness or are at risk of developing mental health issues. Not having access to medication is just one part of the problem. Lack of any kind of support structures and outreach throughout the country makes the situation extremely grave. Recenly, a person called a disability helpline in deep distress. He was calling from another state about his younger brother who had come to Delhi in search of a job a little while ago and, as it happened, had also been diagnosed with TB. He had not answered his phone for two days and with the lockdown it was impossible for the older brother to travel to Delhi. Luckily, volunteers from the helpline tracked down the young man who seemed to have lost all hope of starting a new life. They found him just lying in bed, not having eaten or taken his medication for the past two days. Indeed, the pandemic and the attendant successive lockdowns, loss of jobs, food scarcity, the thought of imminent death, or of losing a loved one have brought mental health issues to the fore front as never before.

The Mental Health Care Act 2017, promises the right to mental health care services in a range of settings and within the community, in other words, care and support to people with psychosocial disabilities at their doorstep. It talks about integrating mental healthcare services into general healthcare services at all levels. Never before has the country needed these services with such urgency as today.[11] Never before have we missed having these services available for the large number of people who are at risk of a mental health disability today.

For children and persons with disabilities, a larger threat also lies in a health system which is highly inaccessible and peopled by medical personnel who are not trained adequately to understand the specific requirements of people with disabilities so as to provide reasonable accommodation during examination and treatment. There is growing fear about the accessibility of quarantine and other COVID facilities services for people with multiple disabilities, deaf and blind people, intellectually disabled people and people who may not be able to communicate verbally. For years, disabled persons and families of children with disabilities have highlighted the deficit-based understanding of disability within the medical system. In situations of emergency, when systems are overwhelmed, devaluations of people can affect decisions about who to save and who to let go.[12]

Children and persons with disabilities are protected under the law and through different guidelines in the event of a disaster. Section 8 of the Rights of Persons with Disabilities Act, 2016 guarantees equal protection and safety for persons with disabilities in these situations.[13] It also mandates Disaster Management Authorities at District/State/National levels to take measures to include persons with disabilities in disaster management activities and to keep them duly informed about these. In September 2019, the National Disaster Management Authority issued National Disaster Management Guidelines on Disability Inclusive Disaster Risk Reduction (DIDRR) in line with the provisions of the law.[14] As the pandemic struck, the Department of Disability Affairs in the Ministry of Social Justice and Empowerment too issued guidelines for people with disabilities.[15]

Some of the important aspects of the advisory include having information dissemination in accessible formats through helplines; training of all persons responsible for handling emergency response on the rights of persons with disabilities; and on risks associated with additional problems for persons having specific impairments. The guidelines advised that:

> Persons with disabilities should be given access to essential food, water, medicine, and, to the extent possible, such items should be delivered at their residence or place where they have been quarantined. Further, States/UTs may consider reserving specific opening hours in retail provision stores including super markets for persons with disabilities and older persons for ensuring easy availability of their daily requirements.[16]

Disability Commissioners in each state were to be the nodal authority with respect to persons with disabilities. District Nodal officers are supposed to have a list of persons with disabilities in the district and monitor their requirements periodically; they should also have a separate list of persons with severe disabilities who need high support in the locality.

The reality, however, presents a different picture. While the guidelines, laws and periodic orders from the government are there to protect children and persons with disabilities, they unfortunately sit on years of weak implementation of laws, and weakened institutions. Delhi, for instance, has functioned without a regular Disability

Commissioner through the whole crisis. The Secretary of the Department for Rights of Persons with Disabilities holds additional charge of the Office of the Chief Commissioner for Persons with Disabilities for the whole country. Despite guidelines and some good practices in states, it has been difficult for persons with disabilities to know where to go and how to access their nodal officers and Disability Commissioners. While organisations in urban areas have exchanged information with each other, it has been very difficult to keep informational channels open and to know what is happening in rural areas.

As Firdaus and his family make their way back to their village in Bihar, what will his chances of accessing rehabilitation and education be? As the country slowly recovers and heals after this unprecedented crisis, it will be time to rethink our priorities. What has emerged with undiluted clarity is that we will have to strengthen and redesign all our institutions so that no one is left behind in times of such crisis.

Notes

1

2 Jeelani, G., Anand, A. & Kumar, A. (2020, March 29). 'Coronavirus in India: How reverse migration is breaching the lockdown'. *India Today*. Accessed 18 May 2021. https://www.indiatoday.in/mail-today/story/coronavirus-in-india-how-reverse-migration-is-breaching-the-lockdown-1660835-2020-03-29

3 Express News Service. (2020, March 20). 'Pension doubled, free food for homeless: Kejriwal announces relief measures amid COVID-19 breakout'. *The New Indian Express*. Accessed 18 May 2021. https://www.newindianexpress.com/thesundaystandard/2020/mar/22/pension-doubled-free-food-for-homeless-kejriwal-announces-relief-measures-amid-covid-19-breakout-2119929.html

4 The Hindu Netdesk. (2020, March 26). 'Nirmala Sitharaman announces ₹1.70 lakh crore package for poor'. *The Hindu*. Accessed 18 May 2021. https://www.thehindu.com/news/national/nirmala-sitharaman-announces-rs-170-lakh-crore-package-for-poor/article31170718.ece

5 Bali, K. (2020, March 27). 'Activists respond to COVID-19 Guidelines and Relief measures for Disabled'. *Kractivist*. Accessed 18 May 2021. https://kractivist.org/activists-respond-to-covid-19-guidelines-and-relief-measures-for-disabled/

6 Statement 32: Percentage distribution of persons with disability by receipt of aid/help and percentage of persons with disability having certificate of disability, Persons with Disabilities In India, NSS 76th Round, 2018.

7 Statement 33: Percentage of persons of age 15 years and above with disability who were working before the onset of disability and their percentage distribution by situation of loss/change of work caused by disability, Persons with Disabilities in India, NSS 76th Round, 2018.

8 Statement 6: Status of education and vocational/technical training, Persons with Disabilities In India, NSS 76th Round, 2018.

9 Statement 36: Percentage distribution of workers in usual status (ps+ss) with disability of age 15 years and above by broad status in employment, by broad industry of work and percentage share of informal sector among regular wage/salaried employees with disability of age 15 years and above in non-agriculture sector, Persons with Disabilities In India, NSS 76th Round, 2018.

10 Sharma, N.C. (2020, June 2). 'COVID-19 Impact: Rural India's other Health Emergencies take a back seat'. *Live Mint*. Accessed 18 May 2021. https://www.livemint.com/science/health/covid-19-impact-rural-india-s-other-health-emergencies-take-a-back-seat-11591068353173.html

11 Ministry of Law and Justice. (2017). *The Mental Healthcare Act, 2017*. New Delhi: Government of India. https://www.prsindia.org/uploads/media/Mental%20Health/Mental%20Healthcare%20Act,%202017.pdf

12 Singh, S. (2020, May 21) Commentary on 'All Bodies': Indian perspective. *Research and Humanities in Medical Education, 7,* 112–115. https://www.rhime.in/ojs/index.php/rhime/article/view/350 The commentary is in response to the graphic titled 'All Bodies' which is accessible at http://rhime.in/ojs

13 Ministry of Law and Justice. (2016). *The Rights of Persons with Disabilities Act, 2016*. New Delhi: Government of India. http://www.deoc.in/the-rights-of-persons-with-disabilitiesrpwd-act/

14 National Disaster Management Authority. (2019). *Disability-Inclusive Disaster Risk Reduction*. New Delhi: Ministry of Home Affairs, Government of India. https://ndma.gov.in/sites/default/files/IEC/Booklets/Disability%20inclusive%20DRR.pdf

15

16 Ministry of Social Justice & Empowerment. (2020, March 27), *DEPwD issues Comprehensive Disability Inclusive Guidelines to States/UTs for Protection and Safety of Persons with Disabilities (Divyangjan) in light of COVID-19*. New Delhi: Government of India.. https://pib.gov.in/PressReleasePage.aspx?PRID=1608495

17

How Did the Forest Dwellers Brave the Pandemic?

SAGAR KUMBHARE

The impact of lockdown is rearing its ugly head in a crucial time in the lives of tribals and other forest dwelling communities in Gadchiroli. Located over 950 km away from Mumbai, in the state's Vidarbha region, this area is densely forested with a population of around 13 lakh. Famous for its high-quality teak wood and other forest produce, at the heart of what is commonly referred to as an 'Left Wing Extremism-affected' area, people here have dealt with lack of employment opportunities, shoddy health facilities, poor quality of education and violence for long. Currently, there is not a single industry in Gadchiroli. The only one that existed was a paper mill based in Ashti in Chamorshi block. But even that was shut down a few years ago for reasons unknown. Thousands of distress migrants travel to distant towns and cities or to agricultural lands in neighbouring states for work from here. For those who stay back, the only possible sources of income are the collection of forest produce and agriculture.

In the nation's heartland, here are a people that already live in the margins. The pandemic added manifold to their precarity. While on one hand, Gadchiroli's remoteness and isolation protected it in the initial months from the virus wreaking havoc, once trickles of distressed migrants started returning to their hamlets, they brought the virus along. And with the abysmal health infrastructure available here, deaths became inevitable. Even then, the death toll here was not enormous. But what hit them harder was the mindless lockdown. It hit their earning season, the time of the year when they collect forest products, what in government parlance is called Non Timber Forest Produce.

In a normal year this helps people earn money in a short period. They use this amount to build or repair their houses, for marriage expenses, education, to start a small business, to purchase agricultural equipment, seeds and fertilisers later during the monsoon, and for daily expenses. But in 2020, collection came to a halt. The PESA coordinator from Gadchiroli said, 'We made necessary arrangements as per the condition and informed contractors to keep hand sanitisers and masks at the procuring sites and to follow the government instructions. But unfortunately, as the number of cases soared in Maharashtra and nearby border states, the government had to stop the procurement of tendu leaves.'

An Example to Follow

Siyaram Halami, Sarpanch of Kukadel village in Korchi block said to us, 'From the last year's income from tendu collection, they have used some amount for a school, small development projects in the village and also during lockdown, they have distributed rations worth of ₹3.55 lakh to the villagers.'

Month	2019	Earnings from the forest collection used for	2020	Earnings from the forest collection will be use for
March	Mahua and other forest based fruits collection.		Because of the strict lockdown in the peak season (End of March and April) therefore, locals did not get a chance to collect Mahua and other forest-based fruits.	
April				
May	Tendu leaves collection		Tendu season curtailed to 7-8 days.	
June		1. Cultivation, 2. Construction/repair, 3. Marriages, 4. Purchasing agricultural equipment, 5. Education, 6. Returning loan money, 7. Daily expenses Etc.		Because of COVID-19 and the strict unplanned lockdown, this year, there is uncertainty about how to bear regular expenses of mentioned activities in 2019 year box.
July				
August				
Sept				
Oct				
Nov				
Dec				
Jan				

'Every year tribal and other forest dwelling communities collect mahua, tembur, saal, charoli, dink, honey, etc. But this year because of lockdown in the peak season (end of March and April) of the collection of forest produce locals did not get a chance to collect it,' added the sarpanch. He described how in every season, it is the collection of forest produce that helps the dependents to pull through the rest of the year. He was apprehensive about the future.

Snehdeep, a local activist from Kamalapur informed us that among the many forest products, it is tendu (used for beedi making) that is the biggest source of income for the tribal and other forest-dwelling communities. He said, 'Every year people earn good amount in this season. If the contractors do not come to purchase or if they curtail the period of tendu plucking, that would affect the livelihood of thousands of families.'

Current Situation of Forest-dwelling Communities

Pengunda is a village located in the dense forest of Bhamragadh block, with a mixed population of the Madia-Gond tribe and other forest-dwelling communities. The entire village is dependent on the forest for their livelihood. Locals visit the nearest market in Chhattisgarh state, and in exchange for the forest produce they procure salt, rice, oil and other useful food material for their families. The Markamis, a family of six members, also earn their living from forest produce in this way. Ramesh, the head of the family told us that since his childhood he has gone to the forest in the morning to collect Charoli (Jungle Berry), Tembur (Diospyrus Melanoxylon), Mahua (Madhuca Longifolia L.), etc. The proceeds from the same ran his family. Further he said, *'Ya varshi je hot ahe te mi ataparyant kadhi ayushyat kadhich pahil navht'* (Whatever is happening in this year, I haven't experienced any such thing in my entire life). 'We lost precious time during the lockdown, we missed collecting the forest produce; we collected tendu leaves but the amount we received from its sale was not enough to sustain my family for an entire year.'

The Warse family in Bellaguda village of Bhamragadh block is facing similar problems. A family of eight members, they are dependent on agriculture. But without the proceeds from the sale of forest products they cannot even buy the inputs for farming. This year, the whole financial cycle has broken down and alone on tendu collection they can't move further. They used some part of their income from NTFP collection for the education of the younger children in the family.

Prashant, from Bhamragadh block said that over the years, the composition of the erstwhile tribal dominant, especially in the villages of Madia community, is becoming heterogeneous. From the state borders of Chhattisgarh and Telangana, the trader's community is settling in tribal villages and influencing the local politics with their money power. Over the years they have come to occupy the most fertile lands. The outsiders recognised how important and valuable the forest produce is, and over the last few years, they have started interfering in local matters and trying to grab control of the local market of forest produce. This is one of the reasons that tribals do not have control over their own forests, rivers and over the prices of the forest produce they gather. Despite progressive Acts like the PESA (Panchayat Extension Scheduled Act) and FRA (Forest Rights Act), the poverty rate among tribals and other forest-dwelling communities is thus unsurprisingly high.

Sachin, a local activist told us that tribals have always been at the receiving end of the so-called development policies or big projects. Even now, everyone is worried about the economic loss caused by the pandemic, but nobody is bothered about how the tribals are managing their lives amid the COVID-induced crisis or what lockdown means for their fragile livelihoods.

He says, '*Aatmanirbhar* (self-reliant) is a word which the PM reiterates in his every speech, and he speaks of making every Indian self-reliant. But in the case of Gadchiroli, despite us having the ability to become self-reliant amid our forests and natural resources, the administration and external forces continue to control the forest in ways that are to our detriment. They don't give space to the locals to decide what is good for them.'

Agony Continued beyond Lockdown

Ramesh Durgam from Sironcha block, a head of a family of five, is a landless farm labour dependent on the forest collection and daily wage work. He belongs to a Dalit community, which operates just short of 9 per cent of this vast land; their population share in rural areas is 18.5 per cent as per the 2011 census. Satyam Gota from Etapally block is a small landholder but he and his family are mostly dependent on the forest collection; he belongs to a Madia Adivasi community which operates about 11 per cent of the land, which is equivalent to their population share in rural areas. But most of this land is in difficult and remote terrain, not accessed by irrigation or even all-weather roads. It includes forest lands operated by communities for subsistence farming. The balance of about 80 per cent of the agricultural land is operated by other castes, either the so-called upper castes or dominant OBCs.

Ramesh Durgam and Satyam Gota are from different parts of Gadchiroli district; they don't know each other but they share the same agony. Both of them lost crucial time when they could have collected the forest products, and it severely affected their livelihoods. There are hundreds of Durgam and Gota families in Gadchiroli who, even in a normal year were already living on the edge, sustaining only on the assurance of their earnings from the forest. The lockdown arrived in their lives as a disaster.

Kisan, a landless farmer from Aheri block said to us that during the lockdown, he did not think about its consequences on his family, which were yet to unfold in the months that followed. First, his older son Pratik (22), who was working in Hyderabad in a tire company, lost his job. Many village youths who had migrated because of the lack of employment opportunities here faced a similar fate. Kisan added that his son used to send home Rs 7000–8000 every month, but without this input, the condition of the family is deteriorating. 'Lockdown affected the collection of the forest products so we could not rely on selling them in a time of crisis. And now in the monsoon, I don't know what to do, I don't have land to cultivate and feed my family. Even my name is not in the BPL list. Now I can only work as an agricultural labourer,' he said.

18

A City Turned into a Wasteland for its Waste Workers

SURESH GARIMELLA AND BALU SUNILRAJ

Moinul, a migrant from West Bengal lived in the slums tucked behind the residential apartments in Kishangarh, Delhi. By the end of April 2020, well into the most stringent lockdown, he had reached out to everyone he could possibly reach out to, just to ensure two meals a day for his family and for others in the slum.

Before the lockdown was announced, working in the waste economy as rag pickers, albeit piecemeal, ensured that Moinul and his neighbours did not have to face starvation. The city's waste took care of their bare necessities. However, with residents in middle-class colonies shutting their doors to outsiders including rag pickers, life took a turn for the worse. In this context, they were rather fortunate to have been able to contact a few civil society actors. The city had overnight turned its back on them. It is difficult to imagine what fate might have awaited them had one of the calls not ensured some ration.

Like Moinul, every waste-economy worker's life contains within it a microcosm of the development trajectory followed by the postcolonial Indian state. The virus succeeded in pushing them over the precarious and rather slippery edge that they had been hanging onto. This is particularly true concerning those who carry out this job in the metropolises of our nation. Most of them are migrants from backward regions in the country. Studies have shown that nearly all of the workers in the waste economy of Delhi were born outside Delhi.[1] Deprived of education and adequate economic opportunities in their home-states, a direct result of the postcolonial capitalist trajectory, which bypassed the concerns of the most marginalised, they are forced to flee and live in precarious conditions in the margins of cities like Delhi. Almost all of them come from the lower castes and other marginalised communities, another reflection of the postcolonial development trajectory, i.e., its caste bias.

With the push for informality being the norm even in the formal sector, one can only imagine the levels of informality present in the waste economy. The state has long forgotten to include them, even in policy designs.[2] They are excluded from access to basic public goods. The only possible benefits are the absence of complete starvation and the availability of a cramped dwelling to live in. Even this bare existence was turned upside down when COVID arrived.

Kishangarh

Like several localities in Delhi, privileged and perilous living conditions exist side by side in Kishangarh. Different strata of population, whether landlords belonging predominantly to dominant caste communities, professionals, academicians and thousands of informal labourers live side by side in this urban village. While the privileged could withstand the impact of the lockdown and occupied themselves with thaalis, lamps and selfies, the case with the labourers was different.

We met labourers who live in Kishangarh while assisting in relief work carried out by CITU (Centre for Indian Trade Unions). Most of them have been living in Delhi since 2010 and have been part of the city's waste economy. Some of them were rag pickers, while others collected waste from nearby residential complexes. The waste collected in this process is sold to a contractor, which provides them with an average wage of Rs 350 per day, far below the minimum wage.[3] As is often the case, a local political leader allowed them to live on his property as tenants. However, the plot was empty when it was given to them. They had to spend their own money to build crumpled dwellings on it. About 60 families live on this plot of land and each family lives in a single 10 feet long and 8 feet wide room. Expectedly, social distancing is an impossibility in these conditions like for most underprivileged Indians living in the cramped underbellies of our cities.

it must be said here that the conditions in which these labourers live had taken a turn for the worse even before the announcement of the lockdown. Since the third week of March 2020, residents of this slum, most of whom were migrants, lost stable employment opportunities. The only avenue of income, albeit limited, was the collection of waste from nearby residential complexes. However, by March end, as the COVID-19 scare reached its peak, residents of these apartment complexes refused entry to outsiders, thereby closing even that avenue of income. It should be noted that it was on 29 March 2020[4] that the government gave a directive that no worker should be dismissed from his/her job. However, like millions in the Indian informal economy who have no identifiable employer, such directives meant nothing beyond a piece of paper for these migrant workers in the waste economy of Delhi.

Without any savings, the only recourse left to them was appealing to state benevolence. The state, however, was criminally absent. The only intervention on the part of the state was the distribution of cooked food packages on a particular day, which many of our respondents said gave them diarrhoea. Azebar Ali states, 'Khana banake packet mein de ke gaye the, raat kho khane ke baad, agla din pura bathroom mein hi bitana pada' (Someone gave and distributed us food packets; I had it in the night, and the whole day, I had to visit the washroom multiple times).

These workers also tried to access the website which the Delhi government had started to distribute ration for those without ration cards. However, to navigate the website was well-nigh impossible for them. They complained to us about how the website would hang frequently and did not process the information which they submitted. This was the experience of Digital India in its national capital.

It was under such conditions that they decided to contact non-state actors and this is how we came in contact with them. Completely overlooked by the state and local political bosses, for the entire period of lockdown, they were dependent on non-state actors for provisions of ration. With the relaxation of the lockdown by the end of May 2020, their employment opportunities revived, although in a limited manner. Living on the margins of the informal economy, there is uncertainty regarding everything, including their current place of residence. With the complete absence of any support, their future in Delhi is dependent on the brutal power relations that exist between the slum and the outside world, the balance of which is not in their favour.

Ruchi Vihar, Rangpuri Pahari

Ruchi Vihar of Rangpur Pahari is a neighbourhood of slum dwellers located right behind Sector E, Pocket 2 of Vasant Kunj. It is located two kilometres away from the Indraprastha gas station, which is situated on the route to Mahipalpur if one were coming from the direction of Vasant Kunj. Opposite the gas station, there is a by-lane through which one can reach Ruchi Vihar. Once you enter this by-lane, which marks the start of Rangpur Pahari, for nearly two hundred meters, the road is well paved. This is unsurprising because there are new DDA apartments here. The state can abdicate its responsibility to the marginalised, but not to the upper middle class. The well-paved road turns into a bowl of dust as one drives beyond these flats. It is as if the hand of the state has miraculously disappeared beyond the boundary wall of the middle-class colony, and one has entered a poor part of a mofussil town in the north Indian plains. This is Rangpuri Pahari, one of the poorest localities in Delhi. Unlike Kishangarh, which is a mixed locality in terms of class, Rangpuri Pahari consists of the most vulnerable population in the capital city. There are several *jhuggis* in the area, in which migrants from the north Indian plains, Jharkhand and Bengal live in tents and other ramshackle dwellings. But even to live in these most inhuman conditions, they have to pay nearly Rs 20,000 to local notables. It is here that we met another set of workers in the waste economy while conducting relief work.

Gorelal came to Delhi in 2006 and has been working as a rag picker ever since. His relative, who migrated before him to Delhi, introduced him to the trade. According to Gorelal, it was the lack of employment opportunities in Bihar which forced him to migrate to Delhi. During his stay in his village, he worked as an agricultural labourer in the fields or did other odd jobs for daily wages. Such jobs, according to him, were irregular and unstable. He came to Delhi in search of stability and development but was pushed into a similar precarity which he faced in Bihar when he started working with his relative as a rag picker.

Before the advent of COVID-19, Gorelal usually worked between 9 am to 4 pm collecting waste from the Mahipalpur locality. In the process, he visited 200–300 houses every day without a break, not even for lunch. Like several other workers in the waste economy, he was engaged in collecting waste under a contractor who paid him a meagre amount of Rs 2000 per month. Even this low paying job as a waste collector was contingent on his servility and submission. Raising his voice for a wage rise or against mistreatment in his place of work was not an option he could afford. The contractor always had one answer, according to Gorelal, if such a situation arose, 'Kaam karna hein tho karo warna tume hatadenge, karne wale bohot hein' (If you want to work, you come, otherwise, you will be dismissed since there are many to take up this job). Naturally, when the lockdown was imposed, the contractor neither supported nor provided any respite to Gorelal and other workers. It should also be noted that Gorelal is the sole breadwinner for his family and usually sends Rs 1000 from his meagre earnings to his parents back in the village.

When the lockdown began, Gorelal who was not a recipient of any PDS schemes, neither in Bihar nor in Delhi, tried to apply for a ration card in Delhi. However, since its procurement required the payment of bribes to several officials, he was unsuccessful. He was also unaware of the food distribution by the Delhi government. The only option, which he availed initially, was the collection of food packets, which were distributed by the police in his colony fifteen days after the lockdown. Since he did not have savings due to the nature of his work, there was almost no money to fall back upon. Even the pickings he collected a few days before the lockdown were left at his home. The contractor whom he usually contacts to sell his pickings to refused to collect them citing his inability to sell them further. The waste supply chain had collapsed.

Despite the tremendous suffering that he underwent during and before lockdown, Gorelal told us that he has no option but to continue working in the waste-economy, in the same unforgiving city. When asked about his registration, he states that the government does not know that he is a 'rag picker'.

Bharathi is also from the same locality. Her parents were daily wage labourers in Delhi and like in Gorelal's case, took to rag picking in the face of the lack of employment opportunities. While Gorelal collected waste from households in Mahipalpur, Bharathi roamed the streets of Mahipalpur collecting waste plastic and other materials. Her day usually starts at 9 am and she collects waste from the streets till 6 pm. When asked about her earnings, she pointed out that, '*Road me dekhte, bag bharthe hue age jate hein, jaha milte hein, waha dekhte jate hein, kisi din miljata hein, kisi din nahi*' (Whatever I find on the road, I pick up and fill my bag. I keep walking, looking and collecting in the bag. Some days, I find enough, other days I do not).

Through rag picking, she usually earned Rs 200–250 in two days. Naturally, her earnings are not sufficient to lead a non-precarious life. Regarding her ordeal in dealing with contractors to whom she sold her pickings, she lamented and pointed out that, '*Ladai bhi nahi kar sakte, dobara mal bhi tho inko hein bechna hein, naliya tho kya karenge*' (I cannot even fight back. Tomorrow, I have to sell it to him only. If he does not buy, what will I do?).

Despite the difficulty in carrying several kilos of waste on her back for long hours on a daily basis, she noted that on most days her collections was not even entirely purchased by the contractor. '*Yeh pura istemal karne ka layak nahi hein*' (A lot of it is not useful). Thus, he would at times reduce a kilo or two from her collection, though by design, she would only collect the stuff which can be sold. '*Kali panni hein, yeh cheez nahi chalega bolke kaat dete hein, Jab hum chnaat ke bhi jate hein, kaat the tho hein hi.*' (This is a black cover, this does not work. Even when we sort the items and go, they reduce the weight stating the items are not worth enough)

When the lockdown was announced, she did not have sufficient savings and as a result, had nothing to eat. She did not receive anything from the government, either in the form of ration or other essentials. Since she was digitally illiterate and did not own a smartphone, she was reliant on a good samaritan to assist her in filling the E-form for ration. Despite this assistance, she did not receive anything even after three months of filling the form.

During the lockdown, like Gorelal, Bharathi also lost her piecemeal savings, increased her debt and survived mainly on food packets distributed by the police and charity organisations. She has an 'intellectually disabled' brother who is dependent on her. Apart from taking care of him, she had to sleep on an empty stomach umpteen times during the lockdown. Before the lockdown, although she earned only for her sustenance, she could at least have two square meals a day.

When we visited her after the lockdown, the prices of the waste she collected and sold had crashed. She lamented that, '*Dukandar kehta hein, mein ithn hi dunga, dena hein tho do, varna wapas le jao*' (The shopkeeper says, I will pay only this much; if you are interested you give, otherwise, take the stuff and leave). She is now forced to sell the waste collection which used to earn her Rs 70–75 rupees a day, for Rs 25–30. Since the number of buyers is limited, she has no option but to sell her pickings at reduced rates.

These narratives point not only towards the suffering that workers in the waste economy faced as a result of the lockdown, but also speak volumes about the structural problems in the Indian informal economy, where the prevailing conditions border on modern-age slavery. Any natural or man-made catastrophe can inflict calamitous blows to their already vulnerable existence. The government ought to have been aware of this before calling for a most stringent lockdown with four hours' notice. Unless of course, those who inhabit the informal economy do not feature in our imagination of the nation.

As is abundantly clear from scholarly studies on informal economy, addressing these problems requires a political will from the governing forces.[5] Sadly, for now, that is nowhere to be seen.

Notes

1 Sarkar, P. (2003). *Solid Waste Management in Delhi–a Social Vulnerability Study*. Proceedings of the Third International Conference on Environment and Health, Chennai, India; Agarwal, A. et al. (2005, April) Municipal Solid Waste Recycling and Associated Markets in Delhi, India. *Resources, Conservation and Recycling 44.1*: 73–90.

2 Bisen, A. (2019) *Wasted: The Messy Story of Sanitation in India, a Manifesto for Change*. New Delhi: Macmillan Publishers

3 Labour Department (2019, October 23) Order No. 12(142)/02/MW/VII/3636. Government of NCT of Delhi. Accessed 2 July 2021. https://labour.delhi.gov.in/sites/default/files/All-PDF/Order_MW2019.pdf

4 Ministry of Home Affairs (2020, March 29) Order No. 40-3/2020-DM-I(A) Government of India https://www.mha.gov.in/sites/default/files/MHA%20Order%20restricting%20movement%20of%20migrants%20and%20strict%20enforement%20of%20lockdown%20measures%20-%2029.03.2020_0.pdf

5 National Commission for Enterprises in the Unorganised Sector (2006). *Social Security for Unorganised Workers: Report*. New Delhi: Government of India.

19

Hunger and Lockdown

Not New to the Tea Garden Workers; Neither is Our Apathy

BANOJYOTSNA LAHIRI

Sunil Oraon (31) from Bhatkhawa Tea Garden of the Dooars had migrated to Jodhpur, Rajasthan to work in the timber line. He, along with 12 others from Alipurduar, was stranded there without work through April and May after the nationwide lockdown owing to the outbreak of Covid-19 pandemic started. At this time, they did not receive any ration. 'We made some distress calls and a local charitable organisation came and gave us cooked food. They assured us they will give us cooked food, whenever we called them,' Sunil said on the phone to me. 'We took their food for about a week. But it felt like we were begging. We are workers and making the call every morning was an affront to our dignity. We wanted ration so that we could cook our own food but did not get any. Now we are buying minimum ration with the little money that we had saved and once we run out of that, we shall have to start begging again.' Sunil's wife

Sapna Oraon is a casual labourer in Bhatkhawa tea garden. Since only permanent workers were being employed in their tea garden in the lockdown, she was not earning at the time of writing this report. When I had spoken to Sunil in May while he was stuck in Jodhpur, he had said to me, 'She is managing on her own. I feel scared to talk to her these days. Both of us, miles apart, are surviving in hunger'

The story of Sunil and Sapna encapsulates the distress that the families of tea garden workers have faced during the lockdown. One of the major sources of income for the tea garden workers in the Dooars is what the family members who have migrated outside for work earn. With the countrywide lockdown and cessation of work of any kind, that source of income had dried up completely. Migrant workers from the Dooars were stranded in various places in the country without any work where they found themselves dependent on the food that was being distributed by governmental and non-governmental agencies as part of relief efforts. This is precisely what they had intended to escape when they had left the tea gardens and set off to look for fresh work opportunities in other parts of the country.

Hunger, lockdown or even social distancing are not new to those inhabiting the tea plantations in West Bengal. They only took on new meaning here post the Corona pandemic. The lush green tea gardens of both Assam and West Bengal have witnessed severe violations of labour rights for centuries. Hunger and starvation stalk the daily lives of the 350,000 workers here who are underpaid, overworked, malnourished even as they work daily in the 294 surviving tea gardens of the Dooars in West Bengal. Moreover, the plantation labourers here have always been forced by the management to maintain social isolation in order to ensure the reproduction of labour forces within the tea gardens. The labour force is not free to switch jobs or even migrate unless they are retrenched or the garden is locked down by the management. Forced migration of other family members and human trafficking of children, especially girls, are, however, common phenomena owing to the abject poverty rampant among the community. The tea gardens lack access to safe and adequate drinking water. Most hospitals and medical facilities in the tea gardens are abysmally ill-equipped lacking qualified healthcare officials or even medicines. The outbreak of a viral epidemic in these remote and underdeveloped areas can easily accelerate into a human catastrophe.

Many tea gardens in West Bengal and Assam did not close down immediately following the announcement of the lockdown and flouting the order kept working till 25 March. As the COVID-19 scare mounted, the tea gardens finally closed. 19 trade unions and organisations made a Joint Deputation to the Chief Secretary of the state demanding full lockdown of the tea gardens with the payment of wages to the workers during this period. The first COVID-19 death of a 44-year-old woman on 30 March in Kalimpong Medical College fortified this demand. But the tea estate owners have had a terrible history when it comes to labour rights. Moreover, they were worried because this is the season of skiffing and plucking the first flush tea leaves that are the most precious, particularly for the Darjeeling variety of tea. Together they quickly did the math and estimated a huge impending loss for the industry. By 29 March, they demanded compensation from the government worth Rs 1455 crore. Leveraging their clout with the government, the tea lobby managed to secure an exception to the lockdown right away. The central government issued a notice on 3 April and announced that only 50 per cent of the workforce could work in the gardens provided proper measures for sanitisation and social distancing were maintained. This was against the rule of the lockdown, as well as the much touted 'Stay Home, Stay Safe' message being sent out all across the country. The tea crops clearly seemed more valuable to the government than the lives of the tea garden workers; this is nothing new, however, since their lives have not mattered to authorities for decades now.

The state government of West Bengal declared on 9 April that 15 per cent of the workforce could be used for skiffing and plucking the first flush leaves. On 11 April, in a fresh notice, they directed that 25 per cent of the labour force could be employed for all activities of the garden, albeit taking necessary precautions. It was decided that the workforce would be employed rotationally. As a result, mostly only permanent workers were employed in most of the gardens.

For the workforce employed in work, social distancing goes for a toss every morning as the workers throng at the tea garden gate or huddle in the shade during lunchtime. 'Some tea gardens have given soap to the workers to wash their hands while in work. Some others didn't bother even with that,' said Rupam Deb, a social activist who works for the rights of tea garden labourers. It was evident that the tea garden management wanted to continue work and ensure the plucking of the first flush tea leaves without any concerns for the risks the workers were being exposed to.

Gradually the tea gardens increased the workforce allowed in the gardens beyond 25 per cent. The workers once again were not in a position to oppose this. Bittu (39), a worker from the Sonali Tea Estate, said the gardens were working as usual. 'Out of 358 permanent workers, 70–80 were working every day earlier, but gradually the number has increased.' While work has resumed, however, the workers' payment has been blocked due to lockdown. Bittu informed us that the management had not released three previous instalments of payments to the workers. Given a choice between hunger deaths and contamination by the virus, the workers had clearly chosen the latter. Contamination is after all left to chance while death from hunger seemed imminent.

For the workers of the tea gardens which had closed down in the recent past, the difficulties are greater. Fifty-four tea gardens had closed in West Bengal between 2000 and 2004. Out of these 47 were subsequently reopened, while six still remain closed, leaving 4,345 workers unemployed. Sushma (42), who worked at Bandapani tea garden that has been closed for eight years now, is one of them. But even as the garden factory bears a haunted look, overtaken as it is by weed and rust, the workers collect raw tea leaves and sell them illegally in the open market through local agents. This has been the practice for the last eight years during the first flush season and it fetches them around Rs 130 per day.

Owing to the lockdown, however, the markets closed, drying up a major source of income which had sustained these out-of-work labourers through the rest of the year. Moreover, the meagre compensation of Rs 1500 per month that they used to receive from the state government as erstwhile workers of a now closed tea garden also ceased after the lockdown was announced. The money is paid quarterly every year and there are no banking facilities in the vicinity of the closed tea gardens. Stuck inside the closed tea gardens without any access to banks or cash, many workers like Sushma were scared that they would not be left with any cash when the lockdown eased. In such a situation, many of them find themselves solely dependent on the ration that the government is providing.

The ration disbursal in the Dooars region is done per family. The registered monthly ration of 20 kg of rice, 15 kg of flour and 3 kg of sugar is given to every family per week irrespective of its size. Larger families normally find it inadequate, but during the lockdown, it was the only source of food for everyone. Both Bittu and Sushma informed us that the government had started charging Rs 13/kg for sugar and soon they would not be in a position to pay this amount any more. Other essential commodities like milk, oil, salt or vegetables had to be procured by them on their own. They were already cutting down on all these elements and were thriving on simplest and blandest of cooking.

The congested workers' colonies of the Dooars have never been conducive to any kind of social distancing. With migrant family members returning in large numbers from various parts of the country, social distancing has become even more of a remote possibility in these overcrowded colonies. The already ill-equipped medical centres are not able to contain the situation and there is a real fear that the gardens could turn into death beds.

The other major source of income for the tea garden workers in Dooars, as mentioned before, is the income of the family members who have migrated outside for work. These migrant workers working elsewhere are in fact the main pillars of economic viability for the families battling the unstable and dwindling sources of income in the tea gardens. With the nationwide lockdown, these workers suddenly lost their sources of income and were left vulnerable in the face of a fast-spreading pandemic. Rahul Oraon (29), for example, worked as a helping hand in a restaurant in Bangalore. He had migrated from Sonali Bagan Tea Garden, where his mother still worked. When the lockdown was announced, he was stuck without work along with four others in Bangalore. They had received rations from the local police station on 7 April and 18 April, which they were surviving on judiciously; what this meant was that they ate only once a day. It goes without saying that they were unable to send any money home. When we spoke to Rahul again in June, he informed us that they were still in Bangalore, waiting to get a place in the Shramik Special Trains that the government had started to take migrant workers back home. Rahul said most of the other migrants have already left for their villages.

'What is the point in staying back here? We work in restaurants. Most of the restaurants here don't know when they will reopen and how many people they would be able to retain. We want to go back home, at least for some months now.' He was hopeful that since people were now going back home, he would be able to board the train back home too. Asked what he would do back home, he responded that he had no clue, but that he was still desperate to leave.

From April 2020 onwards, reverse migration from cities to villages had started on an unprecedented scale. By May itself, Rajesh Roy and Vibhuti Agarwal, in an article in the *Wall Street Journal,* estimated the number of migrants who had returned home to be as high as 10 million people[1]. The first lot of around 4 million walked home, while 6–7 million more were taken back by the 5,200 special trains started by the government. The migrant workers who were one of the major financial supports to the families of tea garden workers, returning unemployed would only add to the existing distress of the tea workers. But they were left with no other choice.

Two Public Interest Litigations were filed in the Supreme Court, on behalf of Labour Unions, the first from Assam and the second from Darjeeling and the Dooars, demanding that the management pay the workers in the lockdown period, ensure their safety from contamination and stop work in the tea gardens. Bandana Rai, a Delhi-based lawyer and social activist filed one petition on behalf of the tea garden workers in the Dooars and Darjeeling. She urged the Supreme Court to intervene and compel the state and central government to roll back the exemption granted to tea gardens from the lockdown, to release payments to the workers including their pending Provident Fund dues and to ensure maximum hygiene and safety in the tea gardens. The Supreme Court did not intervene on behalf of the petition and instructed the petitioner to approach the state authorities instead.

Bandana Rai further wrote to the Chief Secretary of West Bengal on 16 May asking them to immediately stop work in the tea gardens and ensure health and other securities to the workers in the gardens and colonies. On 24 August the lawyers approached the Supreme Court citing a case of contempt to their previous order since the state government had never responded. The Supreme Court ordered the state to file an affidavit. While this back and forth game continued between the judiciary and the executive, the cases of COVID-19 in the district galloped, and stood at 347 in August 2020. The spike was clearly linked to the inflow of migrant workers who entered the district throughout June and July.

'Successive governments over the decades have betrayed the tea garden workers,' Advocate Bandana Rai says, 'They value the tea leaves more than human lives. They sell the tea leaves illegally in the open market for crores of rupees and show low turnout of sales. They cut down on payment of workers and rob them of their basic livelihoods. This has led into abject poverty among the tea garden workers and human trafficking especially of girl children has consistently increased. The lockdown has only added to the woes to the tea garden workers.'

It is evident that the overall situation of the tea garden workers across the Dooars region has only deteriorated during the lockdown. Fear of starvation is the phantom that has relentlessly haunted the workers in the tea gardens all their lives. The fresh anxiety of contamination has only added teeth to that fear.

Notes

1 Roy, R. & Agarwal, V. (2020, May 27). 'Millions of Indians Are Fleeing Cities, Raising Fears of a Coronavirus 'Land Mine' in Villages'. *The Wall Street Journal.* Accessed 21 August 2020. https://www.wsj.com/articles/indias-migrants-head-home-as-lockdown-eases-prompting-fears-of-coronavirus-spread-11590579072

20

Tales from North East Delhi

Living through Communal Violence, a Pandemic and an Apathetic State

VARNA BALAKRISHNAN AND MEERA VISWANATHAN

Communal violence raged across the largely working-class Muslim neighbourhoods of North East Delhi from 24 to 27 February 2020. Houses and shops were burnt, severed bodies were abandoned in drains, thousands were displaced and an entire community fled with their lives clutched in their hands into deeper corners of the urban jungle. When the violence ended, thousands had been left without homes, jobs, savings and sometimes without family members. In the weeks after the violence, many families struggled to find their missing kin and provide care for those injured and hospitalised. The community was in acute need of housing, ration, toiletries, clothes and medicines. They also needed legal support to file for compensation, missing persons reports and for obtaining medico-legal certificates, as well as financial and livelihood strengthening support.

This atmosphere of severe insecurity and anxiety was intensified by the nationwide lockdown in the wake of the COVID-19 pandemic announced on 24 March, less than a month after the violence had subsided. What protections did the world's strictest lockdown provide the survivors of the violence? Livelihoods destroyed by the violence were further debilitated, food insecurity and hunger worsened and health facilities became even more inaccessible. On the one hand, the state and the media wrapped the pandemic with Islamophobia, and on the other, the Delhi Police proceeded to indiscriminately arrest and interrogate Muslim youth in the name of investigating the violence.[1] The meagre sums promised as compensation to those affected remained enmeshed in red tape.

Since the violence broke out, we have been working in different capacities with the people of Mustafabad, one of the most severely affected areas, first, as humanitarian emergency volunteers, supporting rescue and relief and conducting need assessments, and then as community workers with our training in mental health care and research.[2] Javed, Aamir, Heena, Ruksana and others of whom we write here, shared their stories and time with us through this work.[3]

What Does it Mean to Survive Communal Violence?

> *During our home visits, we met four-year-old Fatima from Mustafabad. When we gave her some colours to draw with, she only drew houses. 'All I want is to go back to my house. It's burnt now and I can never go back home, so this is what I want to draw.' Fatima witnessed her home being burnt down in Shiv Vihar. Her family has since taken refuge in a relatively safer neighbourhood nearby.*

Right after the violence, the community's mental health struggles were acute and palpable. Many survivors showed complaints of back aches, stomach aches, panic attacks and insomnia that were clear signs of anxiety and potential Post-Traumatic Stress Disorder. These signs of stress were not limited to those who were direct witnesses of the violence; even hosts of the displaced reported having splitting headaches, panic attacks and an inability to sleep.

As a month passed by, a few families began returning to their broken or looted homes and finding ways to rebuild their lives. Many others were still living in temporary accommodations and a small fraction of them, over a thousand people, were living in the government-run temporary relief camp at Eidgah.

By this time, short-term relief efforts were beginning to lose their value. In the homes where families were hosting violence-affected families, resources had thinned out significantly. With state-assured compensation having reached only a small fraction of families, and livelihood severely shaken, financial resources were also completely draining out. In trying times, it is crucial for the state to step in and provide relief, but in its absence, families were left to the care and efforts of the civil society.

> *'Do you think we like begging and asking for food and money from all of you? All we want is our lives back. We need jobs. We understand that you can't solve all our problems. The government needs to step in.'*
>
> —Irfan, survivor

A Pandemic of Uncertainty

> *'Just when things were starting to get a little better, the lockdown came in and changed everything for the worse.'*
>
> —Aamir, survivor

On the day the lockdown was announced, there was chaos all across Mustafabad. The reluctantly set up and haphazardly run relief camp in Eidgah was closed overnight; most families were given a token sum of Rs 3000 and some ration which barely lasted two days, and asked to fend for themselves even as heavy rains lashed Delhi.[4] One of the residents in the camp recalled this as one of the most traumatic nights of his life. He said, 'I did not know where to go. It was raining heavily and I was homeless with my two little children. We had nowhere to go!' That evening, a team of volunteers worked on finding shelter for those who had been abandoned. Over the lockdown, families affected by the violence were displaced from their homes not once but multiple times. They had to hunt for shelter in their relatives' homes, and in some cases even strangers' houses. Many did not have the money for rent and were facing evictions. The anxiety among families without homes understandably peaked during this time.

In the story of their survival, the night of the Eidgah eviction stands out as a painful reminder of the state's abandonment of the community. When the lockdown came into effect, they became aware that they could expect little from the government, as through this overnight eviction, the government had made its apathy clear. However, the months succeeding the violence also showed them that they cannot survive on civil society's aid alone either.

Food insecurity

As it desperately held onto our relief efforts, we realised that Mustafabad had become a breeding ground for other hidden epidemics. Hunger and desperation for food was common for everyone there, regardless of their relationship with the violence. Widespread public anxiety about an impending food shortage did not help. However, for the violence-affected people, this food insecurity was not new.

A month after the violence, Ruksana and her family were still facing great precarity. In the violence, the majority of their house and her sons' workplace had been burnt down, and their 13 buffalos had been stolen. Through the lockdown, the family of eight lived in the one unburnt room of their house with no income. Conversations with the family during this time largely revolved around where food for the next few days would come from. Ruksana's son Asif regularly stood in line at the mosque nearby where food was being distributed, but would often come back empty-handed. Their money for rations was running out. On some days, a fresh ration delivery would ensure food for a few days, but that would soon run out and the family would be reduced once again to a state of uncertainty. They desperately wanted to start working again, but even several months after the lockdown was lifted, the family continues to have no prospect of livelihood in sight. They have received only Rs 25,000 of the Rs 4,00,000 that they are entitled to as compensation till now. Ruksana's family members continue to wait anxiously to resume their lives, standing inches away from hunger.

Fear of violence

Heena, a 16-year-old resident of Mustafabad, fainted every time she heard a loud noise after the violence in Northeast Delhi. When we met her 10 days after the incident, she said that she could not sleep or eat anything. On 24 February, she had hurt her back while fleeing from her home to escape a fire set alight by an angry mob in her locality. Every day, she fears that someone will chase her. She is scared that she will never be 'normal' again. During the lockdown, these fears intensified. After the violence, several localities and streets began to erect their own protective iron gates. The keys to the gates in Heena's community belong to Hindu families, and this has made her feel even more vulnerable.

Being locked-down in her house this way led Heena to feel constantly threatened, fuelling her paranoia. Such fears of being violently attacked for being Muslim have been permanently etched in the minds of several survivors like her. Her paralysing fear stops her from getting out of her home. She worries that she might be getting ill. Heena's fears are concerning because this constant distress can get hardwired into an individual's psyche and potentially lead to her biggest fear, a serious illness. Since the violence, borders have hardened on religious lines in previously diverse neighbourhoods. Unlike Heena's, several families have chosen to never return to their burnt or looted homes and remain instead in the Muslim neighbourhoods that gave them refuge. The more we speak to people in Mustafabad, the more evident it becomes that this fear is shared, omnipresent and persistent, even now, nearly a year since the violence.

Fear of arrests

As the lockdown intensified and police investigations brought about incessant arrests, members of the community became even more aware of their identity as working-class Muslims. Every day, people were witnessing their friends and neighbours either being taken into custody or being assaulted by the police for 'breaking' the rules of the lockdown. Retired labourer Akram felt he was living a nightmare.

'Kya karein? Inki Sarkar hai. Inki marzi hai. Humare paas sirf duaein hain'. (What can we do? It's their government, it's their whim. All we have are our prayers). Akram found his family and himself in a particularly vulnerable situation. The old man had a fever and was fatigued. When we spoke to him, it had been

over two months since his son, Iqbal, had not returned after leaving to run an errand. He was picked up from the market and arrested on grounds of inciting violence, and has since been sent to jail. While they do have a lawyer now, the family did not have the Rs 2,00,000 that lawyers first asked to get Iqbal released. Akram's is not a family that one would think is in need. 'We have everything—a house, a vehicle—but I feel ashamed of our state now, and to say that we are in need.' With the sole earning member of the family arrested, and a lockdown thrust upon them, the family needs support. Akram is worried for his grandchildren—what does the future hold for them with their father arrested?

During the lockdown, Akram waited for the courts to re-open to see his son. Despite his old age, he continues the fight for Iqbal's freedom, but 10 months after his arrest, Iqbal is still incarcerated. Akram finds solidarity in the stories of many others who have been indiscriminately arrested across Delhi, knowing that his son's arrest is part of a pattern that targets those like him. Akram's health is deteriorating in the meanwhile, but he has little scope or resources to take care of himself.

Loneliness and isolation

We first met Javed a few days after the violence subsided. He had fled along with his family of seven to the relatively peaceful Indira Vihar locality, where they were given safe abode at the house of a local, Shamsad. Javed insisted that he is not a victim of the violence, for he had lost no one in his family to it. However, having escaped with nothing but their lives, the family were in dire need of almost all essentials—from ration to bedding, clothes, utensils and undergarments. His youngest child, a five-year-old, was unwell, possibly with Jaundice. Because of what they had witnessed, the family was in shock. His young daughter had not slept for days.

A few weeks into the lockdown, we caught up with Javed. His family had left town to visit their native village while Javed had stayed behind in Indira Vihar. Although he no longer had the urgent need for relief items as he did a few weeks ago, he was now separated from his family, and still without a source of income. Although his family had witnessed violence that completely disrupted their life, it was his loneliness that Javed talked about when we met him this time.

When we spoke to Javed, he was overwhelmed, scared and extremely concerned for himself and his family. He had never stayed away from them for this long. Having spent many days alone in his small house, little things like finding food, cooking and taking care of himself had become large burdens. He began to display apathy and severe hopelessness. However, through slow and steady support, he began to cope better and reach out to his neighbours.

Javed's loneliness was outside the imagination of the middle class. It was not as glamorous as the ones written about in magazine articles that call for routine and exercise as the antidote to isolation during a pandemic. Javed's isolation was quiet and invisible. Even with the intervention of a trained psychosocial volunteer, it took time for him to speak about his isolation; the stigma around masculinity and vulnerability further added to his hesitation. There are many like him who have not been able to seek mental health support, whose loneliness is an invisible battle. Unfortunately, due to the severe gaps and disparity in mental health support for working-class persons, these struggles remain unknown and unaddressed.

Living in Insecurity

Javed, Amir, Heena, Ruksana, Akram, Fatima and Irfan are only a handful of the thousands of people whose lives were irrevocably changed by the violence in February 2020 and the lockdown from March 2020 onwards. Their stories show us a community grappling with a mental health crisis at the hands of a system that does not see them. The impact of the lockdown is unique and more concerning to those in Northeast Delhi. The community is now living in a state of great fear and anxiety where housing, livelihoods, physical safety, food security and freedom have been rendered precarious, and where faith in the state has eroded beyond repair. In their isolation and in their family homes, there is great uncertainty about what the future holds and if they would ever be able to rebuild what they have lost.

In any situation of violence, the months right after are crucial to healing. However, for the families affected by the Delhi violence, their period of healing was brutally disrupted by the lockdown. Not only did it halt and prolong the healing process, it endangered them further through its Islamophobic and anti-poor narrative. Nearly a year since the violence, the anxiety continues. A team of community workers, who are also from the affected areas, have been working with the survivors to help them with their legal, medical and psychosocial needs. They have observed that the fear of impending violence and the trauma of what they experienced in February 2020 continue to prevent families from bringing their children back to their former homes.

It is crucial to remember that healing cannot happen in an environment of apathy. Through the course of the violence, its aftermath and the pandemic, the community has increasingly felt that there is little that they can expect from the state. The state was not only central to instigating the violence, but was also complicit in its unfolding and apathetic in its aftermath. Despite the many months that have passed since the violence, there has been no official acknowledgement, let alone remorse, for what this community has had to endure. On the contrary, the community that bore the largest losses has now been vilified, and several of those who dissented have been incarcerated.

We have seen how in many crucial instances during the lockdown, the state constantly pushed families into further insecurity. Unsurprisingly, several members of the community now feel abandoned by the state; When Akram said, '*Kya karein? Inki Sarkar hai. Inki marzi hai. Humare paas sirf duaein hain*' ('What can we do? It's their government, it's their whim. All we have are our prayers'), he highlighted a common sentiment. Mental health does not exist in isolation; every aspect of the difficulties communicated in these stories is proof of the oppressive structures that govern the lives of the survivors. In this scenario, identifying, addressing and understanding the psychosocial crisis is crucial. If this is not done, it can morph into larger physical, mental and social concerns, for collective trauma such as this is always transgenerational. This is why, by disrupting and burdening the critical period of healing, the lockdown has jeopardised the entire community's well-being in the long run. Ironically, among the families here, these injustices have overshadowed the fear of the COVID-19 pandemic itself.

> *'I'm not scared of Corona, I've already seen all the misery I can.'*
>
> —*Azeem, survivor*

Notes

1 Mander, H. (2020, April 13). 'The Coronavirus Has Morphed Into an Anti-Muslim Virus'. *The Wire*. Accessed 19 May 2021. https://thewire.in/communalism/coronavirus-anti-muslim-propaganda-india; Naqvi, F. (2020, April 20). 'My Name is Khan and I am Not a Coronavirus Carrier'. *The Wire*. Accessed 19 May 2021. https://thewire.in/communalism/my-name-is-khan-and-i-am-not-a-coronavirus-carrier; Saikia, A. (2020, April 8 8). 'The other virus:

Hate crimes against India's Muslims are Spreading with Covid-19'. *Scroll.in.* Accessed 19 May 2021. https://scroll.in/article/958543/the-other-virus-hate-crimes-against-indias-muslims-are-spreading-with-covid-19

2 We primarily work in the area of Old Mustafabad, where people displaced by extreme violence in the Muslim areas of the neighbouring localities of Shiv Vihar and Karawal Nagar sought refuge. Our work includes a still-active psychosocial support network, consisting of trained community workers whose work and insights have been crucial to this article.

3 The names of all survivors have been changed.

4 J. Anand Mohan & Sinha, J. (2020, March 25). 'Coronavirus: Delhi's Eidgah relief camp cleared out, riot-hit victims hunt for another Shelter'. *The Indian Express.* Accessed 19 May 2021. https://indianexpress.com/article/coronavirus/coronavirus-delhis-eidgah-relief-camp-cleared-out-riot-hit-victims-hunt-for-another-shelter-6329782/

21

Sanitation Workers

At the Bottom of the Frontline against COVID

SAGAR KUMBHARE

A sanitation worker who was assigned to work in Dharavi tested positive. Like most other urban poor families in a megacity like Mumbai, they did not have the square feet that allow for physical distancing. For those from his caste and class backdrop, the 80–100 square feet one-room houses were usually cramped with six to ten people living in shifts. But, during a crisis, as in the current COVID-19 lockdown period, they remained all bundled together for days and months. The victim family was living in one of those proverbial chawls made in colonial times to house workers. This one largely housed sanitation workers. Inadvertently, he ended up spreading it to his wife and she died on 12 April. Thereafter his son-in-law was also infected and then the entire family moved into quarantine.

This case raised concerns around the lives of the sanitation workers through the pandemic. However, the 'social distance' of class and caste ensured that these concerns did not linger for long. Sanitation workers fall in the essential services category. The government seems to have hung a death warrant around their necks sending them to the front to fight Corona without due concerns about their safety.

The Ministry of Health and Family Welfare issued a directive[1] that sanitation workers in hospitals and other places should be provided with personal protective equipment (PPE). But the question is how far have these directives been followed?

In Panna district of Madhya Pradesh, a local activist on 9 March asked the District Collectorate Office to provide protective gear for the sanitation workers as an urgent need given the current situation.

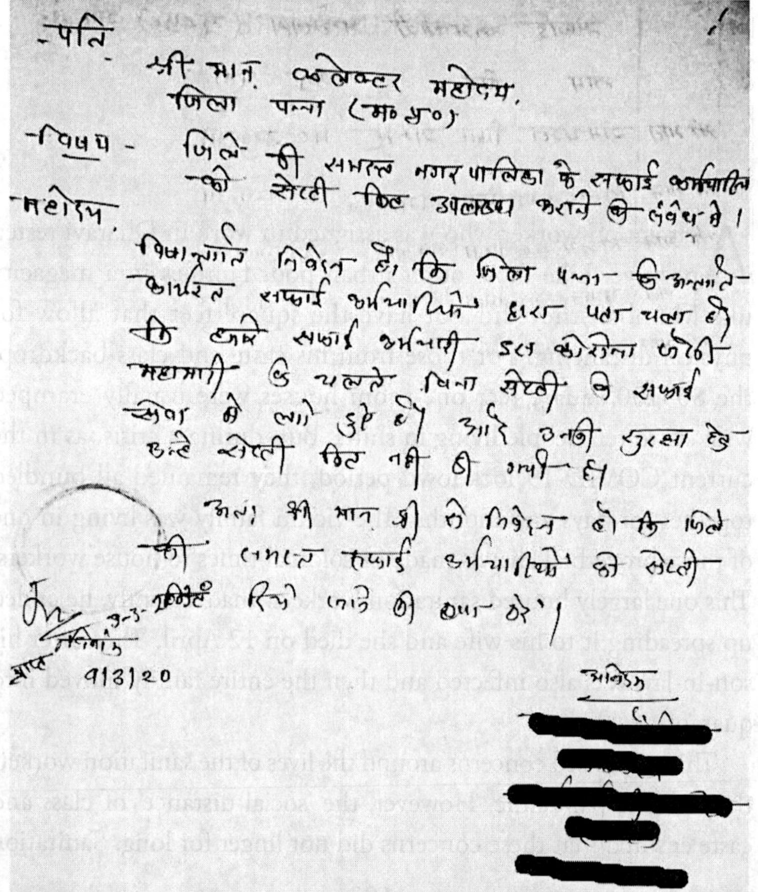

प्रति

श्री मान् कलेक्टर महोदय,
जिला पन्ना (म० प्र०)

विषय - जिले की समस्त नगर पालिका के सफाई कर्मचारियों को सेफ्टी किट उपलब्ध कराने के संबंध में।

महोदय,

विनम्र निवेदन है कि जिला पन्ना के अन्तर्गत कार्यरत सफाई कर्मचारियों द्वारा पता चला है कि उनके सफाई कर्मचारी इस कोरोना जैसी महामारी के चलते बिना सेफ्टी के सफाई सेवा में लगे हुए हैं और उनकी सुरक्षा हेतु उन्हें सेफ्टी किट नहीं दी गयी है।

अतः श्री मान जी से निवेदन है कि जिले की समस्त सफाई कर्मचारियों को सेफ्टी किट दिये जाने की व्यवस्था करें।

9-3-
प्राप्त 9/3/20

आवेदक

After a few days, he received a call from the Collectorate office saying that Madhya Pradesh state currently does not have an 'Urban Development and Housing Minister' and therefore, the state government is not sending money to procure protective equipment. Just like sewer deaths have proved time and again, even the pandemic has not nudged the apathy of political leaders and the administration as far as sanitation workers are concerned.

Sunil Yadav, a sanitation worker and a PhD fellow from TISS, says, 'Everyday sanitation workers get exposed to deadly trash but no special training/guidance is provided to them for how to handle trash.' According to the *New England Journal of Medicine's* study,[2] the coronavirus can survive on plastic and stainless steel surfaces for up to 72 hours, and on cardboard surfaces for up to 24 hours. Nobody knows what kind of waste material is present in dustbins and trash bags that the sanitation workers collect from Indian homes and streets. In India people don't segregate their trash; they mix everything in one bag. Many a time sanitation workers encounter sanitary pads, expired medicine bottles, broken glass and sharp-edged objects in the trash they sort through. Lack of protective gear thus makes sanitation workers' life difficult even in normal time. During a pandemic, they are without doubt even more vulnerable to the virus. Three generations of Sunil Yadav's family[3] have been engaged in sanitation work, all working with the Brihan Mumbai Corporation. During the interview with a web portal, he said 'In such a hopeless atmosphere, my mother wanted me to study. Dr Babasaheb Ambedkar's movement had a great impact on the lives of people, literate or not. Yet I did not know much about Ambedkar, caste and related issues till I was 25. There was no one for guidance, who could have shaped my quest for a dignified life.'

When his father fell ill and suffered paralysis, and it became clear that he could not work anymore, Sunil Yadav got his father's position at BMC. He had now entered a cruel and apathetic world.

He says about that time, 'On the very first day, I thought that the work wouldn't be much difficult. I was assigned the work at "house gully", a narrow place between two buildings in which people put garbage at Grant Road. That day, as I returned home, my entire body was stinking. I was unable to eat because of the horrible stench. My body was aching too. I washed my body several times but the stench did not go.'

Despite knowing how hard Sunil Yadav has worked to uplift his own and other sanitation workers' lives, rather than helping him, BMC created a lot of trouble for him. Despite all these odds, however, he succeeded in securing his seat in TISS for a PhD. As a responsible husband and following the path of Mahatma Phule and Savitribai Phule, he also encouraged and helped his wife to get an education; currently, his wife is pursuing a law degree.

Sanitation workers, almost all of whom are from the Dalit community, are rarely given protective gear. And today even in this pandemic, essentials like masks, gloves and hand sanitisers or just simple soap are not provided.

Rajan, a sanitation worker said, "They gave us some pairs of gloves and a few masks but they were torn after just a day. We asked for more gloves but they said it is going to take time." [4]

A local activist from Panna district of MP said, 'Our people are standing amidst Coronavirus crisis with courage, but there is always a fear in their minds, what if I get infected with Coronavirus? Who will take care of my family and children? Who will feed them?'

So, despite being at the frontlines, sanitation workers are still at the bottom of our priorities. A few days ago, the Delhi CMO's official twitter handle said *'Doctors are on the frontlines of the battle against coronavirus. All doctors serving in Delhi government's Lok Nayak Hospital and GB Pant Hospital on COVID-19 duty will now be housed in Hotel Lalit.'* Similarly, the Uttar Pradesh government has taken over four five-star hotels—Hyatt Regency, Lemon Tree, The Piccadily and Fairfield by Marriott—to lodge doctors. In Mumbai, Taj Hotel, Colaba and Taj Lands End, Bandra have opened for doctors and other health workers. Be it for the corporates or our political leaders, sanitation workers hardly ever feature as frontline workers. It lays bare yet again how caste and class continue to shape our public policy, blinding it to the concerns of some while compelling it to focus only on others.

When I asked Sunil Yadav in a pandemic situation, what had changed for sanitation workers, said he replied, 'Nothing, nobody cares. Here in Mumbai, sanitation workers travel 3 to 4 hours to reach their working place; nobody arranged transportation for us as they did for the doctors and other medical staff.'

Renu Devi used to work as a maid before the lockdown in Dehri, Bihar. When I spoke to her in April she was out of work while her husband was working as a sanitation worker in a hospital earning Rs 7,500 per month. Every day her husband carried an extra pair of clothes to wear at the hospital. Hospital administration needs them to work, but without equipping them with proper protection gear that are required in these times. News like the death of the sanitation chief, Mr Heera Lal, in a premier institute like AIIMS gives a fair idea of the precarity of those engaged in this work at lower levels.

When I again called Renu Devi after a month, she said, her husband had lost his job, and nobody was calling her for any kind of work. She sounded very upset and worried about the future of her children.

Through thick and thin, she has supported her family and community members and made attempts for their upliftment; she believes that only education can empower a community, and therefore, she decided to educate her children. She refused to do dry latrine cleaning and learned to work on a sewing machine to earn money, but because of her social background, not a single woman from the upper caste visits her house to give her clothes to stitch.

During the pandemic, the Indian government and Indian citizens celebrated Corona warriors, but when the lockdown eased, all such celebrations evaporated. Hundreds of sanitation workers, like Renu Devi's husband, lost their jobs after the lockdown. These workers played a crucial role during the lockdown; they collected waste from containment zones, hospitals, even dealt with medical waste. But nobody gave any thought to their future: how their families would survive? how their children would continue their studies?; and how he/she would bear the expenses of the household?

A Legacy of Exclusion

Shivshankar is a father of five daughters and two sons. He used to work at a hotel in Dhanbad as a cleaner. His wife Rekha is also a cleaner working upper-caste Hindu and rich Muslim houses. His older son Virkumar works as a sanitation worker on contract. They earn Rs. 7,000, Rs. 3,000 and Rs. 5,000 per month respectively. But since the lockdown began, they are all without jobs. Shivshankar does not have any money and the PDS rations are far from enough for his family.

Those like Shivshankar find it more difficult during the lockdown as compared with those engaged with government institutions such as a municipality or hospital as the latter at least have work. Shivshankar says, '*Jab sab theek tha tab to kuchh mila nahi, ab kya milega? Ab to sarkar se koi ummeed nahi rakhte hai*' (During normal days we received nothing. So, what can we expect now. We have no hopes from the government). When I asked him why he could not seek help from his employer, he responded, 'I can't ask my employer to provide me with food or give me a salary in advance. I know them personally. Nobody will help me because I am a *Basfor*.'[5]

Shivshankar is merely one of thousands of sanitation workers who starved during the lockdown, and were reduced to begging for food to feed their families. All his life, Shivshankar has struggled for dignity for his community. Whenever he stood up, he was heckled by not only the government institutions but also by society. When I spoke to him during the end of the fourth phase of the lockdown, he said to me, 'Nobody is here to ask them, if they are alive or not? Our existence doesn't matter to these people. Half of the life we spent to serve them, but when we really wanted some help they abandoned us. But we do not have other options; let God decide, what is good for us.'

Indeed, by the end of the fourth phase of lockdown, more than the virus it was the government that had thrown thousands of sanitation workers' families into abject poverty. According to the findings of a 2013 study by the *International Dalit Solidarity Network*, poverty makes lower castes more vulnerable during emergencies. Experience from the 2001 Gujarat earthquake, the 2004 Asian Tsunami and the flooding in Nepal (2008) or in the Indian states of Bihar, Andhra Pradesh, Karnataka and Assam (during 2007–2009), and in Pakistan (2010) has shown that Dalits are more likely to be among the worst affected when such emergencies occur. Nevertheless, they continue to be systematically excluded from relief and recovery efforts due to their inherent socio-economic vulnerability.[6] The pandemic has not changed this grim but unshakable reality.

Raju Basfor (38) from Dhanbad, was working as a sanitation worker along with his two sons, who are 18 and 19 years of age. He lost his wife in 2013, and since then he has raised his four children on his own. The lockdown left him and his sons without jobs and he is not sure whether he will get the same work after the lockdown ends. '*Pehle chhua chhut ke karan hum toilet saaf karte the, ab to mahamari ke chalte log hume aur dur karenge. Abhi bhi hum log ek waqt ka khana kha rahe hai, kabhi kabhi bacche bhi bhukhe sote hai. Iss waqt hum zinda hai na, mar gaye hai*…*bas ek zinda laash ki tarah hai.*' (Because of the practice of untouchability we used to clean toilets but now, due to Covid-19, people will maintain even more distance from us. We are surviving on one meal, sometimes the children have to sleep on an empty stomach. It's like we are the living dead.)

Like the other respondents we spoke to, Raju too tried to contact officers to get some help but as usual they did not respond to his request. At the end of the call in a hard voice he said, '*Hum to kide hai, jis gandagi me paida huve hai usime marenge, par is samaj aur sarkar ke kamkaj me kuchh badlav nahi ayega*' (We are like germs, we will die in the dirt in which we were born, but nothing will change in the world around us).

Caste and Corona

> *'The outcaste is a by-product of the caste system. There will be outcastes as long as there are castes. Nothing can emancipate the outcaste except the destruction of the caste system.'*
>
> *—Dr Babasaheb Ambedkar*

The caste system continues to 'reserve' the sewer and sanitation work for Dalits, be it the Brihanmumbai Municipal Corporation or Nagar Parishad Dehri or the private sector. For instance, around 30,000 sanitation workers are employed by the Greater Mumbai Municipal Corporation and all 30,000 are Dalits. Estimates place 40 to 60 per cent of the 6 million households of Dalit sub-castes to be engaged in sanitation work. While the The Prohibition of Employment as Manual Scavengers and their Rehabilitation Act, 2013 in the 64th year of the Republic formally acknowledged the 'historical injustice and indignity suffered by the manual scavengers', but the persistence of caste has ensured that the implementation of the Act has been far from satisfactory.

As the number of COVID-19 cases in India keeps rising, there is one group that has been left particularly vulnerable. A survey[7] conducted in June 2020 on 214 sanitation workers, mainly in Assam, Madhya Pradesh, Delhi NCR and the Mumbai Metropolitan Region, found that they have been given little protection during this period.[8]

While the 'Pradhan Sevak' participates in a PR exercise like washing the feet of sanitation workers before elections, it is a fact that during 2014–18, the government has not released a single rupee for the rehabilitation of manual scavengers as revealed in an RTI response received by an online web portal.

Radharani (58), a sanitation worker from Khajuraho says, 'From the first day of the lockdown till now, we are working every day to clean this city. We are scared, we are also humans, Corona can infect us also but the government doesn't understand this. I don't like to work here, but I have no options. Even the pandemic failed to make them realise the worth of the sanitation worker.' She adds: *'Sab log CORONA ke dar se ghar me hai, hum to yaha pe usise ladh rahe hai phir bhi humari koi kadar nahi hai'* (Everyone is at home because of the fear of Corona; we are out fighting the virus, but no one seems to want to spare a thought for us).

The novel Coronavirus is against the human race but an unplanned lockdown is against the poor. And as it appears both are poised disproportionately against the Dalits.

What sanitation workers need today are Personal Protection Equipment (PPE), minimum wages, food, insurance, accommodation and transportation like other health workers, mechanisation of their work and solidarity. The Prohibition of Employment as Manual Scavengers and their Rehabilitation Rules, 2013,[9] (under section 4 and 5 of the rules) mandates that the person who is getting the job done must provide the 'protective gear'. However, despite the efforts of many organisations, unions and activists, the government has shown no inclination towards enforcing the law.

Casteist apathy continues unabated in our country and in fact, it has been amplified in the face of the Corona crisis. Nothing

Annexure-I

Status of funds available and expemditure incurred under Self Employment Scheme for Rehabiliation of Manual Scavengers

(in Rupees)

Year	Funds Released by M/o SJ&E	interest earned	Total funds received in the year (2+3)	Total Funds Available (4+ 8 of previous year)	Expenditure Incurred	refund from SCA apex corporation	Net Balance (5-6+7)
(1)	(2)	(3)	(4)	(5)	(6)	(7)	(8)
2006-07	5600,00,000	2,59,898	5602,59,898	5605,19,796	1028,80,000	-	4576,39,796
2007-08	2500,00,000	430,53,004	2930,53,004	7506,92,800	3835,37,244	-	3671,55,556
2008-09	10000,00,000	266,60,241	10266,60,241	13938,15,797	12594,43,894	1170,30,250	2514,02,153
2009-10	5000,00,000	92,25,590	5092,25,590	7606,27,743	4223,27,071	-	3383,00,672
2010-11	-	228,52,455	228,52,455	3611,53,127	594,43,457	2936,14,642	5953,24,312
2011-12	-6000,00,000	464,98,092	-5535,01,908	418,22,404	12,38,952	1096,43,392	1502,26,844
2012-13	-	156,01,535	156,01,535	1658,28,379	1551,27,275	674,78,610	781,79,714
2013-14	5500,00,000	110,02,144	5610,02,144	6391,81,858	1779,39,313	948,43,543	5560,86,089
2014-15	-	535,26,790	535,26,790	6096,12,879	827,50,967	1042,65,732	6311,27,644
2015-16	-	448,76,134	448,76,134	6760,03,778	3778,48,659	627,89,695	3609,44,813
2016-17	-	106,67,901	106,67,901	3716,12,714	1398,98,009	117,66,500	2434,81,205
2017-18 (till date)				2434,81,205			
TOTAL	22600,00,000	2842,23,784			31624,34,841	8614,32,364	

makes this more evident than the fact that when municipal workers expressed the need for sanitisers given the nature of their work in the national capital, they were instead provided with fluorescent jackets so that they could be identified as 'essential' workers from a distance. Sooner or later scientists will invent a vaccine to fight Corona, but as a society, we are far from confronting the viral casteism that continues to determine the fate of millions over generations.

Notes

1 Ministry of Health and Family Welfare. (2020). *Novel Coronavirus Disease 2019 (COVID-19): Guidelines on rational use of Personal Protective Equipment*. New Delhi: Government of India. https://www.mohfw.gov.in/pdf/GuidelinesonrationaluseofPersonalProtectiveEquipment.pdf

2 van Doremalen, N., Bushmaker, T., Morris, D. H., Holbrook, M. G., Gamble, A., Williamson, B. N., Tamin, A., Harcourt, J. L., Thornburg, N. J., Gerber, S. I., Lloyd-Smith, J. O., de Wit, E. & Munster, V. J. (2020, March 17). Aerosol and Surface Stability of SARS-CoV-2 as Compared with SARS-CoV-1. *The New England Journal of Medicine, 382*(16), 1564–1567. https://www.nejm.org/doi/full/10.1056/NEJMc2004973

3 Maitreya Y. (2015, June 3). 'From scavenging to doctoral dreams: An inspiring journey of Sunil Yadav'. *TwoCircles.net*. Accessed 19 May 2021. http://twocircles.net/2015jul03/1435902464.html

4 Majumdar, S. (2020, April 12). 'A Dark Manhole, Caste and Covid-19'. *The Citizen*. Accessed 16 June 2021. https://www.thecitizen.in/index.php/en/NewsDetail/index/15/18584/A-Dark-Manhole-Caste-and-COVID-19

5 *Basfor* is a sub-caste that is considered even lower than the *Valmikis* in the Brahminical caste order.

6 Paul, L. M. (2011). *Addressing caste discrimination in Humanitarian Response*. New Delhi: National Dalit Watch-National Campaign

on Dalit Human Rights. https://idsn.org/wp-content/uploads/user_folder/pdf/New_files/India/2012/IDSN-EU_study_on_CBD_in_humanitarian_response_by_NDW.pdf

7 Nigam, D. D. & Dubey, S. (2020, June). *Condition of Sanitation Workers in India: A Survey During Covid-19 and Lockdown.* New Delhi: India. An Independent Study Report. Accessed 16 June 2021. https://www.academia.edu/43470203/Condition_of_sanitation_workers_in_India_A_survey_during_COVID_19_and_lockdown

8 Ghosh, S. (2020, September 8). 'Little protection for sanitation workers during COVID-19 pandemic, finds survey'. *The Hindu.* Accessed 16 June 2021. https://www.thehindu.com/news/national/little-protection-for-sanitation-workers-during-covid-19-pandemic-finds-survey/article32550790.ece

9 Ministry of Social Justice and Empowerment. (2013). *National Dalit Watch-National Campaign on Dalit Human Rights.* New Delhi: Government of India. http://ielrc.org/content/e1314.pdf (Prohibition of Employment as Manual Scavengers and their Rehabilitation Rules 2013)

22

'Everything in the City Comes at a Price'

Urban Under-class and State Apathy During the COVID-19 Lockdown

BALU SUNILRAJ AND SURESH GARIMELLA

Mofidul, along with other workers, had already booked train tickets to Bengal from Delhi anticipating something akin to a lockdown for 25 March 2020. But given that the Indian Prime Minister is habituated to throwing cruel surprises, Mofidul, like several migrant labourers, was given only four hours of a head start to prepare for the lockdown. As a result, his tickets were cancelled. He lamented that the railway did not even refund the full cost of his ticket: '*IRCTC ne hamara pura paisa bhi nahi wapas kiya; refund kiya lekin pura paisa nahi*' (IRCTC did not even refund us fully. They did refund us, but not the entire amount).

Mofidul is an embroidery worker who came to Delhi from Bengal in 2003. He lives in Shahpur Jat, one of the hotspot settlements for migrant workers in Delhi. Like most workers in the Indian informal economy, Mofidul lived in precarious conditions with meagre wages, congested living conditions and no social security. Along with 18 other workers, Mofidul's home in Delhi was a 15x12 hall, in which they worked, ate and slept. Social distancing was not a privilege he could afford.

Before lockdown, Mofidul used to go to markets such as Chandini Chowk and Karol Bagh in search of orders based on piecemeal contracts and his income was dependent on the orders he procured. Falling sick in such conditions for him would be in itself an expensive affair. Earning only Rs 300 per day before lockdown, he would have to spend nearly a day's wage to visit the local doctor. The only solace among all these difficulties is that he did not face starvation. He managed to meet the basic minimum human need, to have three meals a day, even if nothing else was met. It is in these perilous and uncertain conditions that he entered the lockdown. For one whose life is a never-ending struggle, the impact of the lockdown was devastating.

Life post-lockdown has been a living nightmare for Mofidul and his co-workers. When we spoke to them, they had still not received pending payments from their contractors, which included their wages for the entire month of March 2020. The contractors, it seemed, did not pay heed to the moral sermons of Prime Minister Narendra Modi, to take care of their workers. Their own meagre savings enabled Mofidul and his fellow workers to somehow manage food for the first week. However, after that, they were entirely dependent on private donors to provide them with rations.

Like most migrant workers in the informal economy, there is no institutional support for Mofidul to rely upon, including the ration card. He and his co-workers are not registered with any department of the government nor are they safeguarded by any labour protection laws. Mofidul's landlord was considerate in the first month of the lockdown (April 2020), but after that started demanding payment of rent citing financial problems.

Most nights, Mofidul couldn't sleep till very late. He would be awake pondering about the uncertain future. He says, *'Agar market khula nahi aur 2 mahine kaam nahi milta hein tho ham tho bhuke maar jayenge'* (If the market does not open and we don't get any work for two months, we will die of starvation). The absence of starvation, which was the only respite in his precarious life before the lockdown now seemed like a distant dream.

Trapped in Sarojini Nagar, Away from the State's Gaze

When the lockdown was announced, Abdul Wahab could not leave for his home since the owner of the shop where he worked handed over responsibilities to him. His employer, it should be noted, had quickly moved to the safe havens of his village. Abdul was left alone, with no support. He had to abide by his employer's directions since it was the only measure through which he could hope to rejoin work when the lockdown is lifted. The perks of a contract-less world are that life and security take a backseat when it comes to job security. Abdul said to us, *'Agar abhi rahenge to baad mein hamey kaam dega isi liye ham rah gaye'* (If I stay now, I will have a job later. So I stayed).

Abdul hails from Uttar Dinajpur, West Bengal. He is 24 years old. Like several migrants, he was forced to leave Bengal due to the lack of viable economic opportunities in his state. Abdul's search for work took him to different parts of the country. He used to work in Ludhiana before ending up in Delhi. He came to Delhi eight years ago and became a sales vendor on the street. Later, he started working for a street cart owner, who owned a cart in the Sarojini Nagar Market. He says, *'Naya bande ko dukan lagane mein bohot kathinaye ka saamna karna padta hein'* (It is very difficult for newcomers to open shops). Despite its informality, power relations are a matter of fact even in the streets.

Abdul lives in 'Pillanji Gaon' in a dingy 6x8 room which he shares with six other people. Before the lockdown, he earned Rs 350 a day, which amounted to a meagre Rs 10,000 per month. Half of this money was sent to his parents in the village; he came to Delhi intending to provide at least two meals a day for his parents.

Like most migrants,[1] Abdul did not receive any help from the government in the lockdown period. He says, '*Government ki madad hum tak nahi pahoch paa raha hein*' (Government's assistance has not reached us). This meant complete dependence on private donations since he and his friends ran out of money within a week into lockdown. Already earning far below minimum wages, Abdul did not get any payment in March 2020 due to a lack of sales. The employer, therefore, postponed his payments. Abdul could not pressurise his employer to pay him since that could cost him his job. As is evident from Abdul's case, this deadly combination of informality and the uncertainties of the lockdown can mean the ruination of migrant lives.

Abdul was not alone in facing distress. This was the condition of almost all the migrant labourers who worked in Sarojini Nagar Market. Like all of them, Abdul hoped that the economy would bounce back to normality post-COVID. If not, millions like him would be unemployed. He also hoped to leave for Bengal as soon as the lockdown was lifted. When we spoke to him, he said that the expenses in Delhi were becoming increasingly unbearable for him. He said, '*Shahar mein har cheez ke liye paisa dena padta hein, gaon mein guzara ho jayega, adjust ho jata hein, yaha bohot mushkil ho raha hein*' (We need to pay for everything here. In the village, we adjust, we can sustain ourselves).

Despite all the difficulties he has faced, when we last spoke to him, Abdul continued to pin his hopes on the government.

He believed that only a positive intervention by the government would take care of the market and the economy. He said, *'Abhi toh government ko zimmedari se kaam karna chahiye, khulne ke baad humey government hi kuch kaam dikhani chahiye. Abh ke liye tho hum gaon jake kheti-badi karenge, kisi ke khet mein, majdoori karenge'* (Right now the government should work with some responsibility. After the lockdown lifts, the government should show us some work. For now, we will go to the village and work as labourers in someone's fields.)

But one can't help but wonder whether Abdul's hopes are misplaced, considering the half-baked economic packages of the Indian government that show no intent to increase government spending and rejuvenate the economy.

Longing for his Village in Delhi

Vikram's father is a sharecropper (tenant farmer) and his family consumes a large share of the rice which they produce in the fields. There were no employment opportunities in the village, and Vikram also had the extra responsibility of 'marrying off' his sisters apart from supporting his parents. Therefore, he shifted to Delhi in June 2019 in search of a job. Soon, he started working in a shop in Sarojini Nagar Market.

For Rs 300 per day, Vikram worked for nearly 12 hours every day. Since he was paid daily, Vikram rarely took a day off. The owner was rarely present in the workplace and would only come by the evening to pay the wages. The work in the shop was entirely carried out by Vikram and his co-workers.

Like Mofidul, Vikram's actions and decisions just preceding the lockdown were largely dependent on the instructions given by his employer. The market was closed on 22 and 23 March. The shop-owner, Vikram said, left for his village when this announcement took place. He promised Vikram and the others that he would return within two days. However, soon the lockdown was announced. Vikram and his co-workers did not leave for their home as they had been told that the market would close for only two days. He believed that the decision to close the market was unilaterally taken by the shopkeepers in Sarojini Nagar Market without any consideration for the vast number of workers who are dependent on the market for their sustenance. Through the lockdown, they were all anxious about when the market would reopen and whether they would still have their jobs when it does. When we spoke to him, Vikram said, '*Abhi ummeed nahi hein ki market khulega. Lockdown hatega tho gaon chale jayenge*' (I do not believe that the market will open. When the lockdown lifts will go to the village).

When the lockdown was announced, Vikram had with him merely one thousand rupees, which the shop owner had given to him before he left for his village. However, while he struggled every day to have two meals, what is most worrying for him is the condition of his family back in Bengal. '*Badi chinta hein, wo log bhi nahi kha pa rahe hein*'(I am worried about them. They also have not been able to eat).

Speaking to us, Vikram said that the government should help migrants like him to get back to their villages immediately. He was hoping that he would be able to get back soon and work either as an agricultural labourer or a cycle repair worker. He had no options, but to work in these low paying jobs, even if it would pay less: '*Kaam se kaam khana aur chawal ka nikal jata hein*' (at least we will be able to eat and buy rice). But whether this would translate into a reality is uncertain. Like several migrants, Vikram would also be travelling back to their villages in regions which they left, to begin with, in order to escape the paucity of employment opportunities. Due to the massive labour influx as a result of the reverse migration compelled by the lockdown, he would now be competing with others for low paying jobs, furthering his precarious living conditions. He might even end up without a job since studies clearly show that job loss has been high in rural locations in this time.[2] Continuing to live in the city was clearly unbearable, however; he said to us as we left him, '*Gaon mein thoda theek hein, yahan par pura vyavastha kharab hein*' (In the village it is a little better, here the condition is bad).

State Apathy

The preceding narratives have many things in common. First, even before COVID-19 and the lockdown, these labourers were already victims of unequal power relations in the informal sector, which barely allowed them to survive. While they were exploited to the maximum during 'normal' times, migrant workers in the informal sector, who have nothing to sell apart from their labour-power, were left to starve by their employers during the lockdown. Their experiences are an indictment of successive government policies that allowed for such precarity to emerge. The point we are trying to make here is that the state had already failed them long before the lockdown. The lockdown merely exacerbated the precarious conditions of an extremely vulnerable population.

Second, their dire conditions were a direct result of state apathy. Rather than owning the terrible mistakes on their part, the central government has routinely shrugged off any responsibility. For instance, noted social activists Harsh Mander and Anjali Bhardwaj submitted a PIL in the Supreme Court in the first week of April 2020 to alleviate the migrant crisis. The Home Secretary submitted a status report on this PIL in the Supreme Court. Point 40 of that report is particularly important, an excerpt from which is given below.

> It is submitted in that in view of the aforesaid financial package which takes care of daily needs of every poor person, which

> include migrant workers as well as their respective families in their original villages, there was no necessity for migration of workers to rush to their villages who started shifting from place of their occupation to the place of their residence. Their daily needs were being taken care of wherever they were working and the daily needs of their family members were being taken care of at their respective villages.

These remarks are reflective of the overall nature of the report, i.e., the return of migrant workers to their villages defeats the purpose of the lockdown since they are anyway taken care of in their respective places of occupation. However, as visible from the narrative experiences in this essay, and also from large-scale studies, this cannot be further from the truth. For instance, according to a report prepared by SWAN (Stranded Workers Action Network), 51 per cent of workers who were surveyed had rations left for less than one day, while 72 per cent would run out of food in two days at the time of the survey. This report was released on 15 April 2020.[3] Clearly, not a state of affairs in which 'their daily needs were being taken care of wherever they were working'.

While the central government attempted to paint a rosy picture of migrants being taken care of, in reality, the migrant population struggled daily to make ends meet and were overwhelmingly dependent on non-state donors/actors during the lockdown period. The only variable which has been relevant in mitigating the concerns of the migrants has been the efficiency of state governments and here, the example of Kerala comes to mind.[4]

The Supreme Court, which chooses to take a keen interest in exercises like the NRC, has not only been unconcerned but has been exhibited a troubling elitist mentality on the matter. 'If they are being provided meals, then why do they need money for meals?'[5] said the 'honourable' Chief Justice of India to Prashant Bushan, who was representing Harsh Mander and Anjali Bhardwaj in his PIL on the condition of migrant labourers. However, the aforementioned study and our accounts indicate that migrants are not regularly provided with food by the state. Second, even if migrants were provided with food sufficiently, does it mean the end of the state's responsibility towards them? Are they not deserving of healthcare, monetary compensation due to the loss of working days and job security post-lockdown? Most importantly, is it not the state's responsibility through proactive interventions to ensure that those dependent on the migrants are taken care of? What is completely amiss is that the right to life is also followed by a right to livelihood. In the most shocking episode around this concern, the Karnataka government announced on 18 April 2020 that cash transfer to migrant workers would not be possible since there was no data about them.[6]

Overall, it would seem that migrants are invisible beings, as far as the government is concerned. There is no acceptance of their concerns, struggles, emotions and heart-breaking tragedies. They are barely considered humans. Their concerns to go back to their villages are not to be considered, even when similar concerns of middle-class students stranded in Kota are addressed proactively by the state. In the most insensitive and criminal manner, Home Minister Amit Shah would blame the impatience of some migrant workers for this crisis.[7] Class, it seems continues to make a defining difference when it comes to state action. To sum up, as N.R. Musahar pointed out in his commentary in the *New Left Review,* the Indian government is more than happy to push migrants to 'starvation measures'.[8]

Notes

1 For instance, SWAN report notes that 96% of migrants had not received ration from the government. Joshi, T. (2020, April 27). '96% Migrants Didn't Receive Rations, 90% Didn't Get Wages During Lockdown : Survey'. *HW English*. Accessed 25 June 2021. https://hwnews.in/company-profile-promoters-hw-news

2 The Survey indicates the instance of job loss was significantly in rural location. Of the total respondents in rural location, 92.8% could not find any job during the lockdown. Centre for Equity Studies. (2020). *Labouring Lives: Hunger, Precarity and Despair amid the Pandemic*. New Delhi.

3 Devparna, A. (2020, May 12). 'COVID-19 Lockdown: 50% of stranded migrant labourers have less than Rs 100; 97% didn't get cash transfer from govt, finds report'. *Firstpost*. Accessed on 7 August 2020. https://www.firstpost.com/health/covid-19-lockdown-50-of-stranded-migrant-labourers-have-less-than-rs-100-97-didnt-get-cash-transfer-from-govt-finds-report-8359701.html

4 In the same report submitted by Home secretary to Supreme Court in response to the PIL filed by Harsh Mander and Anjali Bhardwaj, the centre said that 65% of camps for migrants are run in Kerala. The Wire Staff. (2020, April 9). 'Kerala Govt Running 65% of Shelter Camps for Migrants After Lockdown: Centre to SC'. *The Wire*. Accessed 16 June 2021. https://thewire.in/law/kerala-centre-supreme-court-lockdown-migrant-labourers-shelter

5 Legal Correspondent. (2020, April 7). 'If meals are given…: Supreme Court's Query'. *The Telegraph Online*. Accessed 6 August 2020. https://www.telegraphindia.com/india/if-meals-are-given-why-do-they-require-wages-supreme-courts-query-during-coronavirus-lockdown/cid/1762977

6 Press Trust of India. (2020, April 18). 'Karnataka Govt Says no Data on Informal Workers, so Cash Transfer not Possible'. *News Click*.

Accessed 6 August 2020. https://www.newsclick.in/Karnataka-Govt-Says-no-Data-on-Informal-Workers-so-Cash-Transfer-not-Possible

7 Scroll Staff. (2020, June 2). 'Migrant Crisis: Some workers 'lost patience' and started walking, claims Amit Shah'. *Scroll.in.* Accessed 6 August 2020. https://scroll.in/latest/963558/migrant-crisis-some-workers-lost-patience-and-started-walking-claims-amit-shah

8 Musahar N.R. (2020, March 27). 'India's Starvation Measures' *New Left Review.* Accessed 8 August 2020. https://newleftreview.org/issues/II122/articles/india-s-starvation-measures

23

COVID-19 Pandemic

Another Opportunity for the Government to Build the Foundation for Nationwide Implementation of CAA/NRC

BUDDHADEB HALDAR

Just before the Covid-19 outbreak in India, the Bihar government—the first from the NDA camp—passed a resolution against the implementation of the National Register of Citizens (NRC) in the state. Importantly, the Bihar Assembly also passed a resolution seeking implementation of the National Population Register (NPR) as per the format as it was in 2010, and not the souped-up version now prepared by the Centre.

After months of nationwide anti-CAA and anti-NRC protests, 12 states either passed resolutions against both or refused to implement them in their jurisdiction. Such measures put the Indian government led by Prime Minister Narendra Modi on the backfoot. Their defensiveness reflected in the statements made by the leaders of the ruling Bharatiya Janata Party.

For instance, BJP national spokesperson GVL Narasimha Rao claimed on 2 March that 'there is no plan to implement NRC as of now'. He also said that in the future, the NRC would be implemented in a transparent manner after involving all the stakeholders.

However, both inside and outside Parliament, ministers and politicians linked with the BJP continued to campaign to amass support for CAA, NRC and NPR. In the Rajya Sabha, the Home Minister declared on 13 March that no one would be marked 'doubtful' if they are unable to submit the required information demanded during the NRC process. He repeated, 'No document needs to be submitted, and you can give whatever information you have and leave the other questions blank.'

These are just promises, like the ones he had made in Parliament before, a day after which he reiterated that a nationwide NRC would be conducted.

However, despite these contradictory tendencies, the government has been consistent in doing absolutely nothing to amend the regulations governing the CAA, NRC and NPR. As legal experts have pointed out, the laws and regulations covering CAA, NRC and NPR are filled with clauses that are open to discriminatory usage by officials, even in the presence of a benevolent central government.

Now with the Covid-19 pandemic infecting well over 1.6 lakh Indians and a host of other problems in its wake, there has arisen a new tendency: BJP leaders using this moment as an opportunity to strengthen support for the CAA. A case in point is a video posted by BJP Member of Parliament Saumitra Khan, who represents the Bishnupur constituency of West Bengal in the Lok Sabha, on his verified Facebook page. The video features his wife Sujata Khan distributing surgical masks among women. As she distributes relief, she can be heard saying, 'This mask is a gift for you by BJP.... You should wear it all time whenever you go out. You need to live healthy, and most importantly, you know about the CAA. Is not it?'

Khan then pulls up a leaflet and says, 'The law (CAA) is to give you citizenship and not to snatch citizenship from you. No one will be able to remove you from the lap of your mother India…' She goes on: 'You just think why we should shelter Bangladeshis in India? Mother India is our county; it is not a hospice.'

In the same video she suggests that the CAA will 'protect' citizens from infiltrators (read, Muslims) from other countries including Bangladesh, Pakistan and Afghanistan. '…this law has been passed to stop them from coming to India and become settlers here, so they can't remove you from your own country. So, support the CAA,' she can be heard saying.

It is clear that Khan is attempting to generate fear and hatred among Indian citizens by accusing invisible infiltrators from neighbouring countries of wanting to supplant them.

But it is not just one video; hundreds of social media posts in favour of NRC and CAA are going viral. In some, Muslims, Covid-19 and NRC are being linked. For instance, some videos explicitly state that 'Muslims got Coronavirus', and that the NRC is the right 'treatment' for them.

This is a systematic campaign, if one observes the videos in conjunction with several other incidents that have taken place during the Covid-19 lockdown. When the PM announced a one-day janta curfew on 22 March 2020, it was speculated that a nationwide lockdown was already on the cards. This was confirmed when a lockdown for 21 days was indeed announced on the evening of 24 March, effective from 25 March. However, on the morning of 24 March, at around 7 am, the Delhi Police (under central government control) went to the Shaheen Bagh anti-CAA protest site and cleared it within half an hour.

The police also cleared the protest site at the Jamia Millia Islamia campus. Banners, posters, tents and other structures used during the anti-CAA campaign which began on 11 December 2019 were hastily removed. Even a map of India that highlighted the protester's opposition to CAA and NRC, along with a replica of India Gate installed at Shaheen Bagh, were removed, broken and/or disfigured.

The protest graffiti on the walls of Jamia were also disfigured and removed. This was done to all anti-CAA public material/art across the country.

It is indeed surprising that the Indian government, hours before announcing an unprecedented national lockdown to control a deadly pandemic, had its police force dismantling anti-CAA and anti-NRC art installations and graffiti. It is odd that this was considered, in the government's reckoning, as the first and most 'essential government service' while India stood on the brink of a health and economic crisis.

The next shocking step taken by the Centre was to begin arresting activists in connection with the anti-CAA/NRC protests during the lockdown. By the end of March 2020, the Home Ministry had instructed Delhi Police to ensure that arrests related to the communal violence that had broken out in Delhi in late February should not slow down. It was reported that Delhi Police was making six or seven arrests every day and that at least 1,000 people have been arrested or detained in cases related to the Delhi violence.

It is also apparent from reports that a good number of those who have been arrested are Muslim and young activists. For instance, on 1 April 2020, the police arrested Jamia student leader Meeran Haider; on 11 April, another Jamia student leader, Safoora Zargar, who was pregnant at the time, was arrested, and so on. These two and the former JNU student and activist Umar Khalid have been charged under the draconian UAPA (Unlawful Activities Prevention Act, 1967). In their FIR, the police argue that the violence in Delhi was a premeditated 'conspiracy', allegedly formulated by Umar, two others and their unnamed associates.

On 27 April 2020, police raided the house of Kanwaljit Kaur, the Delhi Unit president of the All India Students Association (AISA) and confiscated her mobile phone. On 23 May, JNU students Devangana Kalita and Natasha Narwal, both founding members of Pinjra Tod, were arrested for participating in a sit-in protest against the CAA in northeast Delhi. They were granted bail on that very day by a Delhi court, which had noted that they were 'merely protesting'. However, as has happened to some other student-protesters, within minutes of getting bail, the Crime Branch of the Delhi Police arrested them under charges of 'murder, attempt to murder, rioting and criminal conspiracy'.

The government seems to be using the lockdown as an opportunity to serve its sinister political purposes since there are restrictions in place on legal services under the lockdown and the media is not functioning as in pre-lockdown times either.

In the second week of May, the BJP released a video celebrating its six years in power. This nine-minute video highlights the Citizenship Amendment Act as one of the successes of the second term of the BJP government. Thousands of party members posted this video on their social media profiles. Thus there is no denying that the BJP and politicians affiliated with the ruling party have chosen to gather support for the controversial CAA even while the country is reeling under the Covid-19 pandemic.

It is clear that the nationwide campaigns and protests against CAA and NRC have not made any difference when it comes to the attitude of the government. In December 2019, the Union Cabinet had approved a spending of Rs 3,941 crore on updating the NPR, an exercise which was to be conducted between April and September 2020. The government ignored all the calls to amend the CAA to make it non-discriminatory. And now it is promoting CAA and preparing the ground for implementation of the divisive law and the NPR and NRC on a nationwide scale.

First the budget approval for NPR (the Union Budget has allocated Rs 4,568 crore for 'Census, Survey and Statistics') came amidst nationwide protests against the CAA-NRC-NPR triad. Then, the government decided to use the pandemic-triggered lockdown as a means to gain support for CAA, at a time when the media and citizenry's attention has been diverted by the health crisis. Further, before it took any steps to counter the pandemic, it covered the anti-CAA and anti-NRC paintings and graffiti with paint, and ordered mass arrests of anti-CAA protestors by linking their protests with the Delhi violence. All of this proves its desperation and determination to implement CAA and conduct the NPR process.

The arrests also send a clear message to the activist community that if anybody in post-lockdown India seeks to oppose the CAA and NRC, they will face the same consequences as Meeran Haider, Safoora Zargar, Devangana Kalita, Natasha Narwal and scores of other students.

24

Virtual Classes, Real Divides

University Education in the Lockdown

IMTIAZ QUADRI

The BJP government's only response to the unprecedented humanitarian and economic disaster caused by the Coronavirus pandemic seems to be to 'not waste a good crisis'. Unfortunately for the Indian people, the lessons from this 'good crisis' were learnt much before the pandemic and had only to be hastily implemented when people were safely locked down in their homes. The government's heavy-handed response was complemented by an insensitive society led by the urban middle class impatient with restrictions and seeking an early return to 'normalcy'. For teachers and students in universities, the lockdown posed difficult questions about Education, its ethics and promise of equality, even as attempts were made to tear down public universities in the midst of this 'good crisis'. The immediate occasion for this questioning was the decision by many universities to conduct online exams—in the garb of a step towards the return to 'normalcy'—even as a majority of students protested against the ineffectivity of online classes. This was not surprising since students across the country often had to undertake online learning despite lack of internet connectivity, reading material, college environment and an uncertain academic schedule.

To understand why vice-chancellors are brazenly pushing this idea, it is necessary to understand the background of 'reforms' in education in India, as well as the changing middle-class sensibility and visibility in deciding the status and value of an education. A good education is central to the middle-class value system and their perceptions of upward social mobility. The lockdown revealed an inflexible university education system which exploits and panders to these sentiments while avoiding the difficult task of addressing the discriminatory potential of online education and the old and new forms of inequality this reproduces. Unlike universities, the hardships faced by school and college students went almost unreported. Surveys showed that children from poorer households were forced to drop out of schools to save money, a decision that impacted girl children more than others. In the end this heady rush towards a technocratic dystopia with contactless classrooms, while ignoring the real divides this created among students, was the only outcome of not wasting 'a good crisis'.

Education is Labor Too: Three students, One Complaint

News of students returning from Kota, Rajasthan in state-sponsored buses and trains grabbed headlines as early as 17 April 2020 even as migrant workers were beginning to walk back home under brutalising and fatal conditions. Many people questioned the preferential treatment being given to students over migrants, and not without justification. However, as a teacher I found that this piece of news acted more to obscure the struggles, anxieties and disruptions faced by many more students from weaker sections who were facing new and equally unsettling difficulties.

While everyday life and economic activity stand disrupted teachers and students are facing pressures to continue working, maintain 'productivity', and so on. Even as students have been ferried across the country to ensure their safety, the decision to conduct online examinations shows that they are expected to continue studying even while normal classroom teaching stands suspended. This is based on the questionable belief that work-from-home provides a good-enough or better alternative to classroom teaching. One aspect which separates classroom from online teaching is the space of the classroom and college itself where students can meet fellow students and focus on lessons. As Akanksha[1] from Jammu and Kashmir said to me, the lockdown has effectively cut her off from her classmates, friends and teachers due to the extremely slow 2G internet speeds they have. 'Work-from-home' has meant that her daily routine has been upturned as online classes are being held outside of working hours. Akanksha is now anxious to return to Delhi as soon as the lockdown is lifted to resume preparations for the upcoming MA Entrance and Civil Services Examinations. Akanksha's anxiety is not misplaced. Long periods of lockdown have badly disrupted the academic and exam schedule. She had earlier hoped to have completed her bachelor's examinations by June 2020 and then begin her preparations for the Civil Services examinations. An inability to cope can lead to the real danger of losing an academic year or dropping out of their chosen streams of education as universities insist on holding exams in the online mode despite the odds.

The precarity of pursuing an education is further heightened in Taufiq's story of the lockdown. Taufiq is a undergraduate student of Journalism at Ambedkar College of the Delhi University. He is a resident of Mustafabad in Northeast Delhi and Ambedkar College is the only affiliated college for many students east of the Yamuna. He tells us that he is one of the few students in his extended neighborhood of Mustafabad and Karawal Nagar to gain admission into the college, and how many of his friends have had no other option but to join their family-run businesses of auto spare parts, scrap dealership, etc., for want of educational opportunities. Most of his friends in the neighborhood have completed schooling or graduates at most. His efforts at pursuing an education saw a series of disruptions ever since the introduction of the Citizenship Amendment Act (CAA) in December 2019. Taufiq was a participant at the sit-in dharna against the CAA in Mustafabad and even helped in organising food, shelter, etc., for the protestors. But the CAA protests were hit by the communal rioting which began on 23 February and was especially violent in the Mustafabad area. The communal rioting was one of the worst the national capital had witnessed in decades leaving 53 people dead, hundreds displaced and disrupting the livelihoods of many, including Taufiq's family. For Taufiq, the 2020 academic semester beginning from January overlapped with the anti-CAA protests, communal rioting and the Coronavirus lockdowns in quick succession. Continued precarity, a lack of higher education opportunities and persistent unemployment threaten to push Taufiq away from his educational aspirations and are a source of much anxiety to him. For him and his friends, furthermore, an online education and its assurances of quality and productivity are not without their problems. While supporters of online teaching argue that internet availability in Delhi is wider than its critics allege because many students in the city own smartphones and can thus access the internet, as per a survey conducted by the All India Students' Association (AISA) in Delhi University, as many as 41.2 per cent of students said that they did not attend online classes at all because of poor internet connectivity.

Taufiq's story, however, shows us another problematic aspect of online classes—teaching and learning are affective and emotional labour-intensive processes that require a conducive college atmosphere. Teaching requires constant face-to-face interaction to hold the students' attention, repetition of concepts for clarification, regularity of classes, etc. Similarly, college campuses provide a space for meeting like-minded fellows, for conversations and banter for students. In an online class, this affective and emotional labour is transferred from the teacher, fellow students and the college space onto the student and her/his family. For Taufiq, who is a first-generation learner, this creates new and insidious forms of isolation. Taufiq's father runs a textiles business out of a boutique shop. His older son Shafi* helps his father in running the business. Shafi is also a Bachelor's student at the School of Open Learning (SOL) of Delhi University. Being in his final year, Shafi must prepare for the upcoming online exams while dividing his time between the family business and household chores. For both Taufiq and Shafi the only interaction with their friends is through WhatsApp for sharing books and reading materials. The anxiety to score well despite isolation from fellow classmates and a lack of books can be understood if we look at the increasingly fewer opportunities for employment as a content writer, which is Taufiq's first choice of profession. If, however, he does not manage to secure a job as a content writer, he plans to seek higher education as a researcher. While middle-class values understand education as a means of upward social mobility, for Taufiq it is imperative to secure admission in an MA programme at a reputed college just to ensure that he and his family are not slipping behind or dropping out of the education system altogether. Therefore, Taufiq would prefer to take up employment to 'support his family' after his graduation and pursue an MA degree only if he does not get a job.

Akanksha and Taufiq's precarity, lack of institutional support and dependence on self and family is a condition similar, but less desperate, to conditions facing migrant workers today. But the one comparable aspect between students' and migrant workers' experience has been the inadequacy of villages and towns to provide good education or employment forcing migration to the cities. Many students at Delhi University hail from the NCR, Ghaziabad, Bahadurgarh, etc., and make daily trips to and from the campus. They do not prefer to live in paying guest accommodations in the city. Many other students from villages are still dependent on their families for economic and moral support. For such students, the University is the only toehold they have in the city. As the lockdown showed, they have no institutional support, friends or family for help in an emergency. Vidhi is undergraduate student at the Delhi University who had to leave for her home in Harsana Kalan, Sonepat before the lockdown. She left without her books and has since been unable to access reading material or classes online because of poor internet connectivity. Without a computer she had to rely on her phone for online classes, sometimes without audio. But Vidhi is deeply motivated to use education to support and improve her family's conditions and become 'independent' herself. She says that she prefers to get a job quickly to make some money and allay familial pressure to get married. Her father, an electrical repair mechanic, has been out of work for two months during the lockdown. Despite a high level of motivation, however, she has little support from the University, and the education system at large. Without such support Vidhi has taken it upon herself to follow a strict routine to continue her preparation for the upcoming MA Entrance and Civil Services examinations. 'I begin by reading the newspapers, study my college subjects for two hours and then do my self-preparation for civils,' she says. However, the online exams Vidhi will soon sit for are more a means of signalling a return to normalcy than achieving her aspirations. The cost of such 'normalcy' may well force students from poor and socio-economically disadvantaged families to give up their aspirations, or worse, be forced out of education.

New Educational Policy: Upward Mobility is Bypassing Politics

Akanksha, Taufiq and Vidhi's stories reveal an exclusive education system even under 'normal' circumstances, even as middle-class demands further technocratic 'solutions' to the lockdown. Evidently, the pandemic and lockdown are only the latest in a long series of 'useful crises' to be used to completely transform the education system. The National Education Policy (NEP) adopted in 2019 sought to promote Information and Communication Technology (ICT), SWAYAM Massive Online Open Classes (MOOCs) and a National Repository of Educational Data (NRED) to maintain records of all institutions, teachers and students in digital form. The data record of all students is touted to be a panacea for all educational ills such as school dropouts, low retention rates and educational achievements and even the lack of school buildings and separate classrooms in remote villages. During the epidemic, the rationale of health and safety is a clumsy post-facto rationalisation to further a set agenda of technological 'solutions' to reduce campus education's 'wastefulness.'

It is important to remember that MOOCs were first presented as an alternative in the aftermath of the 2008 financial crisis in America, where they failed. Yet, instead of recognising demands long sought by educationists such as revising teachers' salaries, recruitment and training in use of ICT, the NEP has instead held up venture capitalists such as Byjus Online Classes as examples to emulate. The role of teachers in improving public education will be limited to digitising student performance and curriculum, while Artificial Intelligence (AI) would provide 'automated development of educational content…develop intelligent and interactive tutoring systems…,' etc., finally resulting in the 'rationalisation of teachers… based on analytics of supply-demand gaps across schools'. In this never-ending technology fantasy of endless efficiency and growth, teachers opposed to ICT are being branded as lazy technophobes who do not want to learn newer skills. In reality, teachers are opposed to the potential of centralised control and a one-size-fits-all education model based on treating students as a means for large-scale data aggregation. For a teaching community already burdened with untenured and precarious jobs and cumbersome oversight, the switch to online education understandably poses a new risk of uncontrolled and rapid technological obsolescence.

Till before the economic liberalisation of the 1990s, the value and status of education lay in enabling the vast subaltern masses to gain attributes associated with the middle class; for instance, a white-collar job was seen as a way out of degrading and stigmatised occupations for Dalits. Middle-class values associated with education created subtle hierarchies even before liberalisation. But the paradox lies in the fact that even as the upwardly mobile sections of Dalits, Muslims and women finally inch closer to achieving the attributes of being 'educated', the middle class now redefines status and achievement in terms of the market. Being 'job ready' now requires 'upskilling' and 'reskilling,' often made possible only by degrees from foreign universities. The same middle-class intelligentsia which developed in state-sponsored public universities such as Allahabad University, Osmania University and others since before Independence now champions their slow hollowing out without a trace of irony. Simply put, new middle-class sensibility and visibility has cheated students from the subaltern strata of the recognition of being educated and equal.

Today, the clamour for educational reforms hides a paradoxical reality. On the one hand, public universities rely on hundreds of contractual teachers and deny students from socio-economically weaker sections fellowships, hostels, sometimes even a college campus or building. On the other hand, there are persistent demands for deregulation allowing foreign universities and deemed universities to create 'market-ready' graduates. How did the market acquire such a flexible workforce if the education sector was over-regulated? The lockdown has provided advocates of liberalisation with a pretext to hide their failures, blame them on alleged regulation and to further privatisation. Liberalisation has created hierarchies within the teacher and student community in addition to the variations in curriculum, boards, examinations, etc. Even as ad-hoc teachers hope one day to become permanently employed, guest teachers and research assistants appear no less than a labour aristocracy. If the lockdown and economic downturn are not to result in further job losses and precarity for teachers, then the onslaught on university spaces must be resisted. Therefore, it is necessary to understand what this heady rush to a tech-dystopia of classroom-less, personalised teaching conceals: University campuses are not only physical but also social spaces which engender a student politics, allow for Unionisation and act as sites where students from marginalised sections can assert themselves. If an education were to be an adventure of ideas and fulfil our constitutional vision, virtual education cannot become a real divide in India.

Notes

1 All names have been changed to protect the identity of the respondents.

Epilogue

A Health and Humanitarian Crisis, but Above All the Fallout of a Crisis of Democracy

ANIRBAN BHATTACHARYA, NATASHA BADHWAR, HARSH MANDER

Such are the times that each tragedy gives far less breathing space before it is overshadowed by a graver one. By the time this book goes to press, we have reached newer heights—or lower depths—as a society in familiarising ourselves with death. The second wave of the pandemic has already crashed upon the fragile and long-starved public health system of the country, and it has scattered the hospitals, the overwhelmed crematoriums and burial grounds, as well as the river banks with thousands of body bags. These were many of our poorest who could not afford even a funeral after black-marketing even in firewood: people lost to us who are unaccounted for, unattended, unrecognised and sometimes even unmourned.

In the year before, which the present anthology pertains to, what was ubiquitous was hunger and destruction of millions of lives. This year while hunger and joblessness loom menacingly in the shadows, we are seeing thousands scramble to even breathe as our hospitals run out of oxygen and hospital beds. Compared to last year's peak in September when we were contracting just above 90,000 cases per day, the official figure crossed 4 lakh cases per day in early May 2021. The official death toll stands at 2,78,751. But it is widely known and accepted that most of the disfigured corpses floating in our rivers and the people unable to find a hospital bed are not included in that figure.

Death is all around us. And we are left wondering how we will ever recover from the trauma of the circumstances in which so many of us have struggled to find help. Most of us do not remember this level of dissonance in our lived experience. Add to this another round of knee-jerk ad hoc lockdowns across the country, yet another disruption in the lives of the working poor already living on the edge as a result of the enduring shock of the strictest lockdown on earth enforced last year.

On our phones, there is a constant stream of distress messages from friends and colleagues, most of whom are trying to co-ordinate support for others. And the daily heartbreak, sometimes many times a day, as we hear of our finest, bravest, kindest comrades lost or bereaved. Meanwhile, the government's response has gone through the full spectrum: self-congratulation, arrogance, denial, ignorance and uncanny apathy.

A Crisis of Democracy

As is expected, any criticism of the government at this stage is being derided as 'politicisation' of a tragedy. Such a label, however, is not directed at petty poll promises of 'free vaccines' being dangled in front of the Bihar and Bengal voters during the assembly elections, or the politics of hate that accompanied campaigning. It is reserved rather exclusively for just the difficult questions regarding the regime's handling of the pandemic.

But it is precisely because of the stunning scale of the tragedy that it is imperative to acknowledge that beyond a humanitarian crisis, a health crisis, a bio-economic crisis, in India what we are facing today is above all a fallout of a crisis of democracy, the abandonment of the people by those who we elected to administer us.

It is in times like this that even sceptics should acknowledge that issues like freedom of expression, independence of judiciary, free and vigilant press are not 'elite concerns' of a few 'libtards', or the obsession of just a bunch of annoying 'andolanjeevis' or 'anti-nationals'. It may sound like a stretch, but there is a direct line that connects these so called 'elite concerns' and the aerial images of the mass cremations and burials that we shudder at today.

Things that We have Allowed in Silence

The central government last year did not consult even once the national task force on COVID-19 (comprising 21 leading scientists and epidemiologists from across the country) before announcing the extended national lockdown. This year again, despite members of the task force flagging their concerns well in advance, they were not consulted through the crucial months of February and March as the second wave swelled. And by a member's own admission, the task force has in fact been reduced to a 'rubber stamp' on decisions already taken by politicians. But such gross discrepancies were only greeted by most of us with silent obedient conformity, and among many even with endorsement and appreciation.

The regime, last year, wanted to play to its strength, that is batons instead of brains. The strictest lockdown in the world was epidemiologically unsound and was by design oblivious of the poor. But the untold miseries of the millions on the move, the avoidable loss of lives, the indignity and mass hunger were quickly supplanted with more 'pressing concerns', that of 'drug addiction' among women in Bollywood. We were not only *fine* with this, rather, we were euphoric to see this quite literal witch-hunt play out LIVE on our television sets for months. Reminiscent it was of the blood-sports that were organised to entertain and distract the ancient Romans from the pressing concerns of the day. We hooted and cheered.

Note that these were critical months that could have been used to probe into the inadequacies of our efforts, in identifying the gaps in our preparedness in the first wave and in gearing for the future, i.e., for today. Instead, we prioritised a mandir, a 'dangerous toolkit' of a 22-year-old climate activist and high-voltage election campaigns that kept both the Prime and Home Ministers busy. And the fact is, while such precious time was being squandered, many, if not most of us, cheered along.

Well, if we thought that our failures as citizens, and the failure of our institutions and the media—to question, to prod, to criticise—were to come without a cost, we were wrong. If we thought that by allowing for the diminishing of democracy for a few 'others'—for the minorities, for Kashmiris, for the farmers—we will enhance our own, we were wrong. We are paying for it today, and unfortunately paying too dearly. Tomorrow those who demanded oxygen may also be branded 'anti-nationals'. The chief minister of India's largest state already threatened to arrest people who complain that they could not access oxygen to save the lives of their loved ones.

Instances of our 'Preparedness'

At the end of January, in a premature celebration, at the Davos summit of the World Economic Forum, our PM took a caustic jab at the 'doomsday predictions' by experts that were being made last year about India being the worst affected country. He boasted about what was soon to be his ill-fated 'vaccine diplomacy'. In March, he allowed the Mahakumbh in Haridwar that allowed 35 lakh people to congregate at a time when the number of COVID cases in India were already above 2 lakh. This is estimated to be the largest religious gathering in the world. And what is even more stunning is that as per the religious calendar, the Kumbh was in fact scheduled for 2022, and it was brought forward, presumably to reap the electoral benefits of Hindu consolidation. Even while the second wave had already started bulging, our Health Minister claimed 'we are at the endgame' of the pandemic.

Such statements or gestures go on to prove the absolute apathy of those who were supposed to govern us and save lives. Some may even now say, what can a government do in the face of a disaster of this proportion. Well, to start with, it may choose not to misguide. And most of all, it can pay heed to warning bells, of which there were many.

The Parliamentary Standing Committee on Health as late as November 2020 (after the peak of the first wave) warned of a 'strong need to ensure that the oxygen inventory is in place and oxygen prices are controlled' by tapping into the industrial oxygen supplies. Though still delayed, Maharashtra placed a curb on industrial use of oxygen by 30 March 2021. The union government, for whom the first priority was always 'ease of business', did the same as late as 22 April 2021. So much so that the Delhi High Court, on 20 April 2021, asked the tough question of the government, 'Can we ask patients needing oxygen to hold on till April 22? …we are heading for a bigger disaster as we might end up losing nearly a crore of people. Are we willing to accept that?' And it was not surprising that by 24 April, the Chief Justice of the Supreme Court took over all COVID-related matters prohibiting any of the High Courts from adjudicating on matters related to the pandemic. It is only after senior advocates vocally came out against such a move, that further clarifications were made.

Fallout of an Unhealthy Democracy

In an atmosphere where questioning the PM makes one's patriotic credentials questionable, we accepted the same conditions for questions around the gross opaqueness about the PM CARES funds for COVID relief.

One may very well say, whatever it be, this is not the time to blame a government. And actually we shouldn't. The ones in power had made their priorities clear: corporates over farmers, power over responsibility, polarisation over unity. It is rather the privileged, the super-rich, the educated upper caste middle class, who have failed us. They are the ones who have enjoyed a rather disproportionate space in this unequal country in terms of shaping and amplifying opinion. But soaked in neo-liberal sensibilities and drenched in Hindutva pride, they have abused this space with their silence as well as their complicity.

It is our conformity that has fed the government's fatal complacency. The only antidote was accountability. But unfortunately, all our tools of holding our government to account—be it the media, the autonomy of institutions, a critical civil society, people's movements—have been systematically blunted, eroded, silenced or crushed by this regime. What was promoted instead was rhetoric, prejudice, lies and the opposite of science. So much so that we are faced with a regime that preferred ease of business even at a time when we were desperate in our unease to breathe.

The Path Ahead

If we are to recover from this abyss, then it is high time we acknowledge that our health and well-being are intrinsically related to the health of our democracy. That the much fetishised 'iron hand' of *one* man or *one* voice only stifles alternate views or critical opinion thereby breeding ignorance and complacency.

From where we stand action and solidarity with each other is the only way to dent the hubris that has created the panic we are in. The same social media feed that brings news of devastation is also the location where people are co-ordinating resources to try to save as many lives as possible. All through the second wave, #PakistanStandsWithIndia was the top trending hashtag on Pakistani Twitter, reminding us yet again that iridescent human connections trump political divisiveness.

In his book *If This Is a Man*, Primo Levi, who had survived life in a concentration camp, writes: '...precisely because the Lager was a great machine to reduce us to beasts, we must not become beasts. One must survive to tell the story, to bear witness; and that to survive we must force ourselves to save at least the skeleton, the scaffolding, the form of civilization... We must walk erect, without dragging our feet, not in homage to Prussian discipline but to remain alive, not to begin to die.'

As we stand witness to another phase in human history when cruelty and ruthlessness are being normalised by those in power, we must fight back with the conviction that each individual life is precious. We, as a people must have power over those whom we have elected to govern. We need to keep telling stories that are sought to be buried, asking questions to hold others accountable and lending a hand to those in torment. The good within us must triumph over moral turpitude.

The sense of shock that seems to overwhelm us now has a purpose to serve. Collective grief reminds us of our interconnectedness and how much we are all the same beneath the veneer of race, community and class. Let us resolve to never forget that it is not the COVID-19 pandemic that defeated us. Most deaths that we see as bodies pile up around us are not caused by the deadly and cunningly mutating virus; they have been caused instead by a criminally incompetent and uncaring state. And even more culpably by the insensitivity and reckless arrogance of those who looked the other way when our people needed responsible and compassionate governance the most.

Contributors

Abdul Kalam Azad is a human rights researcher, community organiser and writer. Previously a research fellow with Tata Institute of Social Sciences, he is currently writing his doctoral thesis at VU University Amsterdam. He works primarily on the citizenship crisis in Assam and recently served as one of the co-investigators on the University of York project 'Reimagining Citizenship: The Politics of India's Amended citizenship Laws'.

Amitanshu Verma is a researcher at the Centre for Equity Studies, New Delhi. He has a PhD in Political Science from Jawaharlal Nehru University (JNU) and his research interests lie at the intersection of political economy, local politics and political culture.

Amrita Johri is associated with Satark Nagrik Sangathan (SNS). She is a member of the Delhi Rozi Roti Adhikar Abhiyan, the national Right to Food Campaign and the National Campaign for Peoples' Right to Information (NCPRI).

Anjali Bhardwaj is a founding member of Satark Nagrik Sangathan (SNS), which works closely with residents of slum and low income settlements in Delhi. She is also a founding member of the Delhi Rozi Roti Adhikar Abhiyan, a member of the national Right to Food Campaign and the Co-Convenor of the National Campaign for Peoples' Right to Information (NCPRI).

Anirban Bhattacharya is a researcher and activist and is currently part of the Centre for Financial Accountability, New Delhi. His work is centered around public finance, labour, democratic rights and equality.

Balu Sunilraj is an Assistant Professor of Political Science at Christ University. Before joining Christ University, he worked at Ambedkar University, Delhi and also with the Centre for Equity Studies. He holds a PhD degree in Political Science from the Jawaharlal Nehru University. His research interests include local politics, Left movement in Kerala, state politics and political economy.

Banojyotsna Lahiri is currently a Senior Researcher at the Center for Equity Studies. She has earlier taught sociology in Ambedkar University Delhi, Jamia Millia Islamia and Lady Shri Ram College, Delhi University. She has done her PhD from Centre for Study of Social Systems in Jawaharlal Nehru University.

Buddhadeb Halder is an interdisciplinary researcher presently working as a Post-Doctoral Research Associate with the Arts and Humanities Research Council-funded project titled 'Reimagining citizenship: The politics of citizenship amendment act in India' at the University of York, UK. He holds a PhD in Law, Science and Technology (ICT and Law). He has more than 15 years of work experience with various national and international human rights organisations, including the International Secretariat of Amnesty International.

Harsh Mander is an author, columnist, researcher, teacher and social activist who started the Karwan-e-Mohabbat campaign in solidarity with the victims of communal or religiously motivated violence. He is the Director of the Centre for Equity Studies, a research organisation based in New Delhi.

Mohammed Imtiaz Quadri is Assistant Editor, Economic and Political Weekly. He holds a Ph degree in Political Science from the Centre for Political Studies, Jawaharlal Nehru University. His doctoral research on anti-caste politics in the context of the separate statehood movement in Telangana was published in the Economic and Political Weekly recently.

Kazi Sharowar Hussain is a poet, filmmaker and researcher. His recent collection of poetry *Ghorasalat Etia Nirantar Tupani* was published by Purbayon Publication.

Madhurima Majumder is a researcher based out of Kolkata. She is currently a consultant with the National University of Singapore working on the Southern Collective project. Her present work is on climate induced migration and gender.

Meera Viswanathan is a mental health professional and human rights worker. Her work is centreed around structural violence, trauma and mental health support.

Mihika Chanchani is a researcher based out of Delhi. Her work has centred around communal violence in South Asia, citizenship and statelessness and issues around vulnerable communities in India.

Misbah Rashid is currently working as Assistant Professor, Gitam University, Hyderabad. Previously, she worked as Visiting faculty, Chandigarh University, Chandigarh and Senior researcher at Centre for Equity Studies, New Delhi.

Nandita Haksar is a human-rights lawyer and writer. She has represented workers, women, adivasis, Burmese activists and the people of the Indian Northeast and Kashmir.

Natasha Badhwar is an author, columnist, filmmaker, journalist and media trainer. She is part of the Karwan-e-Mohabbat's campaign for peace, harmony and justice. Her books include *My Daughter's Mum* and *Immortal For a Moment.*

Niyati is a legal researcher, currently working with Centre for Equity Studies, Delhi. Her work is centred around hate crimes, child labour and trafficking, extraordinary laws and violence against women.

Radhika Bordia has worked as a journalist for 25 years. A strong advocate for in-depth reportage, she worked on long format programming at NDTV for two decades. Currently, she is Director, India Programme at the Missouri School of Journalism. She also teaches at the School of Journalism, OP Jindal Global University.

Radhika Mullick Alkazi is the Founder and Managing Trustee of ASTHA, a community based organisation that works with children and persons with disabilities and their families in Delhi and other states since 1993.

Sazid Ali is a researcher at the Centre for Equity Studies, New Delhi. He holds a PhD degree from Centre for Political Studies, Jawaharlal

Nehru University. His research interests lie in themes like democracy, secularism, multiculturalism and minority politics.

Sagar Kumbhare is currently working as a researcher at the Centre for Equity Studies, New Delhi. His work is focused on issues of public policy in relation with caste discrimination and socio-economic exclusion.

Shirin Choudhary is a researcher based out of Delhi. Their work has focused around gender, sexuality, women's work and sexual and reproductive rights. They are interested in research and activism around transgender persons' rights and welfare.

Suresh Garimella is a researcher based in Delhi. He is presently working as a senior researcher at the Centre for Equity Studies. He holds a PhD in History from Jawaharlal Nehru University. His research interests include systemic exclusion, religious polarisation and safeguarding the constitutional rights of the citizens. His work also focuses on tracing the lives and working conditions of various marginalised groups and analysing the changes in the labour policy.

Swati is a Delhi-based advocate and a former legal fellow with Karwan-e-Mohabbat, a people's campaign that supports survivors of hate crimes and injustice with legal, social and livelihood help.

Varna Balakrishnan is a researcher and human rights worker based in New Delhi, focusing on issues of citizenship, communal violence and gender. She has been associated with Karwan-e-Mohabbat, the Centre for Equity Studies and the Institute of Development Studies, UK.